THE COLLECTED WORKS OF

F. A. Hayek

VOLUME VI

GOOD MONEY, PART II
The Standard

PLAN OF THE COLLECTED WORKS
Edited by Stephen Kresge

Volume I	The Fatal Conceit: The Errors of Socialism (1988)
Volume II	The Sensory Order and Other Essays
Volume III	The Trend of Economic Thinking: Essays on Political Economists and Economic History (1991)
Volume IV	The Fortunes of Liberalism and the Austrian School: Essays on Austrian Economics and the Ideal of Freedom (1992)
Volume V	Good Money, Part I: The New World
Volume VI	Good Money, Part II: The Standard
Volume VII	The Demons of Science: On the Uses and Abuses of Reason
Volume VIII	The Demons of Science: Economics and Knowledge
Volume IX	Contra Keynes and Cambridge: Essays, Correspondence (1995)
Volume X	Socialism and War: Essays, Documents, Reviews (1997)
Volume XI	Prices, Production, and Monetary Theory
Volume XII	Investigations in Economics
Volume XIII	The Pure Theory of Capital
Volume XIV	The Road to Serfdom
Volume XV	The Constitution of Liberty
Volume XVI	Philosophy, Politics, and Economics
Volume XVII	Law, Legislation, and Liberty
Volume XVIII	Essays on Liberty
Volume XIX	John Stuart Mill and Harriet Taylor: Their Friendship and Subsequent Marriage
Supplement	Hayek on Hayek: An Autobiographical Dialogue (1994)

The plan is provisional. Minor alterations may occur in titles of individual books, and several additional volumes may be added.

THE COLLECTED WORKS OF

F. A. Hayek

VOLUME VI

GOOD MONEY, PART II

The Standard

EDITED BY

STEPHEN KRESGE

Routledge
Taylor & Francis Group
LONDON AND NEW YORK

First published 1999 by Routledge
2 Park Square, Milton Park, Abingdon, Oxfordshire OX14 4RN
711 Third Avenue, New York, NY 10017

First issued in paperback 2014

Routledge is an imprint of the Taylor and Francis Group, an informa business

British Library Cataloguing in Publication Data
A catalogue record for this book is available from the British Library

ISBN: 978-0-415-03518-7 (hbk)
ISBN: 978-0-415-75529-0 (pbk)

CONTENTS

EDITORIAL FOREWORD

The title of this collection of F. A. Hayek's essays on monetary theory and policy is the title which Hayek had hoped to use for a conclusive summation of his ideas on the subject of money. "I still hope", he confided in an interview with Axel Leijonhufvud in 1978, "to do a systematic book which I shall call *Good Money*. Beginning really with what would be good money—what do we really want money to be—and then going on to the question of how far would the competitive issue of money provide good money in terms of that standard". This book remained unwritten, but the subject had occupied Hayek off and on throughout his career. The essays brought together in the two parts of *Good Money* exhibit the full range of Hayek's views on money—some consistently held, such as the Cantillon effect, and others, such as the apparition of a stable price level, modified or abandoned. Taken all together, the essays provide a solid introduction to aspects of monetary theory often neglected, with insights still applicable to the disordered and bewildering monetary events of the present.

Hayek was born on May 8, 1899, in Vienna. He died on March 23, 1992, in Freiburg im Breisgau in Germany, having lived long enough to see the fall of the Berlin Wall and the vindication of his long struggle against socialism. He had become a British subject in 1938 when he was Tooke Professor at the London School of Economics. After the Second World War, he came to the United States to teach at the University of Chicago from 1950 to 1962. As an economist, Hayek is among his peers perhaps the least confined to a view of the world which seeks to identify a model of an economy with a single nation. He was quick to learn languages—Swedish and Italian among them—and quick to spot the evils of coercion which lurk within nationalistic pretensions.

Hayek made his first visit to the United States in 1923, where he responded to the controversies of the day with an insight into monetary theory as to the crucial role of *time* in any concept of equilibrium. Once it is understood that prices change over time, the order in which prices change in response to changes in the supply of money cannot be ignored.

This insight was a new departure both for Hayek and for economics. The aftermath of the First World War brought to the forefront of the concerns of central bankers and economists the difficulty of stabilizing the value of currencies, both in terms of a domestic price level and in terms of other currencies. Hayek criticized the goal of an artificial stabilization of the value of money, resting his argument on a pioneering demonstration of the need for intertemporal equilibrium in the formation of which money must remain neutral.

By 1937, the views on monetary policy which Hayek criticized were largely discredited by events. In a lecture on "Monetary Nationalism and International Stability" he drew attention to what we now know to be the prime cause of the economic distress of the 1930s—the failure to maintain an international monetary standard. Yet all too quickly the scourge of belligerent nationalism had forged the calamity to come, and after the Second World War the US dollar, tied loosely to gold, became the accepted international standard. By 1973, the dollar was no longer tied to gold, and much of the world experienced levels of inflation not seen since the period following the First World War. Hayek concluded that national governments could not be relied upon to provide good money. He offered a bold proposal for the denationalization of money: People should be allowed to choose the money they prefer to hold; governments should compete with private issuers to supply money.

Between his 1937 argument for fixed exchange rates and his later proposal for competing currencies, Hayek put forward a proposal for a commodity reserve currency. Money would be backed by stored commodities in some fixed proportion, and money could be exchanged for a fixed unit of these commodities, or if it were found more profitable to do so, commodities could be offered for storage in exchange for money. Two advantages were claimed for this system: an automatic limit on the supply of money and a counter-cyclical mechanism for limiting the trade cycle.

At this writing, the world seems to be slipping back into the monetary expediency of nationalist controls; governments are again intervening in currency markets, stock markets, and banking. The value of money and the level of interest rates are subject to bouts of uncertainty not seen since the 1920s and 1930s. Good money is once again an elusive goal. In perhaps only one respect are monetary conditions greatly changed from those which formed the context in which Hayek wrote: Communications are swifter, to the degree that adjustment to unforeseen change may be instantaneous—for better or worse. The danger is that we will be overwhelmed by 'information' the significance of which we cannot know, since we have lost the standards by which we judge. Hayek's essays are an invaluable contribution to a theoretical and historical perspective which we may call upon to sort out the good money from the bad.

The essay "A Commodity Reserve Currency" was, surprisingly, catalyst to the Collected Works of F. A. Hayek. Just how this came about is, in its own not insignificant way, an example of Hayek's concept of 'spontaneous order'. The initial impulse came from Walter Morris, who attended the keynote address given by Hayek at the convocation of the Open Society and Its Friends in New York in November 1982. Morris was an admirer of Benjamin Graham, whose book *Storage and Stability* was one of the sources of Hayek's essay. In what was to be only the first of many acts of generosity, Morris then brought together, at a dinner party in honor of Hayek, W. W. Bartley III; Irving Kahn, who has recently seen Graham's *Storage and Stability* back into print; and, among others, this editor. The talk at the dinner party was about Hayek's ideas, notably his proposal for the denationalization of money.

In the following year, Walter Morris supplied the enthusiasm, good will, and persistence that convinced Hayek and Bartley that a collected works must be produced to acquaint the present generation with Hayek's thinking and to preserve for future generations a legacy which we can now see is nothing less than an introduction to the development of the modern world. We owe to Walter Morris and to the Morris Foundation, for its continuing financial support of the project, an immense debt of gratitude. The editor wishes to express his personal appreciation to Walter for the untiring support he has provided in some difficult times.

In bringing order to the unwieldy bounty of words that somehow manage to become the manuscripts of the collected works, Gene Opton, who has been assistant editor from the start, has been indispensable. Routledge and the University of Chicago Press, Hayek's longtime publishers, are due our appreciation for their support, with particular thanks going to Alan Jarvis and Penelope Kaiserlian. For their help with Part Two of *Good Money,* the editor thanks his research assistant, Elisa Cooper; Bruce Caldwell, for spotting certain incautious conclusions and other possible muddles; and Denis O'Brien for his thorough and knowledgeable criticism of the Introduction. We would like to thank the Institute of Economic Affairs for permission to reprint "The Denationalization of Money", and to express our appreciation to Lord Harris, John Blundell, and the late John Wood for their support of the Collected Works. We would also like to thank Anthony S. Courakis and the estate of John Hicks for permission to print a letter from Hicks to Hayek. For permission to reprint "The Future Unit of Value", we would like to thank Kluwer Law

International; and for permission to reprint "Toward a Free Market Monetary System", we thank Burton S. Blumert and the Center for Libertarian Studies.

Stephen Kresge
Big Sur, California

INTRODUCTION

One of the more dramatic images that Hayek has left us from his long life—he was born in Vienna in 1899 and died in Freiburg, Germany in 1992—was the preparation he made in 1939 for a possible escape from Nazi-controlled Austria which he wanted to visit before the outbreak of war. Although by then he was a British subject and could travel with a British passport, "I didn't want to be suspected of having any special privileges with the Germans", he remembered. "I knew those mountains so well that I could just walk out. I knew [the mountains in Carinthia] well enough, even better than the Vorarlberg-Switzerland boundary".[1] Those boundaries, indeed all of the boundaries of Eastern Europe which had to be established following the collapse of the Austro-Hungarian empire, lay at the core of much of the horror inflicted on the twentieth century.

Vienna had saved Europe from the invading Ottoman Turks in 1683; the First World War—in which Hayek fought for Austria—had its origins in the conflict of nationalist and imperial pretensions growing within the declining Ottoman empire. One of the more perceptive writers of the inter-war period prefaced a warning with a prophetic anecdote:

> In 1886 a young Englishman, son of Joseph Chamberlain, was sent to Paris by his family to prepare for a career in public affairs. One day, at the Ecole des Sciences Politiques, he heard the lecturer on diplomatic history, Albert Sorel, make this pronouncement: 'On the day when the Turkish question is settled Europe will be confronted with a new problem—that of the future of the Austro-Hungarian Empire'. But what perturbed young Austen Chamberlain was not the possibility that the Austro-Hungarian Monarchy might collapse and its dominions disintegrate. It was that Sorel went on to draw a conclusion most discomfiting to any thinking Englishman. The young man, destined to be Foreign Secretary of his country, heard the French professor describe the disintegration of

[1] F. A. Hayek, *Hayek on Hayek,* Stephen Kresge and Leif Wenar, eds (Chicago: University of Chicago Press, and London: Routledge, 1994), p. 137.

> Austria-Hungary as a possible preliminary to the break-up of the British Empire.
>
> Sir Austen Chamberlain said that he never forgot Sorel's warning. The former Foreign Secretary of the United Kingdom was not happy about the disruption of the Austro-Hungarian political and economic unity, sanctioned by the victorious Allies in the Peace Treaties. He became towards the close of his life increasingly unhappy about the future of maimed and lamed Austria, threatened by Germany's Third Reich. But, perhaps fortunately, he did not live to see what happened to Europe in 1938. For then what his French professor had feared half a century earlier came to pass. The last vestiges of the Austro-Hungarian Empire, the small independent states reared on its ruins and in its place, collapsed before two short and sharp German diplomatic assaults.[2]

Suppose that one knew nothing of history and had before one only two maps of the world: one map drawn at the end of the nineteenth century and the other at the end of the twentieth. One fact would be clearly visible: The empires of the European powers which covered the world at the end of the nineteenth century had vanished by the end of the twentieth. Knowing nothing of history, one could not know how this happened, or even if it mattered. Without history, the present division of the world into numerous independent states becomes a political and economic fact, without causes and, one might suppose, without consequences. One consequence is that each of these now independent states had to develop means to maintain internal order and coherence; resolve conflicts that arose from past legal, religious, or ethnic differences; and establish new currencies for internal use. But with the establishment of new boundaries comes the challenge of communicating *across* borders, the difficulty of conducting trade when independent currencies may be linked by no common standard. With a little investigation of the monetary conditions that prevailed in the nineteenth century, the map reader would learn that the imperial currencies had possessed a common standard—the gold standard—which did not survive their collapse. What did these now-independent countries put in the place of the abandoned standard to make it possible to conduct trade across new boundaries?

John Hicks has observed that "Monetary theory is less abstract than most economic theory; it cannot avoid a relation to reality, which in other economic theory is sometimes missing. It belongs to monetary history, in a way that economic theory does not always belong to economic his-

[2]Graham Hutton, *Danubian Destiny* (London: George G. Harrap, 1939), pp. 5–6.

tory. . . . So monetary theories arise out of monetary disturbances".[3] Hayek concurs: "In the past, periods of monetary disturbance have always been periods of great progress in [monetary theory]. The Italy of the sixteenth century has been called the country of the worst money and the best monetary theory".[4]

The collapse of the gold standard during the first World War contributed to two calamitous monetary disturbances of the mid-twentieth century: the inflation—hyperinflation in Germany and Austria—immediately following the war, and the deflation and depression in much of the world in the 1930s. At the end of the First World War, confined within the narrow boundaries of the left-over Austria, the Vienna in which Hayek began his university studies found itself near starvation and without electricity. With the dissolution of the Hapsburg empire, Vienna could no longer obtain from within its own domain Hungarian wheat or Czech coal. The boundaries which confined Austria to its hapless condition were imposed upon it by the terms of the Treaty of St. Germain, largely dictated by the determination of the French to create Slav states to contain a resurgent Germany.

With gold and other financial reserves exhausted by the war, the new republican government of Austria, under attack by socialists, resorted to printing money, banknotes which were no longer acceptable in the regions upon which Vienna depended for provisions. The resulting inflation destroyed much of the professional middle class—the class to which Hayek belonged—which had loyally purchased government bonds to finance the war effort. To say that Hayek was affected by this financial catastrophe is only to acknowledge the obvious; of more importance for the role it played in the development of his economic theories was the insight he gained thereby into the multiple effects—sometimes crude and immediate, but often subtle and prolonged—that inflation inflicts upon a society. The fate of Austria in the twentieth century also left Hayek less eager to accept the borders of nations imposed by governments of questionable legitimacy as also determining the boundaries of economies.

This introduction to Hayek's ideas about money is in large measure directed to the map reader that each of us becomes when exploring unfamiliar territory. Hayek's monetary theory rested on assumptions about

[3]John Hicks, "Monetary Theory and History—An Attempt at Perspective", in *Critical Essays in Monetary Theory* (London: Oxford at the Clarendon Press, 1967), p. 156.

[4]F. A. Hayek, *Prices and Production* (London: Routledge & Kegan Paul [1931], 2nd edition, 1935), p. 2.

the workings of a non-monetary economy (which, perforce, would be in theory only) that we cannot take for granted in current economic thinking, which neglects much of the implications of the ancient debate over just why and how money 'matters',[5] and which assumes only that money is provided by governments and that only our expectations about increases or decreases in the supply of money matter. Embedded in this approach is the assumption that the supply of money is an exogenous variable, that is, an institutional matter, but the demand for money can be construed as amenable to theoretical analysis. This modest approach to money is perhaps the result of a certain fatigue with the inconclusive debates between 'monetarists' and 'Keynesians' which petered out in the 1980s when no empirical regularities could be found between increases in the supply of money and employment.[6]

Hayek's intellectual heritage came from two primary sources, the Austrian tradition of Menger and Mises, and the 'classical' tradition of Adam Smith and David Hume, to which Hayek added Richard Cantillon and Henry Thornton.[7] In his approach to money Hayek retained a theory of value based on the subjective choices of individuals; but value theory survived in the macroeconomics of the 'monetarists' and the 'Keynesians' only through questionable methods of composition: the use of statistical

[5]Charles P. Kindleberger traces common elements of a debate over money as far back as the sixteenth century and continuing in following centuries in debates between, for instance, Lowndes and Locke, the Banking and Currency Schools in Britain, and between Friedman and Keynes. "But the dichotomy is not between any particular views of those great economists. It is rather far more general, between one school worried about inflation and deflation of prices and the quantity of money, and the other more about output and employment. . . ". *Keynesianism vs. Monetarism and Other Essays in Financial History* (London: George Allen & Unwin, 1985), p. 1.

[6]The debate was launched with *Studies in the Quantity Theory of Money*, Milton Friedman, ed. (Chicago: University of Chicago Press, 1956). Friedman wrote of a surviving tradition at the University of Chicago ". . .in which the quantity theory [of money] was connected and integrated with general price theory and became a flexible and sensitive tool for interpreting movements in aggregate economic activity and for developing relevant policy prescriptions". Milton Friedman, "The Quantity Theory of Money: A Restatement", *ibid.*, p. 52. The emphasis here, in contrast to Hayek, is on aggregate economic activity. The statistical investigation of aggregate economic activity in an attempt to find predictable regularities began with Wesley Clair Mitchell and the founding of the National Bureau of Economic Research where Milton Friedman began his career. On Hayek's relationship to Mitchell, see *Good Money, Part I*, Introduction.

[7]Carl Menger (1840–1921) was the founder of the Austrian school of economics, which traced the source of economic value to the subjective choices of individuals; Ludwig von Mises (1881–1973) directly influenced Hayek through his writing on money and socialism, as well as through personal contact and discussion, most notably in a seminar which gathered together several of the most promising young economists of the period. See F. A. Hayek, *The Fortunes of Liberalism* (1992), Peter G. Klein, ed., being vol. 4 of the Collected

aggregates or theoretical 'functions'. Here the primary influences—those which set macroeconomists apart from their predecessors—included American institutionalists from whom was developed a methodology that depended upon statistical aggregation.[8] It is not easy to characterize Hayek's dislike of the uses made of statistical inferences, but he suffered serious aggravation when what he regarded as particular and necessarily individual economic choices were conflated by mechanical numerical means into the methodological solecism of 'aggregate demand'.[9]

In 1930, Irving Fisher presented a concise justification of the reasoning that permitted him to substitute for the subjective qualities of individual choices the real goods which individuals received; and for this real income its cost in money, which permitted Fisher to construct the statistically contrived indices which are now used to determine the 'value' of money.[10] This reasoning owed as much to the growing 'positivistic' bent

---

Works of F. A. Hayek (Chicago: University of Chicago Press, and London: Routledge), Part One.

Adam Smith (1723–1790) is honored as the founder of classical economics and, with David Hume (1711–1776), is the leading figure in the Scottish enlightenment. Richard Cantillon (c.1680–1734) received belated recognition for his pioneering account of the way money effects changes in an economy. Henry Thornton (1760–1815) came to be regarded as the foremost monetary theorist of the nineteenth century. On Cantillon and Thornton, see F. A. Hayek, *The Trend of Economic Thinking* (1991), W. W. Bartley III, and Stephen Kresge, eds, being vol. 3 of the Collected Works of F. A. Hayek, op. cit.

[8]An overlooked link between Keynes and the American monetarists was John Rogers Commons (1862–1945), who taught at the University of Wisconsin from 1903 to 1945 and was the leading exponent of an institutionalist view of economics, particularly in respect to the role of laws and legal institutions. Hayek was influenced by his view of Federal Reserve policy—see *Good Money, Part I,* chapter 2. According to Robert Skidelsky, Commons was an important if unacknowledged influence on Keynes; Keynes wrote to Commons in 1927 that "there seems to me to be no other economist with whose general way of thinking I feel myself in such general accord". See Robert Skidelsky, *John Maynard Keynes, The Economist as Savior, 1920–1937* (London: Macmillan, and New York: Allen Lane, Penguin Press, 1992), p. 229. Skidelsky observed that "Psychological and institutional *observation* was the foundation of Keynesian economics. . . Keynes always stressed the crucial importance of 'vigilant observation' for successful theory-construction—theory being nothing more, in his view, than a stylised representation of the dominant tendencies of the time, derived from reflection on the salient facts". *Ibid.*, pp. 220–221.

[9]"If, therefore, monetary theory still attempts to establish causal relations between aggregates or general averages, this means that monetary theory lags behind the development of economics in general. In fact, neither aggregates nor averages do act upon one another, and it will never be possible to establish necessary connections of cause and effect between them as we can between individual phenomena, individual prices, etc. . . .". F. A. Hayek, *Prices and Production,* op. cit., pp. 4–5.

[10]"To recapitulate, we have seen that the enjoyment income is a psychological matter, and hence cannot be measured directly. So we look to real income instead; but even real income is a heterogeneous jumble. It includes quarts of milk, visits to the moving picture

of the social sciences, particularly behavioral psychology (which eventually succeeded in transforming hedonistic individuals into calculating 'agents'), as it did to the failure of prior attempts to compare interpersonal utility. Hayek was prepared, as were his fellow proponents of marginal utility theory, to reason in terms of real incomes, but not at a level of aggregation that would deny the very basis of utility. Hayek's monetary theory is, however, directed to exposing the deficiencies in any attempt to make money costs and incomes serve as unqualified surrogates for real income.

The sticking point is that if the distribution of income in any of the three 'modes' is to be equivalent to the distribution of income in the other two, then what is logically true of any one theory of distribution of income must hold for the others. Otherwise, contradictions may arise to the effect that a gain of real income might entail a loss of subjective income, and likewise with money income.

Hayek began his theoretical investigations with an attempt to introduce time and money into a theory of value the formal demonstration of which was based on a simultaneous solution of equations of an indefinite but finite number of 'indifference curves' representing subjective preferences for real goods.[11] The solution to the given set of equations, in which a 'numeraire' is randomly or arbitrarily selected, constitutes equilibrium for the system, and although Hayek does not in his early essay on the subject provide a technical description of such a theory of value it is clear that for his purposes it could not vary in any significant way from the accepted theory of general equilibrium. Given the assumption of simulta-

house, etc., and in that form cannot be measured easily or as a whole. Here is where the cost of living comes in. It is the practical, homogeneous measure of real income. As the cost of living is expressed in terms of dollars it may, therefore, be taken as our best measure of income *in place of* enjoyment income, or real income. Between it and real income there are no important discrepancies as there are between money income and real income. Money income practically never conforms exactly to real income because either savings raise money income above real income, or deficits push money income below real income". Irving Fisher, *The Theory of Interest* (New York: Macmillan, 1930), p. 12. Fisher's methodological bent did not lead him to pose the question whether the non-conformity of money and real income through the possibility of savings or deficits might not be traceable to a non-conformity between real income and the subjective basis of individual choice. The possibility reenters monetary discussion through questions of foresight and risk.

[11] In a letter to W. C. Mitchell, June 3, 1926, Hayek wrote, "It seems to me now as if pure theory had actually neglected in a shameful way the essential differences between a barter economy and a money economy and that especially the existing theory of distribution needs a thorough overhauling as soon as we drop the assumption of barter and pay sufficient regard to *time*". The text of the letter may be found in *Good Money, Part I*, op. cit., Introduction.

neity, one cannot quarrel with the logic of a general equilibrium solution to the problem of how prices are formed; but there cannot therein be introduced any such concept as a price *level,* since in the theory to which Hayek refers, goods are traded simultaneously for goods.[12]

Hayek's first approach to monetary problems was to search for a way to neutralize the effects of supply of and demand for money which were independent of or at odds with the supply and demand for real goods: a concept of 'neutral' money.[13] As it works out, this becomes a strict interpretation of a quantity theory of money, virtually paradoxical in that no change in the supply or demand for money could take place without affecting *relative* prices; that is, it could not be neutralized. His most succinct statement of this view can be found in a letter to John Hicks, written long after his original work on monetary theory and trade cycles, but in response to new questions about that work. He wrote to Hicks that in an economy reacting to an influx of new money

> it seems to me altogether impossible that all prices rise (or fall) at the same time and in the same proportion. But if they change in a certain order of succession, however rapidly the individual changes may follow upon each other, but each as a consequence of another having changed before, it must be true that so long as the process of change lasts the relations between the prices will be different from what it has been before the process of change in the quantity of money has started or will be after it has ceased. This is what already Cantillon and Hume objected [to] in the crude Lockean quantity theory and what seems to me equally to apply to any argument assuming that during a process of inflation or deflation relative prices will continue to be determined by real causes only.[14]

Hayek challenged the automatic application of quantity theories, particularly when embodied in indices of prices, with what we may call the

[12]"From the moment at which the analysis is no longer concerned exclusively with prices which are (presumed to be) simultaneously set, as in the elementary presentations of pure theory, but goes on to a consideration of the monetary economy, with prices which necessarily are set at successive points in time, a problem arises for whose solution it is vain to seek in the existing corpus of economic theory". F. A. Hayek, "Intertemporal Price Equilibrium and Movements in the Value of Money", *Good Money, Part I,* chapter 5, p. 187.

[13]See *Good Money, Part I,* chapter 6.

[14]F. A. Hayek, letter to John Hicks, December 2, 1967. The full text of the letter together with a letter from John Hicks to Hayek is printed in this volume as an addendum to chapter 1. The correspondence was initiated by Hicks when he undertook a reassessment of Hayek's theory of trade cycles, published as "The Hayek Story" in John Hicks, *Critical Essays in Monetary Theory,* op. cit. Most of the correspondence has been preserved in the Hayek archive at the Hoover Institution, Stanford University.

Cantillon effect.[15] His quarrel with quantity theorists is about the path that monetary change must follow from one point of time to a subsequent one.[16] He insisted that conditions of real production, particularly the formation of capital, inhibit an instantaneous and uniform adjustment of prices in response to monetary changes. Here, too, do the Keynesians and monetarists differ, particularly in respect to the rate of interest as a function of real investment.[17]

A careful reader of Hayek's work may note one omission: He does not apply the Cantillon effect to financial assets, such as stocks, bonds, mortgages, etc., the prices of which, given the means for supplying new money and credit to an economy, are likely to be immediately responsive. Applying the Cantillon effect to these prices does not invalidate any of Hayek's conclusions about the effects of purely monetary changes on real economic values; rather it strengthens his claims about disturbing effects of changes in liquidity, the false expansions of an elastic currency.

For a quantity theory of money to have any explanatory content, boundary conditions must be supplied: Initial conditions of the stock variables must be ascertained together with some specification of their price interrelationships within a set period of time. Simply put, the determination of boundary conditions is both a theoretical problem (which all formal treatments of economic variables must specify) and a practical and

[15]Following Mark Blaug: "[T]he Cantillon Effect, which denies 'the homogeneity postulate' by asserting that changes in the price level produced by cash injections vary with the nature of the injection, and that the change in absolute prices is almost always associated with alterations in relative prices". Mark Blaug, *Economic Theory in Retrospect,* 3rd edition (Cambridge: Cambridge University Press, 1978), p. 159.

[16]The strict form of the so-called equation of exchange (MV=PQ), raises the troubling possibility that the advocates of stabilization of the value of money, beginning with Irving Fisher, rested their case on an equation that is unstable. The variable of velocity (of money transactions) is a function of time, that is, a rate or flow. Whereas the combined sum of prices and quantities exchanged may be either a flow, that is, something equivalent to 'national' or 'domestic product' or it may be a stock, a simple aggregation measured at some point in time. The form of the equation does not tell us which is to be the case. In any case, as long as there remains one time-dependent variable, the equation produces the anomaly that it must be true for some given period of time but cannot be found to be true at any one instant of time. In their eagerness to utilize indices of prices to measure changes in the value of money, Fisher and his followers neglected this logical point, which means that the determination of boundary conditions is always arbitrary.

[17]As Skidelsky points out, "Keynes would develop a distinction between interest as the 'price of money' and the 'natural rate' (though he abandoned the term) as the 'price of capital'. Hayek's role in the Keynesian Revolution was thus to force out of him the logical distinction between a money and a 'real exchange' economy". Robert Skidelsky, *John Maynard Keynes, The Economist as Savior, 1920–1937,* op. cit., p. 458. As to how the forcing was done, see F. A. Hayek, *Contra Keynes and Cambridge* (1995), Bruce Caldwell, ed., being vol. 9 of the Collected Works of F. A. Hayek, op. cit.

political problem which markets and governments must confront. It is a problem of considerable complexity, as Hayek noted in a later essay on the topic of complex phenomena:

> What we single out as wholes, or where we draw the 'partition boundary', will be determined by the consideration whether we can thus isolate recurrent patterns of coherent structures of a distinct kind which we do in fact encounter in the world in which we live.[18]

The economist, then, speaks of 'economies' or of 'markets' or 'communities', taking for granted that these abstractions exist in some actual location; terms such as 'region', 'domain', even 'nation' are used without specifying how the boundaries of any space-time location are determined. Yet in the political realm, boundaries become only too specific, to the point where it may be virtually impossible to adopt a model of social and economic behavior that is applicable to a region which is not confined within a national boundary to one which is. The difficulty increases when we must identify regional or national boundaries along with temporal divisions. Eventually, the theorist must bow before history.

Monetary Nationalism

In 1937, Hayek was invited to Geneva to give five lectures "on some subject of distinctly international interest". Published under the title of *Monetary Nationalism and International Stability* (included in this volume as chapter 1), the lectures are in large measure an extension of Hayek's ideas of the 1920s about the methods of monetary control—then generally referred to as 'stabilization'—applied to the difficulties of the international exchange of currencies. These ideas had their roots in a PhD thesis Hayek began, but did not complete, at New York University in 1923–24. The title of the thesis was, "Is the function of money consistent with an artificial stabilization of its purchasing power?" The essays collected in *Good Money, Part I* are largely directed to this topic and are decidedly critical

[18]F. A. Hayek, "The Theory of Complex Phenomena", [1964], reprinted in F. A. Hayek, *Studies in Philosophy, Politics and Economics* (Chicago: University of Chicago Press, and London: Routledge & Kegan Paul, 1967), p. 27. Compare also Nicholas Georgescu-Roegen, "As is natural we should begin with the basic co-ordinates of the analytical representation, its boundary which completely identifies the process—*no boundary, no process*. . . . And it goes without saying that the boundary must have two dimensions, a geographical one and a temporal one, both finite if we wish to use this construction for economic policy". "Time in Economics", in Harald Hagemann and O. F. Hamouda, eds, *The Legacy of Hicks* (London and New York: Routledge, 1994), p. 245.

of theories underlying various proposals for monetary policies directed to the stabilization of some average price and/or wage level.

Hayek defined monetary nationalism as the "doctrine that a country's share in the world's supply of money should *not* be left to be determined by the same principles and the same mechanism as those which determine the relative amounts of money in its different regions or localities".[19] Whatever that mechanism is—he does not provide a description—we are encouraged to draw the conclusion that if stabilization is problematical for a closed system, however its boundaries are determined, it would surely be more problematical when attempted in terms of two or more currencies.

Hayek takes for granted that the benefits of international trade accrue generally; he writes of "sharing in the advantages of the international division of labor".[20] His basic assumption is that "it is clear that changes in the demand for or supply of the goods and services produced in an area may change the value of the share of the world's income which the inhabitants of that area may claim".[21] By 'world's income' (a concept open to challenge by the proponents of monetary nationalism on the grounds that by far the larger component of income cannot under any terms be shifted from region to region), Hayek means real income, the actual goods and services produced and consumed by the world's population. His argument throughout these lectures follows the course of his previous work on monetary theory, that the equivalence of real income and money income (*pace* Fisher) is assymetrical: Changes in real conditions of production, consumption, and saving must determine the values expressed in money wages and prices and that monetary means cannot be used to induce, alter, or compensate for real economic changes. In his earlier argument for 'neutral' money, he held an even stronger position: Any use of money, because of the elasticity of its supply, would distort the structure of relative prices in ways that underlying 'real' conditions would not support. This elasticity of the supply of money comes into the discussion of *Monetary Nationalism* through the mechanism of 'liquidity': the equivalence and convertibility of forms of currencies and credit. He observes that, "It is probably much truer to say that it is the difference between the different kinds of money which are used in any one country, rather than the differences between the moneys used in different countries which constitutes the real difference between different monetary systems".[22]

[19]This volume, chapter 1, p. 41.
[20]This volume, chapter 1, p. 84.
[21]This volume, chapter 1, p. 50.
[22]This volume, chapter 1, p. 45.

By the fifth lecture, Hayek "hope[s] at least to have shown three things: that there is no rational basis for the separate regulation of the quantity of money in a national area which remains a part of a wider economic system; that the belief that by maintaining an independent national currency we can insulate a country against financial shocks originating abroad is largely illusory; and that a system of fluctuating exchanges would on the contrary introduce new and very serious disturbances of international stability".[23]

He made clear at the beginning of his lectures that he would not discuss specific circumstances of the time, excusing himself from any analysis of particular institutions or techniques then proposed or in use. To our great benefit, Hayek's choice left the discussion free to move along purely theoretical lines, remaining as relevant to world monetary conditions at the end of the century as it was in the early years following the breakdown of the gold standard.

He does not foresee the revival of the gold standard; its ideal working is likely to be frustrated—as it was before and after the First World War—by the existence of separate national reserves. These create

> the problems which arise out of the fact that the so-called gold currencies are connected with gold only through the comparatively small national reserves which form the basis of a multiple superstructure of credit money which itself consists of many different layers of different degrees of liquidity or acceptability. It is, as we have seen, this fact which makes the effects of changes in the international flow of money different from merely interlocal shifts, to which is due the existence of separate national monetary systems which to some extent have a life of their own. The homogeneity of the circulating medium of different countries has been destroyed by the growth of separate banking systems organized on national lines. Can anything be done to restore it?[24]

The aim, so Hayek reminds us, "must be to increase the certainty that one form of money will always be readily exchangeable against other forms of money at a known rate, and that such changes should not lead to changes in the total quantity of money".[25] The solution Hayek offers in these lectures is largely an institutional one. "The rational choice would seem to lie between either a system of 'free banking', which not only gives all banks the right of note issue and at the same time makes it necessary for them to rely on their own reserves, but also leaves them free to choose their field of operation and their correspondents without re-

[23]This volume, chapter 1, p. 86.

[24]This volume, chapter 1, pp. 87–88.

[25]This volume, chapter 1, p. 93.

gard to national boundaries, and on the other hand, an international central bank. I need not add that both these ideals seem utterly impracticable in the world as we know it".[26] In the world at the end of the twentieth century, the European community has come to a similar conclusion, but has decided that an international central bank with a uniform currency—the Euro—can be made to work. Hayek, as we shall see, came to believe that no central bank subject to political influence could be relied upon to provide money of constant value. History is on Hayek's side (though we should not risk the solecism of historicism); monetary nationalism, whether mercantilism or the ever-popular 'dirty float' of exchange rates, buttressed with tariffs, subsidies, and capital controls, has been the rule.

Portraits of rulers were not stamped on coins for aesthetic reasons. Control of the currency was and remains as much an imperative for governments as control of borders, and except for those times when governmental authority collapses, borders and currencies have been coextensive. The gold standard was largely a British pound standard, sustained by imperial trade and the skills—and honour—of the City of London. Both were protected by the British navy, and when the navy lost its dominance in the world, the pound gave way to the US dollar. Yet it may be argued that the City of London and the gold standard were the most successful institutions the world has developed for overcoming the resistant difficulties of transmitting goods and capital across the boundaries of states and cultures. One cannot fail to hear in Hayek's writings a sense of betrayal in the collapse of the gold standard and the return of monetary nationalism. He blamed Keynes and his followers; but theirs was the mildest of the forms of national monetary control, based on a justification that even Hayek conceded was respectable, though he disputed it.[27]

The arch nationalist of the interwar period was Hjalmar Schacht of Germany, whose methods have since been adopted by virtually every authoritarian regime.[28] Schacht forced all foreign exchange transactions to be made through the Reichsbank and used his control of foreign exchange and bank reserves to dictate capital investment within Germany.

[26]This volume, chapter 1, p. 88.

[27]"[The argument] must rest, and indeed it does rest, on the assumption that there is a particularly close connection between the prices—and particularly the wages—within the country which causes them to move to a considerable degree up and down together compared with prices outside the country. . . . I regard it as the only argument on which the case for monetary nationalism can be rationally based". F. A. Hayek, this volume, chapter 1, p. 44.

[28]Hjalmar Horace Greeley Schacht (1877–1970) served in the Weimar Republic as Currency Commissioner and President of the Reichsbank from 1924 to 1930. Hayek credits him with ending the German hyperinflation, although parts of the program were in place before Schacht took office. "None of these apologists", Hayek wrote later, "of the inflationary policy was able to propose or apply measures which made it possible to terminate the

What remains of interest in this otherwise discreditable experiment was that by stages he was forced from a policy resembling a pure quantity-of-money approach, based on a fixed gold exchange ratio, to engaging in the *disaggregation* of credit: rationing the supply of foreign exchange to pay debts. Schacht devised various categories of German marks including the *Reisemark* (for travel), the *Registermark* (for investment or export goods), and the *Askimark* (for support of people or causes),[29] thereby illustrating the importance of the Cantillon effect.[30]

One positive achievement came out of the prolonged Schacht campaign to convince the Allied powers that Germany could not pay reparations for the war: the establishment of the Bank for International Settlements. The Committee of Experts on Reparations which met in Paris in 1929 acknowledged that the scale of debts and the size of the claims for reparations could not be met through usual channels without disrupting exchange rates and trade. A bank was organized to accept payment of German reparations in marks, stretched out over a thirty-five year period, with payment to creditors in their own currencies, financed through capital contributions and the issuance of bonds. All participants were required to maintain gold-backed currencies, and the accounts of the bank were to be kept in a stable unit, the gold franc. There were strong expectations at the time that the bank would function as an international clearing bank, working to harmonize monetary and trade policies.[31]

---

inflation, which was finally done by a man who believed in a crude and primitive version of the quantity theory, Hjalmar Schacht". See F. A. Hayek, *New Studies in Philosophy, Politics, Economics and the History of Ideas* (Chicago: University of Chicago Press, and London: Routledge, 1978), p. 198. Schacht began with a firm dedication to the gold standard, but to revive the German economy and to avoid the payment of reparations he later instituted strict exchange and credit controls, believing that productive investment should take precedence over government borrowing and expenditure with the singular exception of military expenditure. Schacht regained the presidency of the Reichsbank in 1933 but was forced out by Hermann Goering in 1937 when he refused to continue financing the Nazi military build-up. See Amos E. Simpson, *Hjalmar Schacht in Perspective* (The Hague: Mouton, 1969).

[29] John Weitz, *Hitler's Banker, Hjalmar Horace Greeley Schacht* (Boston: Little, Brown, 1997), p. 155. Weitz also quotes an apocryphal story: invited by an American banker to come to New York where there was lots of money to see real banking, Schacht replied, "No, come to Berlin. We have no money at all. *That's* real banking". *Ibid.*, p. 207.

[30] In a lead article, *The Economist* pointed out that "in 1923 [Schacht] proclaimed that what is not economically possible cannot be accomplished by any monetary magic. In 1933 it was the other facet of the truth which needed emphasis: that if a thing is economically possible, financial means for carrying it out can be found". The same article also observed that "it is he who has been the chief technician of the Nazi trading methods, whose ingenuity is admired in foreign countries as much as their immorality is reprobated". *The Economist*, January 28, 1939.

[31] Owen D. Young, head of the American delegation to the Committee of Experts on Reparations, regarded the establishment of the Bank for International Settlements as the most important accomplishment of the conference; but the American government would

In most respects the bank would have satisfied the conditions Hayek outlined in his lectures on monetary nationalism for a solution to the liquidity problems of incompatible credit structures in separate nations.[32]

As events turned out, the Bank was woefully undercapitalized and too restricted by political conflict at a critical juncture—primarily by French insistence that Austria not enter into a customs union with Germany—to perform as expected. When the time came to staunch the run stirred by the collapse of the Credit-Anstalt bank in Austria,[33] the Bank's lending capability was too little and too late; as panic spread, the Bank could do little more than save itself, as banks are wont to do in troubled times. The crux of the matter, which no bank ever wants to be the last to face, is that liquidity cannot be attained by all, all at the same time.[34]

To fully appreciate Hayek's later work on monetary theory and policy in its historical context, it might be well to remind ourselves just what is entailed by the predicament that there cannot be an increase of liquidity for a community as a whole. (By 'liquidity' is meant the conversion of any asset, note, debt, inventory, or real estate into cash: that is, the most immediately acceptable form of money; internationally, this means the

---

not permit official participation in the bank, maintaining a stubborn refusal to acknowledge any link between debts and reparations. As one press report stated, "America's large holdings of gold mean that we do not need this bank, so that for the present we shall have none of it, refusing the directorship offered to the Federal Reserve System". (Edwin L. James, *The New York Times*, June 8, 1929, pp. 1–2.) Two years later, America discovered to its dismay that its gold holdings were not large enough to resist a simultaneous internal and external liquidation.

[32]In 1939, Hayek sold to the Bank for International Settlements an extensive collection of rare books pertaining to monetary history and theory.

[33]Too little attention had been paid to the plight of the former Hapsburg empire by the Allied powers; the balance sheet of the Credit-Anstalt in 1930 was as large as the state of Austria's, since the bank had been forced to take over a fair number of weak Austrian banks. Collapse was almost inevitable since many of the 'assets' of the bank were in non-Austrian parts of the former empire and could not be liquidated. Fear of a renewed inflation led to a flight from the Austrian schilling, which spread to Germany and led England to abandon the defense of the pound. The opinion is widely held that the collapse of the Credit-Anstalt triggered the onset of the financial depression of the 1930s as well as the end of the gold standard. See Aurel Schubert, *The Credit-Anstalt Crisis of 1931* (Cambridge: Cambridge University Press, 1991).

[34]As Barry Eichengreen observed, "But with the world supply of monetary gold fixed at a moment in time, not all countries could substitute gold for foreign exchange reserves simultaneously. They were forced to raise central bank discount rates and restrict domestic credit in a desperate effort to acquire gold from one another. Between the ends of 1931 and 1932, the reserve losses of the remaining gold standard countries were double the reserve gains of countries with depreciated currencies". Barry Eichengreen, *Golden Fetters, The Gold Standard and the Great Depression, 1919–1939* (Oxford and New York: Oxford University Press, 1992), p. 291.

most acceptable common currency, which under the gold standard was gold.) For any one person to liquidate an asset, some other person must provide the cash; assuming no new money can be created, it is impossible for everyone to increase liquidity. The belief that what is possible for one must be possible for all is often referred to as the 'fallacy of composition'. Indeed, the statement does take that logical form, but it is not identical: The fallacy of composition is to assume that what is *true* of the part is also true of the whole. The economic predicament that resembles this fallacy is logically weaker, but theoretically more interesting. One of the more important contributions economists can make to our understanding of economic possibilities is to work out the implications of this 'predicament' of composition; it occurs not just in the context of liquidity but in any attempt by individuals to alter or expand or reduce their financial or economic activity.

On the other side of the ledger, as it were, is found the not-unfamiliar possibility that the 'whole' (of some set of economic transactions) may be greater than the sum of its 'parts'; that is, that the net effect of a series of transactions may have consequences greater, or other, than those derived from any single act within the series. These two statements of the formal or logical relationship of parts and wholes are useful in understanding how at least two categories of unintended consequences come about. How it is, so to speak, that no good deed goes unpunished. On a theoretical level, the prospect of the predicament/fallacy of composition presents a serious challenge to any theory of economic equilibrium which relies on *simultaneous* transactions.

In his work on monetary theory and trade cycles, Hayek reaches his conclusions through an analysis of the means by which the parts of the economy—the individual saver, lender, producer, and consumer—find themselves out of equilibrium with the whole—the net effect of decisions to save, invest, and consume. His candidate for the initiating event in the upswing of a trade cycle is the reduction of the monetary rate of interest below the natural rate of interest, a concept which he adapted from Thornton and Wicksell. Credit creation by banks produces the elastic currency which distorts the price relationships within the 'real' economy. But it is not the volume of loans extended by any *one* bank that is the source of the ensuing difficulty. "The main reason for the existing confusion with regard to the creation of deposits is to be found in the lack of any distinction between the possibilities open to a single bank and those open to the banking system as a whole".[35] The consequence of that lending, equivalent to 'forced' saving, is an oversupply of capital goods relative

[35]F. A. Hayek, *Monetary Theory and the Trade Cycle* [1933] (Clifton, N.J.: Augustus M. Kelley, 1975), pp. 152 ff.

to consumer goods, the value of which is lost when the forced saving comes to an end.[36]

This brief explication is little more than a hint of the whole of Hayek's theory; it is mentioned here only to indicate that at bottom he attempted to work out the consequences—we may certainly regard them as unintended—of the predicament of composition. It was his differing conclusions as to the consequences of that predicament that brought him into conflict with Keynes, who approached the same predicament with a very different sense of how the monetary limits to liquidity and production could be managed to allow the 'whole' to become greater than the sum of its parts.[37] Should we not be surprised that their respective analyses were both set in motion by the same event and at least one common assumption?

The event in question was the action of the US Federal Reserve banks to manage an excess of gold reserves following the First World War. Keynes claimed that the United States "buried" the gold—that is, did not let it have its full effect on monetary growth and prices; Hayek disputed this conclusion.[38] The importance of the event lay in their common view that it was not possible to simultaneously stabilize the domestic price level and the foreign exchange rate. At issue was the relative value of the pound and the US dollar, and, as it turned out, the fate of the gold standard.

Hayek believed that his English colleagues, in pressing for a mild form of monetary nationalism, were led astray by a singular event: the return to gold by the British pound in 1925 at prewar parity with the US dollar.

[36]For many critics, the puzzle in Hayek's theory was why an increase in demand for consumers' goods did not lead to an increased demand for producers' goods. But Hayek explained, "The confusion on this point seems to result from a very common mistake—that of applying what is true of a single industry to industry as a whole. While, of course, the relative magnitude of the demand for equipment for a particular industry will depend upon the demand for the product of that industry, it is certainly not true to say that the demand for capital goods in general is directly determined by the magnitude of the demand for consumers' goods". F. A. Hayek, *Prices and Production,* op. cit., p. 143.

[37]Peter Clarke has made this point clearly: "What simple basic conception impressed itself upon Keynes's mind during 1932, allowing him to make sense in a new way of the relation between income and expenditure and between saving and investment? . . .It was the distinction between what was true for the individual and what was true for the community as a whole which constituted that linchpin of the analysis. . . . [I]t identified as fallacious the claim, for example, that because individuals might benefit from cutting wages, everyone could beneficially do so at once: or that because any individual could achieve liquidity of investment, it was possible for the community as a whole. This 'fallacy of composition', however, plays a larger part than has been recognized in the structure of the *General Theory.* It is built into the architecture of the work as a whole". Peter Clarke, *The Keynesian Revolution in the Making 1924–1936* (Oxford: Oxford University Press, 1988), pp. 269–270.

[38]See F. A. Hayek, *Good Money, Part I,* op. cit., chapters 2 and 3.

"In consequence", he wrote "to restore equilibrium, it was necessary to reduce *all* prices and costs in proportion as the value of the pound had been raised. . . . It was not a case where with given exchange rates the national price or cost structure of a country as a whole had got out of equilibrium with the rest of the world, but rather that the change in parities had suddenly upset the relations between all prices inside and outside the country".[39] Implicit in this distinction is the assumption of the assymetrical relation of monetary effects and real causes; "as if", Hayek points out, "there were any reason to expect that as a rule there would arise a necessity that the price and cost structure of one country as a whole should change relatively to that of other countries".[40]

The competitive devaluations of currencies which followed England's departure from gold demonstrated in yet another form the predicament of composition: It is not possible for all currencies at once to be overvalued against each other. All currencies cannot be both overvalued against all other currencies and against the prices of commonly traded commodities. In the 1920s, Keynes insisted that the Federal Reserve policy of 'sterilizing' gold reserves left the dollar undervalued against the pound. In the 1930s, the net effect was that all currencies appeared to be overvalued against gold. How did Britain, and those who had followed her first onto the gold standard and then off, get into this predicament? An answer to that question means going back to John Locke.

There are those who will believe that going back to John Locke at the end of the seventeenth century is going further back than is strictly necessary for an introduction to Hayek's ideas on money. But if the goal is to find a reliable means of providing 'good' money, then we must pay atten-

[39]This volume, chapter 1, p. 67. Hayek's treatment of the return to gold in 1925 and of Keynes's role in the decision is somewhat quizzical. On more than one occasion, Hayek appears to blame Keynes for not being persuasive enough to prevent a return to gold at an overvalued parity with the dollar, and particularly for not using a statement of Ricardo's which, Hayek implies, might have been sufficient to turn the tide. See this volume, chapter 3, p. 127.

[40]This volume, chapter 1, p. 68. In support of this position, Hayek points out in a note that "the propensity of economists in the Anglo-Saxon countries to argue exclusively in terms of national price and wage levels is probably mainly due to the great influence which the writings of Professor Irving Fisher have exercised in these countries. Another typical instance of the dangers of this approach is the well-known controversy about the reparations problem, where it was left to Professor Ohlin to point out against his English opponents that what mainly mattered was not so much effects of total price levels but rather the effects on the position of particular industries". *Ibid.*, p. 69n. Curiously Hayek does not cite Ohlin's major contribution to the theory of international trade: Bertil Ohlin, *International and Interregional Trade* (Cambridge, Mass.: Harvard University Press, 1933).

tion to the problem which Locke confronted and why his argument, which, though successful, led to a remarkable failure.

At the end of the seventeenth century, three factors in England's international payments had left the shilling seriously debased: A large indemnity from Spain paid in silver had raised prices; the East India Company drained silver from England to pay for imports; and the government was forced to pay for military costs on the continent. Because of the debased coinage, the discount on British notes left the government seriously embarrassed. William Lowndes, Secretary of the Treasury, recommended a recoinage of the shilling, but with a silver content 20 per cent less than the old shilling. John Locke countered with an argument to the effect that as the value of a shilling derived from its silver content, and as one ounce of silver must always be equal to another, the shilling could not regain its former value with less silver.[41] Locke's argument carried the day, and the result was deflation, a continued drain of silver, and its eventual replacement by the gold standard.

Locke's argument prevailed largely as a matter of principle, despite its wobbly economics. The importance of the choice made by the British government, to hold to a standard of value in which rents and contracts were agreed to, must not be underestimated. For once, a government elevated principle above expedience in monetary matters, establishing a precedent which later British governments felt compelled to uphold; on the first occasion, after the Napoleonic wars, and once again after the First World War. The happy result in the nineteenth century was to establish London as the financial center of the world; the unhappy result in the twentieth century was to mimic the deflation which followed Locke's recoinage in 1695; by 1931, England left the gold standard and surrendered two centuries of financial dominance.

Locke took for granted the use of silver as a standard of value, established through a social process he referred to as 'consent'. But although silver might be the standard of value, the shilling was the standard of payment in which contracts were drawn, rents were paid, and prices were compared. The shilling was assumed to contain a fixed weight of silver, thus fixing the link between the standard of value and the standard of payment. But over time individual coins could lose much of their silver

[41] Locke had earlier offered a lucid explanation, the first in English, of a quantity theory of the relation of money to prices which recognized the effects of the velocity of circulation. His recoinage proposal failed to take into account the fact that debased coins were circulating at a value higher than their silver content. Hayek wrote a full account of this crucial episode in monetary history, published as chapter 9 of F. A. Hayek, *The Trend of Economic Thinking*, op. cit. On John Locke (1632–1704) see Karen I. Vaughn, *John Locke: Economist and Social Scientist* (Chicago: University of Chicago Press, 1980).

content, thus producing the 'bad' money which would continue to circulate while the 'good' money would be withdrawn into more profitable uses elsewhere.

Locke's argument stopped short of the real problem: How is the treasury to determine what is the proper weight of silver for each shilling when the total number of possible shillings relative to the total amount of silver available is not known? Any miscalculation on this point would lead to a shift in either exports or imports of silver (and the exports would be in the form of shillings) and a consequent rise or fall in prices. This difficulty, which for convenience we may refer to as *Locke's problem,* is the dilemma for all monetary standards and monetary policy; it is particularly troubling when it comes to finding exchange ratios for currencies which do not have a common standard.

Locke wished to restore an historical ratio of silver to shillings which was no longer appropriate to England's circumstances. In particular, the East India Company found it profitable to import goods from India which it paid for with silver; the Indians preferred the silver to anything else England could offer.

The drain of precious metals to the East was a constant problem for Europe. As Alfred Crosby notes, "Western Europe did not have great deposits of easily mined gold and silver, and therefore, when it took the hook of a cash economy, did not have enough precious metal of its own for its economy to function efficiently. The West suffered from a chronic balance-of-payments problem until some time in the sixteenth century. Specie flowed from Northern Europe to the Mediterranean ports and thence to trading partners in the East. In the 1420s, Venice exported something like fifty thousand ducats a year to Syria alone. The flow of gold eastward was so steady and lasted for so long that the Spanish had a special name for it: *evacuacion de oro*".[42]

The first great windfall of silver and gold from the New World and the continuous outflow of precious metals to the East served as the beginning and end points of Europe's monetary development, the economic reality with which theoretical discussion contended; starting with Hume's and Cantillon's descriptions of the 'quickening' of trade from an influx of new money, to the dispute between the Currency and Banking schools over the issue of bank notes.[43]

[42]Alfred W. Crosby, *The Measure of Reality: Quantification and Western Society, 1250–1600* (Cambridge: Cambridge University Press, 1997), p. 73.

[43]Hayek observed, "In his 1844 publication, [Thomas] Tooke had already argued that the movement of precious metals between two countries did not necessarily affect the actual quantity of money in ciculation even under a purely metallic currency, since imported and exported metals were usually drawn from reserves rather than from circulating metal. In

Keynes had India in mind when he blamed 'liquidity preference' for disappointing the profit expectations of entrepreneurs (read 'traders', prior to the industrial revolution). After Europe had squandered its money in the First World War—all that pirated gold returned to the New World—Keynes regarded the prudence of the US Federal Reserve in respect to its uncertain reserves as the equivalent of hoarding. Hayek, on the other hand, believed that eventually the gold would burn a hole in the Federal Reserve's pocket, and Hume's specie-flow movement would have its effect; as a purely monetary phenomenon, it would be self-reversing. In the event, Hjalmar Schacht devised the means to finance the Nazis in Germany, and the question became moot. The rest of the world had once again to find the means to pay for war, embracing the very techniques they had so deplored when Schacht made use of them.

A Commodity Reserve Currency

Hayek and Keynes agreed about a means for Britain to pay for war, a method of utilizing individual savings which would avoid the more draconian forms of rationing and price control, but they did not concur over how to fund the debts incurred; that is, the return of savings to individuals.[44] At bottom lurked the fear of another depression and their differing views of the link between national monetary policies and international exchange rates. The government did not take their advice. By 1943, it was possible to think about what shape an international order would assume after the war. Hayek put forward the concept of a new reserve currency, which could be adopted internationally, the basic unit of which would be redeemable in a fixed combination of warehouse warrants for a quantity of storable commodities.[45]

Keynes published Hayek's article, "A Commodity Reserve Currency", in the *Economic Journal* and added a short note by way of comment, "The Objective of International Price Stability". This note elicited letters from

[John] Fullarton's work, this view was elaborated into his notorious theory of hoards, which functions as a regular 'deus ex machina' in his struggle against the quantity of money. The hoards presumably sop up excess quantities of money and release them again into circulation when demand for money increases. Fullarton's peculiar theory probably stemmed from his banking experiences in India, whose population has always been inclined to put aside large stores of precious metals for times of emergency and to return them to circulation after bad harvests, etc.". F. A. Hayek, *The Trend of Economic Thinking,* op. cit., pp. 240–241.

[44] Hayek's reviews of Keynes's proposal are printed in *Socialism and War* (1997), Bruce Caldwell, ed., being vol. 10 of the *Collected Works of F. A. Hayek,* op. cit.

[45] Hayek's proposal was derived from two books sent to him by Jacob Viner: Benjamin Graham, *Storage and Stability* (New York: McGraw-Hill, 1937), and Frank D. Graham, *Social Goals and Economic Institutions* (Princeton: Princeton University Press, 1942).

both Benjamin Graham and Frank Graham, the latter of which was printed in the *Economic Journal,* together with a brief reply from Keynes.[46]

In light of the international monetary arrangments which fell (or were pushed) into place after the war, Hayek's presentation of the two Grahams' commodity reserve proposal and the discussion it provoked might seem to warrant little more than polite acknowledgment, a minor footnote in the annals of monetary alchemy.[47] In form, the proposal was entirely too reasonable; politically, it was clearly not an idea whose time had come. However, considering where the world is now—floating currencies and an International Monetary Fund which seems to function as some sort of amalgam of stern governess and tooth fairy—it is worth taking a closer look at some of the implications of the commodity reserve currency proposal, and Keynes's response to it.

By 1943, Keynes was preoccupied with the precariousness of Britain's finances; he knew better than anyone, having managed day-to-day currency balances for the Treasury during the First World War, that Britain was dependent on the United States.[48] His first priority was to keep the cost of that dependency as low as possible. Thus his demurrer in his letter to Benjamin Graham, that it was a mistake for him to comment on Graham's proposal since he was not free to publish the more detailed work he was doing on the subject 'behind the scenes'.

He did not, then, address the specific merits or weaknesses of Hayek's proposal but simply criticized the substitution of stored commodities for a gold reserve as a new attempt to impose fixed exchange rates on national

[46]F. A. Hayek, "A Commodity Reserve Currency", *Economic Journal,* June–September, 1943, vol. 53, no. 210; printed this volume, chapter 2. J. M. Keynes, "The Objective of International Price Stability", *Economic Journal,* June–September, 1943, vol. 53, no. 210; reprinted in J. M. Keynes, *The Collected Writings of John Maynard Keynes,* Donald Moggridge, ed. (Cambridge: Cambridge University Press and Macmillan for the Royal Economic Society, 1971–1989), vol. 26, *Activities, 1941–1946: Shaping the Post-War World, Bretton Woods, and Reparations* (1980), pp. 30–33. Keynes's letters to Frank Graham and Benjamin Graham, dated December 31, 1943, are reprinted in *Ibid.,* pp. 34–38. Frank Graham's response was printed as "Keynes vs. Hayek on a Commodity Reserve Currency", *Economic Journal,* December 1944, pp. 422–429, together with a brief note by Keynes.

[47]Hayek's article "A Commodity Reserve Currency", together with excerpts of works by Frank D. Graham and Benjamin Graham, was submitted by the (US) Committee for Economic Stability (under the auspices of the Social Science Research Council) to the International Monetary and Financial Conference at Bretton Woods, New Hampshire, in 1944. The proposal did not receive the attention it deserved.

[48]Keynes later wrote that "[i]n the last war, the greatest bone of contention arose out of the fact that, in effect through the pegged dollar rate for sterling, we were using our credits from the American Treasury to support the value of sterling throughout the world". J. M. Keynes, "Operations on Other Fronts—February to June 1940", in vol. 22, *Activities 1939–1945: Internal War Finance* (1978), *The Collected Writings of John Maynard Keynes,* op. cit., p. 171.

economies. What Keynes wanted—and his own scheme for a Clearing Union would be a way for Britain to run a massive overdraft against the United States—was an international currency scheme which would "prevent not only those evils which result from a chronic shortage of international money due to the draining of gold into creditor countries but also those which follow from countries failing to maintain stability of domestic efficiency costs and moving out of step with one another in their national wage policies without having at their disposal any means of orderly adjustment".[49] There is something cavalier in the implication that creditor countries should not be entitled to payment ("draining of gold into creditor countries"—it's that burying of the gold again). Time and patience do not permit us to sort out the implications of Keynes's notion of "efficiency", even though his rejection of a commodity reserve currency hinged on it; "each national price level is primarily determined by the relation of the national wage level to the national efficiency".[50] But whatever it is, it could only be determined by the relation of the wage to the price of the product of the labour, and if that product is traded internationally, it is hard to see how *national* efficiency could produce anything but a comparative advantage or disadvantage. The great merit of the commodity reserve proposal is that it would tend to stabilize the prices of basic commodities; Keynes evidently feared that it would stabilize prices *below* the level at which British labour was fixed. Thus he overlooked the value of the proposal as a counter-cyclical means of reducing fluctuations in employment which stemmed from the over-production of commodities and their subsequent liquidation. Hayek was certainly attracted to the proposal for that very possibility: "Instead of a rise in prices and a consequent increase in output as demand increased, and *pari passu* with the return into circulation of the accumulated money hoards, raw commodities would be released from the stocks and the money received for them impounded. The savings made by individuals in the form of cash during the slack period would not have run to waste but would be waiting in the form of raw commodities ready to be used".[51] To a surprising degree, a commodity reserve currency would eliminate most of the causes of the trade cycle which Hayek had analyzed in his earlier work.[52]

[49] J. M. Keynes, "The Objective of International Price Stability", op. cit., p. 32.

[50] *Ibid.*, p. 31.

[51] F. A. Hayek, this volume, chapter 2, p. 112.

[52] Some corroboration of this view is found in Hayek's early work on theories of 'stabilization' and US monetary policy. (See *Good Money, Part I,* chapters 1 and 2.) The key role was played by the New York call money market in which country banks lent their reserves between crops. In surplus years, this lowered the money rate of interest which led to over-

The more surprising hypothesis which emerges from this possibility—that it was the connection of gold reserves to credit for commodity production that was the perpetrator of the trade cycle—is that the First World War simply accelerated a trend that was already at work in the world economy, connected with the evolution of transportation from steam and horsepower to petroleum-driven engines. Consider the implications of the anguished cry of Richard III: "a horse, a horse, my kingdom for a horse". To put it in the pedestrian terms of supply and demand: if wishes were horses, then beggars would ride; the point being, what does it take to supply a horse. What it takes is time, and the number of horses (the amount of horsepower) the world could command for any period of time is limited by the breeding cycle of horses. This cycle set a fundamental limit to growth for the world economy for any period of time; industrialization, and particularly the invention of the internal combustion engine and motor vehicles, removed that limit. This had a dramatic effect on the production of coal, oil, and grain. The demand for grain for animal feed fell, the demand for coal began to drop, and the demand for oil surged.[53] The secular trends of changes in economic values involved in this shift meant that the cost of adaptation for Britain was higher than for the United States, which could bring unused land and resources into production rather than have to shift from present use to new use. The cost differential over which Keynes temporized was opportunity cost.

The attractiveness of a commodity reserve currency is that it provides a physical link between real income and the money used to measure it. The problem is not in the way such a reserve would function to stabilize

---

investment; when the country banks called back their money and interest rates rose to protect reserves, the result was the loss of earlier investment, the so-called 'forced savings'. It was possible to construct indices which demonstrated a direct link between gold prices and commodity prices. See George F. Warren and Frank A. Pearson, *Gold and Prices* (New York: John Wiley & Sons, and London: Chapman & Hall, 1935). Perhaps Jevons and H. L. Moore, who claimed that the trade cycle was caused by cycles in agricultural production due to weather changes were not so wrong. Whatever the link, since the 1930s, governments have been unable to let agriculture fend for itself in a free world market.

[53]The trade figures for the United States for 1923–1924 (at the end of the period during which Keynes believed the United States was burying gold) are revealing. According to the Federal Reserve Bulletin for June 1924, the largest single trade deficit for any one country was with the Straits Settlements, largely for the import of rubber. See also a recent chart for coal production in Britain, which shows that production peaked in 1913 with 290,000,000 tons and is now reduced to approximately 49,000,000 (*The Economist*, December 20, 1997, p. 78). Denis O'Brien reminds the editor that in 1947 the Labour government of Britain forced the introduction of tractors, which led to the wholesale slaughter of farm horses.

commodity prices but in determining which commodities should be included in the reserve in what proportion and at what initial price and quantity.

In an extended critical review of the proposal written in 1951, Milton Friedman argued that a commodity reserve currency could not stabilize prices because the technical difficulties of managing the reserve could not be overcome and the ensuing cost of maintaining the reserve would be unacceptable, because it would be greater than the gains from the counter-cyclical benefits of the reserve. However, the technical difficulties—having mostly to do with the different rates of technological productivity for the separate commodities which compose the currency 'unit' and with short-term variations in agricultural production—are the same for the use of any index-based measurement of value.[54]

The weakness of the commodity reserve currency proposal is its measure of uncertainty for the *relative* prices of the individual commodities which comprise the stored 'unit'. As outlined by its proponents, stability of the price of the unit requires offsetting price changes among the individual components. Locke's problem finds no solution in this remedy, if the cost of stability of prices is disequilibrium in one or another commodity markets. A possible remedy which was not considered by either proponents or critics (no doubt because it may have undesirable effects of its own) would be to fix the ratio of the components of the unit not by quantity but by value; the percentage of the whole allotted to each commodity would be fixed by the value of the commodity as expressed by quantity × price, in proportion to its value in the economy as a whole. Changes in the price of any one commodity would lead first to changes in the quantities of that commodity offered for or withdrawn from storage; only when conditions were such that quantity adjustments of individual commodities sufficient to retain a fixed value in proportion to the whole could not prevent a price change for the whole unit would the money supply be affected. Depending on how successfully the initial composition of the unit reflected supply and demand equilibrium in the whole economy, an

[54]"A currency unit fixed in composition would no longer appropriately represent total output; the fraction of the output devoted to monetary use would vary from commodity to commodity so that technological change could have differential effects on the currency unit; and the elasticity of current supply would be reduced. In view of the small fraction of the current output of each product that would have to be devoted to monetary use, none of these effects would be serious until a very considerable period had elapsed. What they illustrate is simply the impossibility of a complete solution of the index-number problem". Milton Friedman, "Commodity-Reserve Currency" [1951], in *Essays in Positive Economics* (Chicago: University of Chicago Press, 1953), p. 214.

allocation of components within the unit in proportion to value might well approximate a state of monetary neutrality.

Even this modification could not protect the scheme from unforeseen change if an economic change were large enough and prolonged enough—such as the substitution of oil for coal and wheat—to circulate currency without adequate reserves or to leave commodities in storage in permanent surplus. It is the uncertainty of the future which ultimately renders Locke's problem insoluble. For as Hayek says, "Yet there are times when the desire of individuals to put themselves in a more liquid position expresses a real social need. There will always be periods in which increased uncertainty about the future will make it desirable that a larger portion of our assets should be given forms in which they can be readily converted to the needs of what are still unpredictable circumstances".[55]

"The importance of money", Keynes declared, "essentially flows from its being a link between the present and the future".[56] But liquidity, as John Hicks observed, "is not a property of a single choice; it is a matter of a sequence of choices, a related sequence. It is concerned with the passage from the known to the unknown—with the knowledge that if we wait we can have more knowledge".[57] Money, so we may suppose, evolved as the commodity of choice to take with us to the border between the known and the unknown.

Denationalization of Money

The commodity reserve currency proposal did not lack antecedents, the nearest of which, both in time and intent, was the Sub-Treasury Plan in America (named with deliberate association to the US Independent Trea-

[55] F. A. Hayek, this volume, chapter 2, p. 108.

[56] But Keynes also believed that "it is by reason of the existence of durable equipment that the economic future is linked to the present". For durable equipment, substitute storable commodities, and we may find that the commodity reserve proposal is a plausible method of linking both commodities and money in the same future, which could minimize the effects of liquidity that Keynes inveighed against: "Of the maxims of orthodox finance none, surely, is more anti-social than the fetish of liquidity, the doctrine that it is a positive virtue on the part of investment institutions to concentrate their resources upon the holding of 'liquid' securities. It forgets that there is no such thing as liquidity of investment for the community as a whole. The social object of skilled investment should be to defeat the dark forces of time and ignorance which envelop our future". J. M. Keynes, *The General Theory of Employment, Interest, and Money* [1936], reprinted as vol. 7 (1973) of *The Collecting Writings of John Maynard Keynes*, op. cit., pp. 146, 155, 293.

[57] John Hicks, *The Crisis in Keynesian Economics* (Oxford: Basil Blackwell, 1974), pp. 38–39.

sury System in use from 1846 to 1921), put together by the National Farmers Alliance and other populist groups in 1889.[58] Commodity prices had suffered a steady decline from the 1870s on, as world gold production failed to keep pace with economic growth, particularly in the United States. The extension of railroads had brought new land into production; in the South, land was largely farmed by tenants: Credit—the deplorable share-cropping system—replaced the fertility of land as the determinant of marginal productivity. Owing to their widespread indebtedness, farmers were forced to sell their crops at harvest, each driving down the price for the others. The Sub-Treasury scheme proposed to offer loans to farmers upon deposit of grain and cotton for storage; warehouse certifcates were negotiable but had to be redeemed within one year.

Its advocates failed to persuade the government to fund the plan, largely because their calculations of its cost and its inflationary potential were wildly unrealistic. But the plan brought to the surface the populist American distrust of bankers, gold, and foreign powers. Although political agitation for cheap money died down after the increase of gold production in the 1890s, the distrust remained, to surface in the isolationist positions of the 1920s (the refusal to allow official government participation in the Bank for International Settlements, for example) and the convolutions of the 1930s, most fatefully in the confiscation of monetary gold by the government in 1934, the prohibition of "gold clauses" in contracts, and the quixotic scheme for raising commodity prices by raising the price of gold. By its daily purchases in the gold market, the US Treasury outbid the rest of the world for all gold offered for sale; the price of gold rose, the dollar was devalued, the Treasury booked a two-billion-dollar gain on the confiscated gold, commodity prices did not rise, and even with a newly fixed price, the United States continued to acquire most of the gold offered for sale in the world, which anchored the domestic currency out of sheer weight, for which no dollars, except those held by foreigners, would ever be redeemed.

One might well wonder what the bumpkins thought they got for surrendering their gold. What they got was something they believed gold would not buy: protection against the skulduggery of bankers and railroads and the vagaries of time and weather. The government offered insurance; for bank deposits, for crops, for old age, for unemployment, and so on. Giving up privately owned monetary gold in exchange for government-provided insurance was not as irrational then as it may seem

[58]See William P. Yohe, "An Economic Appraisal of the Sub-Treasury Plan", published as an Appendix in Lawrence Goodwyn, *Democratic Promise, The Populist Moment in America* (New York: Oxford University Press, 1976).

later on. There is a statistical reality behind the choice, the 'Law of Large Numbers'.[59]

It operates in two dimensions in financial arrangements; the first is the familiar principle at work in all insurance coverage, to distribute a risk of loss over a sufficiently large number of possibilities in order to lessen the probability of any one loss exceeding the return from the remainder. The second dimension is the 'netting out' of any series of obligations, offsetting the balance from any one exchange within a series or group against the other balances within the same group. It is the first aspect of the law of large numbers which banks use to minimize their loss from loans; it is the second which banks use to conserve their reserves against withdrawal of deposits.

What makes a risk of any unwanted occurrence other than a random possibility is the determination of boundary conditions, the specification of a location and a time frame in which one either does or does not want something to occur. Boundary conditions enable us to assess the probability of risks; the organization of institutions enables us to extend or transcend boundaries of time and place to redistribute the hazards of various risks. A simple point needs to be emphasized: Banks and insurance companies earn their keep by reducing potential losses to individuals in a way that individuals themselves cannot. But the risk of loss—from catastrophe, folly, deceit, or depredation—remains; banks, or governments, minimize the cost of risk to the individual, but they do not eliminate the cost of risk overall. In the end, the loss must be paid for. When governments provide explicit or implicit guarantees to bank depositors for the security of their deposits, the cost of losses from bad risks is redistributed. This raises the possibility of what is called 'moral hazard': Free of responsibility for the safety of individual deposits, bankers may take greater investment risks with these deposits to increase their own profits. The greater hazard is that when governments are forced to make good on all the guarantees offered to the citizenry, governments will simply print money to do so.

We then have to contend with the passage from one boundary to another where no government can enforce jurisdiction. The piper is always paid; the question is how, and in what currency. In 1976, as inflation seemed endemic, Hayek faced the question head-on. In what is certainly the most daring monetary proposal of his career, he called for governments to surrender their monopoly of money and allow whatever money people choose to accept to circulate however and wherever it listeth. This

[59]John Hicks has noted the importance of the 'Law of Large Numbers' for the development of banking and insurance, which in turn were crucial to the evolution of trade. See John Hicks, *A Theory of Economic History* (Oxford: Oxford University Press, 1969), p. 79.

would mean that a single currency could be used in more than one country, and that more than one currency could circulate in any one country.

The scheme is not, as some would have it, utopian; rather, it is at the other end of the scale, hyper-realistic, in the manner of the child who pointed out that the emperor had no clothes. If governments were to follow Hayek's recommendation to put no impediment in the way of privately issued currencies, they would have to forego taxing the issuance of currency whether from domestic or foreign sources; the fiercely defended privilege of 'seigniorage' would be surrendered; the printing press would be shut down, and with it all pretense that governments possess resources other than those provided by their citizens. It would then be obvious that the insurance against risks that the Americans in 1934—and the rest of the world after 1973—accepted in exchange for gold was simply a grandiose scheme of self-insurance where all the profits went to the managers of the 'company'.

Hayek's proposal assumes that *competition* in the issuance of currencies will produce what governments cannot: good money. In a market free of taxes and tariffs and subsidies, would not people choose money which is stable in value as long as it were not subject to some sort of default on the part of the issuing agency? Still, there is a thorny question of what standard would be used to determine stability of value. (Hayek proposes an index of widely traded basic or raw commodities.[60]) Also to be considered are what are now called 'network effects', the advantage to individuals that come from being linked to others in a common system, such as a telephone network. The primary advantage of money over barter is to reduce the cost of time and effort of locating a suitable trading opportunity. There are those who would argue that using multiple currencies is a step backward towards barter, increasing the cost of discovering the merit of any exchange. People accept money which is acceptable. Money is a medium like language; it matters how many people can communicate in that language. It matters less that they speak it well, than that they can communicate at all.

Whether people would prefer a money of constant value but limited acceptability, or the reverse, would seem to be an empirical matter.[61]

[60]Hayek did not regard such an index as the only or even the best standard the market might turn to. In conversations with the editor, he envisioned other possibilities, such as a mix of commodities and currencies; he also entertained the possibility that the issuing agency might not be a traditional bank, but perhaps one of the large issuers of credit cards, where a new currency would come about as a means of guaranteeing forward rates of exchange between national currencies.

[61]Hayek reminds us: "For what follows it will be important to keep in mind that different kinds of money can differ from one another in two distinct although not wholly unrelated

These are complex issues, perhaps not amenable to a theoretical determination.

The concept of competing currencies does, however, force us to revise our understanding of the 'quantity' theory of money. As Hayek points out: "But if the different currencies in circulation within a region have no constant relative value, the aggregate amount in circulation can only be derived from the relative value of the currencies and has no meaning apart from it. . . . [T]here are always significant differences in the demand for different forms of money and money substitutes of varying degrees of liquidity".[62] We can demonstrate that in respect of a quantity theory of the relation of money to prices there is no difference in theory between an arrangement where currencies do not trade in different locations and where more than one currency trades in a single location, as long as in the first case there is at least one commodity which trades in both locations and as long as currencies are freely convertible. The possibility of flexible exchange rates together with a variable price for a common commodity means that no change in the supply of any one currency could produce a determinate change in either the exchange rate or the price of the commodity.[63] We are led inexorably back to the dilemma which Hayek identified in 1923 and of which *The Economist* does not tire of reminding us: monetary policy cannot simultaneously stabilize domestic prices and foreign exchange rates.[64]

---

dimensions: acceptability (or liquidity) and the expected behaviour (stability or variability) of its value. The expectation of stability will evidently affect the liquidity of a particular kind of money, but it may be that in the short run liquidity may sometimes be more important than stability, or that the acceptability of a more stable money may for some reason be confined to rather limited circles". This volume, chapter 4, p. 163.

[62]This volume, chapter 4, p. 180. In his 1937 lectures, Hayek observed that "changes in liquidity preference as between different kinds of money are probably a much more potent cause of disturbances than the changes in preference for holding money *in general* and holding goods *in general*. . . ". This volume, chapter 1, p. 90.

[63]As Hayek observes, "It remains true, however, that so long as good and bad currencies circulate side by side, the individual cannot wholly protect himself from the harmful effects of the bad currencies by using only the good ones in his own transactions. Since the relative prices of the different commodities must be the same in terms of the different concurrent currencies, the user of a stable currency cannot escape the effects of the distortion of the price structure by the inflation (or deflation) of a widely used competing currency". This volume, chapter 4, p. 191.

[64]"Today's global capital market only rules out sooner what has always been impossible in the longer term—namely, treating interest rates and the value of the currency as entirely separate instruments matters. Globalisation has not altered the basic limits: monetary policy can be used to regulate the domestic economy or to regulate the exchange rate, but it cannot successfully accomplish both goals at once". *The Economist*, December 6, 1997, p. 89.

Hayek would not want to deny that the problem to be solved (providing money of stable value) and the means for doing it (expanding or contracting notes and loans) is the same for a central bank or a private bank granted a similar opportunity. The position of the central bank of, say, Singapore is not unlike the position of a private issuer of currency in Hayek's proposal. The difference is whether competition between currencies within a given location would be a more effective spur to good money than the self-imposed restraint of a national monopolist who dare not ignore the rate of foreign exchange. In the end this would seem to be an empirical question; the members of the European monetary union have chosen to subordinate national monopolies to a new monopoly over all members. They will now have to find out what happens to the prices of commonly traded goods and services. There is, however, one important difference between a national monopoly of money and a denationalized currency which may prove all-important. Currencies which compete for acceptance across national boundaries must necessarily alter or extend, and possibly even eliminate altogether, the boundaries which separate financial markets.

Any currency-issuing agency which hopes to stay in business by maintaining a stable value for its currency can only do so through the ability to quickly expand or contract its assets to match changes in its outstanding liabilities (which is the currency it is providing).[65] The old bugbears of the seasonal flow of funds, changes in the flow of trade, natural or man-made disasters—all of these must be managed on the money market, which means that someone else must accept the agency's asset as a liability.[66] Just as the market for commodities is not confined to any one nation, money markets which must exchange currencies cannot be bounded by geographical or political limits, as we now know from the many abject failures that have followed Hjalmar Schacht's. We may argue that what success there has been in providing good money can be traced to the efficiency of a particular money market: London in the nineteenth century, New York after the Second World War. Failures may be found in the restric-

[65] As Hayek cautions: "The dealings of an issue bank in other currencies would therefore never be a purely mechanical affair (buying and selling at constant prices) guided only by observed changes in the purchasing power of the other currencies; nor could such a bank undertake to buy any other currency at a rate corresponding to its current buying power over the standard batch of commodities; but it would require a good deal of judgement effectively to defend the short-run stability of one's own currency, and the business will have to be guided in some measure by prediction of the future development of the value of other currencies". This volume, chapter 4, p. 170.

[66] If governments could ever lose their mercantilist leanings, they could offer to money markets secure instruments, with debt denominated in a currency not of their own making. The liquidity provided by government debt is perennially useful in managing the statistical possibility of the predicament of composition.

tions placed on markets by inept or grasping governments: for example, the present conduct of the Japanese Ministry of Finance; the weird conjunction of American and Soviet maneuverings around and about the time of the Vietnam War, and the behaviour of the French in virtually any crisis one cares to name.[67]

The dependence of central banks on money markets became indissoluble when the dollar was no longer redeemable for gold at a fixed price. Milton Gilbert pointed to the key difference, that "gold was the only asset that was not matched by a liability, whereas dollar assets had to have their counterpart in liabilities of either a borrower in the money market or a bank".[68] In this manner, by first forbidding the redemption of its money into gold by its own citizens and then refusing redemption to foreign holders of dollars, unthinkable to earlier generations, the Americans, with the complicity of other government treasuries, put paid to Locke's problem. As long as anyone is willing to accept dollar-denominated liabilities as assets, the process may continue without limit, and we need not trouble ourselves about quantity. All that remains in this system of accounting is what used to be thought of as 'velocity'. It is precisely here that the Cantillon effect remains in the picture. To the degree that markets are imperfectly linked, price adjustments will be disproportionate to changes in the supply of money and credit.[69]

[67]The story of the rise and fall of the world's monetary system since the Second World War, if not well known, is at least well reported. Two episodes deserved more publicity. The first is how the Soviet Union began the process of denationalizing money by moving their dollar accounts from the United States to London, thereby starting the eurocurrency market which eventually drove the United States off the gold standard (in 1973), as the amount of dollars abroad grew beyond redemption. The multiplication of world reserves rose precipitously from the actions of central banks who deposited dollars with the Bank For International Settlements which in turn invested them in the eurodollar market from whence they ended up back in the reserves of central banks. In response, Paul Volcker, then US Treasury Undersecretary, produced a plan which neatly captured folk wisdom, that what goes around comes around. The Volcker plan attempted to distribute some of the pain of balance of payments adjustment to the creditor countries, and in this, as Robert Solomon points out, it "bore a striking resemblance to the Keynes plan of 1943. . . . [I]n this case, those who forgot history managed to reconstruct it. The concerns of the United States in the early 1970s were in many ways like those Keynes tried to cope with in the early 1940s". See Robert Solomon, *The International Monetary System, 1945–1981* (New York: Harper & Row, 1982), p. 242. On the US government resistance to facing its predicament, particularly its stubborn refusal to raise the dollar price of gold, see Milton Gilbert, *Quest for World Monetary Order* (New York: John Wiley, 1980). See also Leland Yeager, *International Monetary Relations: Theory, History, and Policy*, 2nd edition (New York: Harper & Row, 1976).

[68]Milton Gilbert, *Quest for World Monetary Order*, op. cit., p. 31.

[69]A new model to account for how the system works has been put forward by Richard A. Werner: "The new approach suggests (1) to replace the standard definition of the money supply as deposits with a definition based on credit creation; (2) that the standard 'quantity theory of money' is a special case of a more general disaggregated quantity theorem, which

The world has changed in the twenty-odd years since Hayek wrote *Denationalization of Money:* The costly failures of socialism have revived a belief in the efficacy of markets; nationalistic enterprises buttressed by trade and capital controls have had to make way for competition; even monetary policy has had to accommodate market forces. Except for the United States, much of the world has had to accept some denationalization of currencies where fluctuating exchange rates reduce much of the control of national money monopolies. This is a world of uncharted depths and currents; as Hayek pointed out in 1937, "changes in liquidity preference as between different kinds of money are probably a much more potent cause of disturbances than the changes in the preference for holding money *in general* and holding goods *in general*. . .".[70] We may extend the notion of different kinds of money to include different currencies; certainly currency trading now makes up a considerable portion of bank income. In the present world of floating exchange rates, commodity prices across boundaries have tended to be more stable than currencies whose fluctuations have become a major source of disturbance to international equilibrium.

In what sense can we conceive of a price *level* in this environment? Hayek did not work out all the reciprocal implications of the possibility of competing currencies for a price level as a measure of the stability of the value of money. A yen-based index of prices, for example, is useless for measuring any change in a price level measured in dollars, since any change in the exchange rate of dollars and yen will, owing to the Cantillon effect, alter relative prices before it will effect the general price level. Such an effect on relative prices would also be likely with changes in exchange rates of competing currencies.

There is also a change in the way prices are now being set in markets which is made possible by electronic commerce and the information available on the Internet. Prices for standard commodities and even branded or rare items can now be set in several inventive ways of matching buyers and sellers in electronic auctions or offers of spot (time-limited) pricing. This sort of development, where prices may vary from moment to moment, will make price indices impossible to compile and useless as a guide to measuring changes in the value of money.

---

distinguishes between credit creation used for 'real' and 'financial' transactions; a sudden rise of the latter may be induced by banks, which results in asset price bubbles; and (3) that excess credit creation entering the 'financial circulation' is likely to spill over abroad as foreign investment and hence determine capital flows". Richard A. Werner, "Towards a New Monetary Paradigm: A Quantity Theorem of Disaggregated Credit, with Evidence from Japan", *Kredit und Kapital,* vol. 30, no. 2, 1997, pp. 276–308.

[70]This volume, chapter 1, p. 90.

The issuer of a denationalized (that is, used across national boundaries) currency could offer the holder of that currency some stability in the face of risks other than general or indexed price changes. For the individual, the risk from inflation or deflation does not come from the general rise or fall of prices, but from the possibility of a disparity between his or her own costs and income. If the issuer of a private currency, through portfolio balancing of probable risks spread over large numbers, succeeded in protecting the individual enterprise against adverse changes in its own position, it might well discover the means to establish its currency. The burden of opportunity cost for the individual would then be shared with the currency-issuing agency, which could distribute risk across any number of boundaries.[71]

In advancing such a radical proposal as the denationalization of money, which would require changes in many existing institutions, Hayek has been accused of a kind of covert 'constructivism'.[72] There is some truth to this criticism, but it is by no means the whole truth of the matter. Hayek has recalled that he first became aware of the social disposition he termed 'constructivism' in a lecture by W. C. Mitchell, who certainly did feel that such an approach was the most positive one to adopt in the face of economic difficulties: "The most hopeful sign in our dealings with the economic difficulties of 1920–21 is that many men in public and in private stations have taken the constructive attitude, considering the future as well as the present, thinking about prevention as well as cure". The passage from Mitchell to which Hayek most took exception was: "For since the money economy is a complex of human institutions, it is subject to amendment. What we have to do is to find out just how the rules of our

[71] A solution to this problem would also address one of the criticisms of Hayek's proposal made by Milton Friedman. He wrote, "The fundamental problem is that in the present circumstance of the world there are no assets which banks could acquire to match purchasing-power obligations. Let a bank undertake to pay out money which will have a fixed purchasing-power, how can it be sure to guarantee that result? Only if it can match those liabilities with assets which can be assured of fixed purchasing-power. That will be possible when and only when governments in turn issue purchasing-power securities". Milton Friedman, "Currency Competition: A Sceptical View", in *Currency Competition and Monetary Union*, Pascal Salin, ed. (The Hague: Martinus Nijhoff, 1984), p. 43.

[72] See for example, Milton Friedman and Anna J. Schwartz: "[Hayek's] latest works have been devoted to explaining how gradual cultural evolution—a widespread invisible hand process— produces institutions and social arrangements that are far superior to those that are deliberately constructed by explicit human design. Yet he recommends in his recent publications on competitive currencies replacing the results of such an invisible hand process by a deliberate construct—the introduction of currency competition". "Has Government Any Role in Money?", *Journal of Monetary Economics*, vol. 17, 1986, p. 60.

own making thwart our wishes and to change them in detail or change them drastically as the case may require".[73]

But the rules to which Mitchell refers are not really of 'our' own making; they are rules which have been imposed by those who seized the monopoly of money. They are, so to speak, the house rules, which we must accept if we are to play at all. In this game there are only two rules: money may be only what government says it is, and government will also—we know not how or why—say how much of it there is. Hayek's daring monetary proposal is a call to start over, to stop the cheating and being cheated that the present situation leads to.

Consider that if the authorities were actually following rules in the formation and implementation of monetary policy, there would be no need to conduct meetings in secrecy. The Federal Reserve Board needs the money market to make its control of the money supply effective; but if the market were kept apprised of the Board's thinking, no one in the market would hold bonds or cash whose value could be changed by the vote of the Federal Reserve Board. For the system to work, some 'mark' has to bet against the house.

This is not a system that works by rules any more than the CIA or KGB follow rules. Both 'intelligence' agencies and central banks gain their control of events through their power to acquire information about events as, or—so they hope—before, they happen. Hayek argues that only the competition of the market can produce the knowledge that is necessary to provide money that holds its value in a world of uncertainty. And only the risk of private capital can ensure the accountabilty that leads to the correction of mistakes before irreversible damage has been done to the economy.

The following remarks, written by a former Director of the Division of Research and Statistics for the Board of Governors of the Federal Reserve System, are worth repeating, since the present Board seems to have drifted far from its origins:

> Statistics are necessarily expressed in totals and subtotals, while the course of human events is shaped by many millions of individual decisions which may not always fit into statistical categories. The broader the totals, the more violence they may do to reality. . . . Proposals based on a facile interpretation of aggregate figures are likely to suggest measures that would influence the totals on the supposition that all component

[73]Hayek's review of the article by W. C. Mitchell in which these passages are found is printed as chapter 1 in *Good Money, Part I.* Hayek's recollection that Mitchell was catalyst for the concept of constructivism is in his essay "The Errors of Constructivism", *New Studies in Philosophy, Politics, Economics and the History of Ideas,* op. cit., p. 3, note 3.

> parts have similar characteristics. Conclusions based on impersonal aggregates may lead to policies that have disastrous personal consequences to many groups. . . . Policy based on aggregates and aimed at shaping them tends towards an ever-increasing degree of centralized action. In a preface to a German edition of his *General Theory,* Keynes indicated that his analysis (based as it is largely on totals) can be made to fit conditions in a totalitarian state much more easily than in one where free competitive enterprise prevails under a large measure of *laissez faire.* A democratic approach to public problems must stress the fact that economic totals are only aggregates of millions of parts which may differ from each other in as many respects as they parallel each other, or even more. Mistakes made by individuals may offset each other, but mistakes based on totals leave no room for offsetting factors, and may be disastrous.[74]

Hayek's proposal for a denationalized currency is a call to dislodge the monopoly which now controls our money, and which is guided only by 'rules of thumb'. With the standard of value which once guided monetary policy now locked away in treasury vaults or sold surreptiously to a gullible (or prescient) market, no further evolution of that standard is possible. If *Denationalization of Money* does not succeed in opening monetary standards to competition, it has at least succeeded in opening the debate.

Stephen Kresge

[74] E. A. Goldenweiser, *American Monetary Policy* (New York: McGraw Hill, 1951), pp. 2–3.

ONE

MONETARY NATIONALISM AND INTERNATIONAL STABILITY[1]

Preface

The five lectures which are here reproduced are necessarily confined to certain aspects of the wide subject indicated by the title. They are printed essentially as they were delivered and, as is explained in the first lecture, limitations of time made it necessary to choose between discussing the concrete problems of the present policy of Monetary Nationalism and concentrating on the broader theoretical issues on which the decision between an international standard and independent national currencies must ultimately be based. The first course would have involved a discussion of such technical questions as the operations of Exchange Equalization Accounts, Forward Exchanges, the choice and adjustment of parities, cooperation between central banks, etc., etc. The reader will find little on these subjects in the following pages. It appeared to me more important to use the time available to discuss the general ideas which are mainly responsible for the rise of Monetary Nationalism and to which it is mainly due that politics and practices which not long ago would have been frowned upon by all responsible financial experts are now generally employed throughout the world. The immediate influence of the theoretical speculation is probably weak, but that it has had a profound influence in shaping those views which today dominate monetary policy is not open to serious question. It seemed to me better therefore to concentrate on these wider issues.

This decision has permitted me a certain freedom in the discussion of alternative policies. In discussing the merits of various systems I have not felt bound to confine myself to those which may today be considered practical politics. I have no doubt that to those who take the present trend of intellectual development for granted much of the discussion in the following pages will appear highly academic. Yet fundamentally the alter-

[1]First published in 1937 as Publication No. 18, The Graduate Institute of International Studies, Geneva (Geneva, London, and New York: Longmans, Green, 1937; reprinted, Augustus M. Kelley, 1964). —Ed.]

native policies here considered are no more revolutionary or impracticable than the deviations from traditional practice which have been widely discussed and which have even been attempted in recent years—except that at the moment not so many people believe in them. But while the politician—and economist when he is advising on concrete measures—must take the state of opinion for granted in deciding what changes can be contemplated here and now, these limitations are not necessary when we are asking what is best for the human race in general. I am profoundly convinced that it is academic discussion of this sort which in the long run forms public opinion and which in consequence decides what will be practical politics some time hence. I regard it therefore not only as the privilege but as the duty of the academic economist to take all alternatives into consideration, however remote their realization may appear at the moment.

And indeed I must confess that it seems to me in many respects the future development of professional and public opinion on these matters is much more important than any concrete measure which may be taken in the near future. Whatever the permanent arrangements in monetary policy, the spirit in which the existing institutions are administered is at least as important as these institutions themselves. And just as, long before the breakdown of the international gold standard in 1931, monetary policy all over the world was guided by the ideas of Monetary Nationalism which eventually brought its breakdown, so at the present time there is grave danger that a restoration of the external apparatus of the gold standard may not mean a return to a really international currency. Indeed I must admit that—although I am a convinced believer in the international gold standard—I regard the prospects of its restoration in the near future not without some concern. Nothing would be more fatal from a long-run point of view than if the world attempted a formal return to the gold standard before people had become willing to work it, and if, as would be quite probable under these circumstances, this were soon followed by a renewed collapse. And although this would probably be denied by the advocates of Monetary Nationalism, it seems to me as if we had reached a stage where their views have got such a hold on those in responsible positions, where so much of the traditional rules of policy have either been forgotten or been displaced by others which are, unconsciously perhaps, part of the new philosophy, that much must be done in the realm of ideas before we can hope to achieve the basis of a stable international system. These lectures were intended as a small contribution to this preparatory work which must precede a successful reconstruction of such a system.

It was my good fortune to be asked to deliver these lectures at the *Institut Universitaire de Hautes Etudes Internationales* at Geneva. I wish here to express my profound gratitude for the opportunity thus afforded and for the sympathetic and stimulating discussion which followed the lectures. My thanks are particularly due to the directors of the Institute, Professors [William E.] Rappard and [Paul] Mantoux, not only for arranging the lectures but also for undertaking their publication in the present series.

I am also indebted to a number of my friends and colleagues at the London School of Economics, particularly to Dr. F. Benham, Mr. F. Paish, Professor Robbins, and Mr. C. H. Secord, who have read the manuscript and offered much valuable advice as regards the subject matter and the form of exposition of these lectures. This would certainly have been a much bigger and much better book if I had seen my way to adopt and incorporate all their suggestions. But at the moment I do not feel prepared to undertake the larger investigation which my friends rightly think the subject deserves. I alone must therefore bear the blame for the sketchy treatment of some important points and for any shortcomings which offend the reader.

I hope however it will be borne in mind that these lectures were written to be read aloud and that this forbade any too extensive discussion of the more intricate theoretical points involved. Only at a few points, I have added a further explanatory paragraph or restored sections which would not fit into the time available for the lecture. That this will not suffice to provide satisfactory answers to the many questions I have raised I have no doubt.

F. A. Hayek
London School of Economics and Political Science
May 1937

Lecture 1. National Monetary Systems

I

When I was honoured with the invitation to deliver at the Institut five lectures "on some subject of distinctly international interest", I could have little doubt what that subject should be. In a field in which I am particularly interested I had been watching for years with increasing apprehension the steady growth of a doctrine which, if it becomes dominant, is likely to deal a fatal blow to the hopes of a revival of international economic relations. This doctrine, which in the title of these lectures I have described as 'Monetary Nationalism', is held by some of the most brilliant and influential economists of our time. It has been practiced in recent years to an ever-increasing extent, and in my opinion it is largely responsible for the particular intensification of the last depression which was brought about by the successive breakdown of the different currency systems. It will almost certainly continue to gain influence for some time to come, and it will probably indefinitely postpone the restoration of a truly international currency system. Even if it does not prevent the restoration of an international gold standard, it will almost inevitably bring about its renewed breakdown soon after it has been re-established.

When I say this I do not mean to suggest that a restoration of the gold standard of the type we have known is necessarily desirable, nor that much of the criticism directed against it may not be justified. My complaint is rather that most of this criticism is not concerned with the true reasons why the gold standard, in the form in which we knew it, did not fulfill the functions for which it was designed; and further that the only alternatives which are seriously considered and discussed completely abandon what seems to me the essentially sound principle—that of an international currency system—which that standard is supposed to embody.

But let me say at once that when I describe the doctrines I am going to criticize as Monetary Nationalism I do not mean to suggest that those who hold them are actuated by any sort of narrow nationalism. The very name of their leading exponent, J. M. Keynes, testifies that this is not the case. It is not the motives which inspire those who advocate such plans, but the consequences which I believe would follow from their realization, which I have in mind when I use this term. I have no doubt that the advocates of these doctrines sincerely believe that the system of independent national currencies will reduce rather than increase the causes of international economic friction; and that not merely one country but all will in the long run be better off if there is established that freedom in national monetary policies which is incompatible with a single international monetary system.

The difference then is not one about the ultimate ends to be achieved. Indeed, if it were, it would be useless to try to solve it by rational discussion. The fact is rather that there are genuine differences of opinion among economists about the consequences of the different types of monetary arrangements we shall have to consider, differences which prove that there must be inherent in the problem serious intellectual difficulties which have not yet been fully overcome. This means that any discussion of the issues involved will have to grapple with considerable technical difficulties, and that it will have to grapple with wide problems of general theory if it is to contribute anything to their solution. My aim throughout will be to throw some light on a very practical and topical problem. But I am afraid my way will have to lead for a considerable distance through the arid regions of abstract theory.

There is indeed another way in which I might have dealt with my subject. And when I realized how much purely theoretical argument the other involved I was strongly tempted to take it. It would have been to avoid any discussion of the underlying ideas and simply to take one of the many concrete proposals for independent national currency systems now prevalent and to consider its various probable effects. I have no doubt that in this form I could give my lectures a much more realistic appearance and could prove to the satisfaction of all who have already an unfavourable opinion of Monetary Nationalism that its effects are pernicious. But I am afraid I would have had little chance of convincing anyone who has already been attracted by the other side of the case. He might even admit all the disadvantages of the proposal which I could enumerate, and yet believe that its advantages outweigh the defects. Unless I can show that these supposed advantages are largely illusory, I shall not have got very far. But this involves an examination of the argument of the other side. So I have come rather reluctantly to the conclusion that I cannot shirk the much more laborious task of trying to go to the root of the theoretical differences.

II

But it is time for me to define more exactly what I mean by Monetary Nationalism and its opposite, an International Monetary System. By Monetary Nationalism I mean the doctrine that a country's share in the world's supply of money should *not* be left to be determined by the same principles and the same mechanism as those which determine the relative amounts of money in its different regions or localities. A truly International Monetary System would be one where the whole world possessed a homogeneous currency such as obtains within separate countries and where its flow between regions was left to be determined by the results of the action of all individuals. I shall have to define later what exactly I mean by a homogeneous currency. But I should like to make it clear at the outset that I do not believe that the gold standard as we knew it conformed to that ideal and that I regard this as its main defect.

Now from this conception of Monetary Nationalism there at once arises a question. The monetary relations between small adjoining areas are alleged to differ from those between larger regions or countries; and this difference is supposed to justify or demand different monetary arrangements. We are at once led to ask what is the nature of this alleged difference? This question is somewhat connected but not identical with the question what constitutes a national monetary system, in what sense we can speak of different monetary systems. But, as we shall see, it is very necessary to keep these questions apart. For if we do not we shall be confused between differences which are inherent in the underlying situation and which may make different monetary arrangements desirable, and differences which are the consequence of the particular monetary arrangements which are actually in existence.

For reasons which I shall presently explain, this distinction has not always been observed. This has led to much argument at cross purposes, and it is therefore necessary to be rather pedantic about it.

III

I shall begin by considering a situation where there is as little difference as is conceivable between the money of different countries, a case indeed where there is so little difference that it becomes doubtful whether we can speak of different 'systems'. I shall assume two countries only and I shall assume that in each of the two countries of which our world is assumed to consist, there is only one sort of widely used medium of exchange, namely coins consisting of the same metal. It is irrelevant for our purpose whether the denomination of these coins in the two countries is the same, so long as we assume, as we shall, that the two sorts of coins are freely and without cost interchangeable at the mints. It is clear that the mere difference in denomination, although it may mean an inconvenience, does not constitute a relevant difference in the currency systems of the two countries[2].

[2]Since these lines were written a newly published book has come to my hand in which almost the whole argument in favour of Monetary Nationalism is based on the assumption that different national currencies are different commodities and that consequently there ought to be variable prices of them in terms of each other (Charles Raymond Whittlesey, *International Monetary Issues* (New York and London: McGraw Hill, 1937)). No attempt is made to explain why or under what conditions and in what sense the different national moneys ought to be regarded as different commodities, and one can hardly avoid the impression that the author has uncritically accepted the difference of denomination as proof of the existence of a difference in kind. The case illustrates beautifully the prevalent confusion between differences between the currency systems which can be made an argument for national differentiations and those which are a consequence of such differentiations. That it is "only a difference in nomenclature" (as Professor Gregory has well put it) whether we express a given quantity of gold as Pounds, Dollars, or Marks, and that this no more constitutes different commodities than the same quantity of cloth becomes a different commodity when it is expressed in meters instead of in yards, ought to be obvious. Whether different national currencies are in any sense different commodities depends on what we

In starting from this case we follow a long established precedent. A great part of the argument of the classical writers on money proceeded on this assumption of a "purely metallic currency". I wholly agree with these writers that for certain purposes it is a very useful assumption to make. I shall however not follow them in their practice of assuming that the conclusions arrived [at] from these assumptions can be applied immediately to the monetary systems actually in existence. This belief was due to their conviction that the existing mixed currency systems not only could and should be made to behave in every respect in the same way as a purely metallic currency, but that—at any rate in England since the Bank Act of 1844—the total quantity of money was *actually* made to behave in this way.[3] I shall argue later that this erroneous belief is responsible for much confusion about the mechanism of the gold standard as it existed; that it has prevented us from achieving a satisfactory theory of the working of the modern mixed system, since the explanation of the role of the banking system was only imperfectly grafted upon, and never really integrated with, the theory of the purely metallic currency; and that in consequence the gold standard or the existence of an international system was blamed for much which in fact was really due to the mixed character of the system and not to its 'internationalism' at all.

For my present purpose, however, namely to find whether and in what sense the monetary mechanism of one country can or must be regarded as a unit or a separate system, even when there is a minimum of difference between the kind of money used there and elsewhere, the case of the "purely metallic currency" serves extraordinarily well. If there are differences in the working of the national monetary systems which are not merely an effect of the differences in the monetary arrangements of different countries, but which make it desirable that there *should* be separate arrangements for different regions, they must manifest themselves even in this simplest case.

It is clear that in this case the argument for a national monetary system cannot rest on any peculiarities of the national money. It must rest, and indeed it does rest, on the assumption that there is a particularly close

make them, and the real problem is whether we should create differentiations between the national currencies by using in each national territory a kind of money which will be generally acceptable only within that territory, or whether the same money should be used in the different national territories.

[3][Hayek wrote a complete account of the significance of the Bank Act of 1844 and the debate between the Currency and Banking Schools which led up to it. See F. A. Hayek, *The Trend of Economic Thinking,* W. W. Bartley III and Stephen Kresge, eds, being vol. 3 of the Collected Works of F. A. Hayek (Chicago: University of Chicago Press, and London: Routledge, 1991), chapter 12. —Ed.]

connection between the prices—and particularly the wages—within the country which causes them to move to a considerable degree up and down together compared with prices outside the country. This is frequently regarded as sufficient reason why, in order to avoid the necessity that the "country as a whole" should have to raise or lower its prices, the quantity of money in the country should be so adjusted as to keep the "general price level" within the country stable. I do not want to consider this argument yet. I shall later argue that it rests largely on an illusion, based on the accident that the statistical measures of price movements are usually constructed for countries as such; and that in so far as there are genuine difficulties connected with general downward adjustments of many prices, and particularly wages, the proposed remedy would be worse than the disease. But I think I ought to say here and now that I regard it as the only argument on which the case for monetary nationalism can be rationally based. All the other arguments have really nothing to do with the existence of an international monetary system as such, but apply only to the particular sorts of international systems with which we are familiar. But since these arguments are so inextricably mixed up in current discussion with those of a more fundamental character it becomes necessary, before we can consider the main arguments on its merits, to consider them first.

IV

The homogeneous international monetary system which we have just considered was characterised by the fact that each unit of the circulating medium of each country could equally be used for payments in the other country and for this purpose could be bodily transferred into the currency of that country. Among the systems which need to be considered, only an international gold standard with exclusive gold circulation in all countries would conform to this picture. This has never existed in its pure form and the type of gold standard which existed until fairly recently was even further removed from this picture than was generally realized. It was never fully appreciated how much the operation of the system which actually existed diverged from the ideal pure gold standard. For the points of divergence were so familiar that they were usually taken for granted. It was the design of the Bank Act of 1844 to make the mixed system of gold and other money behave in such a way that the quantity of money would change exactly as if only gold were in circulation; and for a long time argument proceeded as if this intention had actually been realized. And even when it was gradually realized that deposits subject to cheque were no less money than bank notes, and that since they were left out of the regulation, the purpose of the Act had really been defeated, only a few modifications of the argument were thought necessary. Indeed in general this argument is still presented as it was originally constructed, on the assumption of a purely metallic currency.

In fact however with the coming of modern banks a complete change had occurred. There was no longer one homogeneous sort of money in each country, the different units of which could be regarded as equivalent for all relevant purposes. There had arisen a hierarchy of different kinds of money within each country, a complex organisation which possessed a definite structure, and which is what we really mean when we speak of the circulating medium of a country as a 'system'. It is probably much truer to say that it is the difference between the different kinds of money which are used in any one country, rather than the differences between the moneys used in different countries, which constitutes the real difference between different monetary systems.

We can see this if we examine matters a little more closely. The gradual growth of banking habits, that is the practice of keeping liquid assets in the form of bank balances subject to cheque, meant that increasing numbers of people were satisfied to hold a form of the circulating medium which could be used directly only for payments to people who banked with the same institution. For all payments beyond this circle they relied on the ability of the bank to convert the deposits on demand into another sort of money which was acceptable in wider circles; and for this purpose the banks had to keep a 'reserve' of this more widely acceptable or more liquid medium.

But this distinction between bank deposits and 'cash' in the narrower sense of the term does not yet exhaust the classification of different sorts of money, possessing different degrees of liquidity, which are actually used in a modern community. Indeed, this development would have made little difference if the banks themselves had not developed in a way which led to their organisation into banking 'systems' on national lines. Whether there existed only a system of comparatively small local unit banks, or whether there were numerous systems of branch banks which covered different areas freely overlapping and without respect to national boundaries, there would be no reason why all the monetary transactions within a country should be more closely knit together than those in different countries. For any excess payments outside their circle the customers of any single bank, it is true, would be dependent on the reserve kept for this purpose for them by their bank, and might therefore find that their individual position might be affected by what other members of this circle did. But at most the inhabitants of some small town would in this way become dependent on the same reserves and thereby on one another's action,[4] never all the inhabitants of a big area or a country.

It was only with the growth of centralized national banking systems that all the inhabitants of a country came in this sense to be dependent on the same amount of more liquid assets held for them collectively as a national reserve. But the concept of centralization in this connection must not be interpreted too narrowly as referring only to systems crowned by a central bank of the familiar type, nor even as confined to branch banking systems where each district of a country is served by the branches of the same few banks. The forms in which centralization, in the sense of a system of national reserves which is significant here, may develop, are more varied than this and they are only partly due to deliberate legislative interference. They are partly due to less obvious institutional factors.

For even in the absence of a central bank and of branch banking, the fact that a country usually has one financial center where the stock exchange is located and through which a great proportion of its foreign trade passes or is financed tends to have the effect that the banks in that centre become the holders of a large part of the reserve of all the other banks in the country. The proximity of the stock exchange puts them in a position to invest such reserves profitably in what, at any rate for any single bank, appears to be a highly liquid form. And the greater volume of transactions in foreign exchange in such a centre makes it natural that the banks outside will rely on their town correspondents to provide them with whatever foreign money they may need in the course of their business. It was in this way that long before the creation of the Federal Reserve System in 1913 and in spite of the absence of branch banking there developed in the United States a system of national reserves under which in effect all the banks throughout their territory relied largely on the same ultimate reserves. And a somewhat similar situation existed in Great Britain before the growth of joint stock banking.

But this tendency is considerably strengthened if instead of a system of small unit banks there are a few large joint stock banks with many branches; still more if the whole system is crowned by a single central bank, the holder of the ultimate cash reserve. This system, which today is universal, means in effect that additional distinctions of acceptability or liquidity have been artificially created between three main types of money, and that the task of keeping a sufficient part of the total assets in

[4]Compare on this and the following Lionel Robbins, *Economic Planning and International Order* (London: Macmillan, 1937), pp. 274 et seq.

liquid form for different purposes has been divided between different subjects. The ordinary individual will hold only a sort of money which can be used directly only for payments to clients of the same bank; he relies upon the assumption that his bank will hold for all its clients a reserve which can be used for other payments. The commercial banks in turn will only hold reserves of such more liquid or more widely acceptable sort of money as can be used for interbank payments within the country. But for the holding of reserves of the kind which can be used for payments abroad, or even those which are required if the public should want to convert a considerable part of its deposits into cash, the banks rely largely on the central bank.

This complex structure, which is often described as the one-reserve system, but which I should prefer to call the system of national reserves, is now taken so much for granted that we have almost forgotten to think about its consequences. Its effects on the mechanism of international flows of money will be one of the main subjects of my next lecture. Today I only want to stress two aspects which are often overlooked. In the first place I would emphasize that bank deposits could never have assumed their present predominant role among the different media of circulation, that the balances held on current account by banks could never have grown to ten times and more of their cash reserves, unless some organ, be it a privileged central bank or be it a number of or all the banks, had been put in a position to create in case of need a sufficient number of additional bank notes to satisfy any desire on the part of the public to convert a considerable part of their balances into hand-to-hand money. It is in this sense and in this sense only that the existence of a national reserve system involves the question of the regulation of the note issue alone.

The second point is that nearly all the practical problems of banking policy, nearly all the questions with which a central banker is daily concerned, arise out of the co-existence of these different sorts of money within the national monetary system. Theoretical economists frequently argue as if the quantity of money in the country were a perfectly homogeneous magnitude and entirely subject to deliberate control by the central monetary authority. This assumption has been the source of much mutual misunderstanding on both sides. And it has had the effect that the fundamental dilemma of all central banking policy has hardly ever been really faced: the only effective means by which a central bank can control an expansion of the generally used media of circulation is by making it clear in advance that it will not provide the cash (in the narrower sense) which will be required in consequence of such expansion, but at the same time it is recognised as the paramount duty of a central bank to provide that cash *once* the expansion of bank deposits has actually occurred and the public begins to demand that they should be converted into notes or gold.

I shall be returning to this problem later. But in the next two lectures my main concern will be another set of problems. I shall argue that the existence of national reserve systems is the real source of most of the difficulties which are usually attributed to the existence of a national standard. I shall argue that these difficulties are really due to the fact that the mixed national currencies are not sufficiently international, and that most of the criticism directed against the gold standard *qua* international standard is misdirected. I shall try to show that the existence of national reserve systems alters the mechanism of the international money flows from what it would be with a homogeneous international currency to a much greater degree than is commonly realized.

V

But before I can proceed to this major task I must shortly consider the third and most efficient cause which may differentiate the circulating media of different countries and constitute separate monetary systems. Up to this point I have only mentioned cases where the ratio between the monetary units used in the different countries was given and constant. In the first case this was secured by the fact that the money circulating in the different countries was assumed to be homogeneous in all essential respects, while in the second and more realistic case it was assumed that, although different kinds of money were used in the different countries, there was yet in operation an effective if somewhat complicated mechanism which made it always possible to convert at a constant rate money of the one country into money of the other. To complete the list there must be added the case where these ratios are variable: that is, where the rate of exchange between the two currencies is subject to fluctuations.

With monetary systems of this kind we have of course to deal with differences between the various sorts of money which are much bigger than any we have yet encountered. The possession of a quantity of money current in one country no longer gives command over a definite quantity of money which can be used in another country. There is no longer a mechanism which secures that an attempt to transfer money from country to country will lead to a decrease in the quantity of money in one country and a corresponding increase in the other. In fact, an actual transfer of money from country to country becomes useless because what is money in the one country is not money in the other. We have here to deal with things which possess different degrees of usefulness for different purposes and the quantities of which are fixed independently.

Now I think it should be sufficiently clear that any differences between merely interlocal and international movements of money which only arise as a consequence of the variability of exchange rates cannot themselves be regarded as a justification for the existence of separate monetary systems. That would be to confuse effect and cause—to make the occasion of difference the justification of its perpetuation. But since the adoption of such a system of 'flexible parities' is strongly advocated as a remedy for the difficulties which arise out of other differences which we have already considered, it will be expedient if in the following lectures I consider side by side all three types of conditions under which differences between the national monetary systems may arise. We shall be concerned with the way in which in each case redistributions of the relative amounts of money in the different countries are effected. I shall begin with the only case which can truly be described as an international monetary standard, that of a homogeneous international currency. Consideration of this case will help me to show what functions changes in the relative quantities of money in different regions and countries may be conceived to serve; and how such changes are spontaneously brought about. I shall then proceed to the hybrid 'mixed' system which until recently was the system generally in vogue and which is meant when, in current discussion, the traditional gold standard is referred to. As I said at the beginning, I shall not deny that this system has serious defects. But while the Monetary Nationalists believe that these defects are due to the fact that it is still an international system and propose to remove them by substituting the third or purely national type of monetary system for it, I shall on the contrary attempt to show that its defects lie in the impediments which it presents to the free international flow of funds. This will then lead me first to an examination of the peculiar theory of inflation and deflation on which Monetary Nationalism is based; then to an investigation of the consequences which we should have to expect if its proposals were acted upon; and finally to a consideration of the methods by which a more truly international system could be achieved.

Lecture 2. The Function and Mechanism of International Flows of Money

I

At the end of my first lecture I pointed out that the three different types of national monetary systems which we have been considering differed mainly in the method by which they effected international redistributions of money. In the case of a homogeneous international currency, such a redistribution is effected by actual transfers of the corresponding amounts of money from country to country. Under the 'mixed' system represented by the traditional gold standard—better called "gold nucleus standard"—[the redistribution] is brought about partly by an actual transfer of money from country to country, but largely by a contraction of the credit superstructure in the one country and a corresponding expansion in the other. But although the mechanism and, as we shall see, some of the effects of these two methods are different, the final result, the change in the relative value of the total quantities of money in the different countries, is brought about by a corresponding change in the quantity of money, the number of money units, in each country. Under the third system, however, the system of independent currencies, things are different. Here the adjustment is brought about, not by a change in the number of money units in each country, but by changes in their relative value. No money actually passes from country to country, and whatever redistribution of money between persons may be involved by the redistribution between countries has to be brought about by corresponding changes inside each country.

Before, however, we can assess the merits of the different systems, it is necessary to consider generally the different reasons why it may become necessary that the relative values of the total quantities of money in different countries should alter. It is clear that changes in the demand for or supply of the goods and services produced in an area may change the value of the share of the world's income which the inhabitants of that area may claim. But changes in the relative stock of money, although of course closely connected with these changes of the shares in the world's income which different countries can claim, are not identical with them. It is only because people whose money receipts fall will in general tend to reduce their money holdings also and vice versa that changes in the size of money stream in the different countries will as a rule be accompanied by changes in the same direction in the size of the money holdings. People who find their income increasing will generally at first take out part of the increased money income in the form of a permanent increase in their cash balances, while people whose incomes decrease will tend to postpone for a while a reduction of their expenditure to the full extent, preferring to reduce their cash balances.[5] To this extent changes in the cash balances serve, as it were, as cushions which soften the impact and delay the adaptation of the real incomes to the changed money incomes, so that in the interval money is actually taken as a substitute for goods.

But, given existing habits, it is clear that changes in the relative size of the money incomes—and the same applies to the total volume of money

[5]For a full description of this mechanism, see for example Ralph G. Hawtrey, *Currency and Credit* [1919], 3rd edition (London: Longmans, 1928), pp. 41–63.

transactions—of different countries make corresponding changes in the money stocks of these counries inevitable; changes which, although they need not be in the same proportion, must at any rate be in the same direction as the changes in incomes. If the share in the world's production which the output of a country represents rises or falls, the share of the total which the inhabitants of the country can claim will fully adapt itself to the new situation only after money balances have been adjusted.[6]

Changes in the demand for money on the part of a particular country may of course also occur independently of any change in the value of the resources its inhabitants can command. [These changes] may be due to the fact that some circumstances may have made its people want to hold a larger or smaller proportion of their resources in the most liquid form, that is, in money. If so, then for a time they will offer to the rest of the world more commodities, receiving money in exchange. This enables them, at any later date, to buy more commodities than they can currently sell. In effect they decide to lend to the rest of the world that amount of money's worth of commodities in order to be able to call it back whenever they want it.

II

The function which is performed by international movements of money will be seen more clearly if we proceed to consider such movement in the simplest case imaginable—a homogeneous international or 'purely metallic' currency. Let us suppose that somebody who used to spend certain sums on products of country *A* now spends them on products of country *B*. The immediate effect of this is the same whether this person himself is domiciled in *A* or in *B*. In either case there will arise an excess of payments from *A* to *B*—an adverse balance of trade for *A*, either because the total of such payments has risen or because the amount of payments in the opposite direction has fallen off. And if the initiator of this change persists in his new spending habits, this flow of money will continue for some time.

But now we must notice that because of this in *A* somebody's money receipts have decreased and in *B* somebody's money receipts have increased. We have long been familiar with the proposition that counteracting forces will in time bring the flow of money between the countries to a stop. But it is only quite recently that the exact circumstances de-

[6]Perhaps, instead of speaking of the world's output, I should have spoken about the share in the command over the world's resources, since of course it is not only the current consumable product but equally the command over resources which will yield a product only in the future which is distributed by this monetary mechanism.

termining the route by which this comes about have been satisfactorily established.[7] In both countries the change in the money receipts of the people first affected will be passed on and disseminated. But how long the outflow of money from *A* to *B* will continue depends on how long it takes before the successive changes in money incomes set up in each country will bring about new and opposite changes in the balance of payments.

This result can be brought about in two ways in each of the two countries. The reduction of money incomes in country *A* may lead to a decrease of purchases from *B*, or the consequent fall of the prices of some goods in *A* may lead to an increase of exports to *B*. And the increase of money incomes in country *B* may lead to an increase of purchases from *A* or to a rise in the prices of some commodities in *B* and a consequent decrease of exports to *A*. But how long it will take before in this way the flow of money from *A* to *B* will be offset will depend on the number of links in the chains which ultimately lead back to the other country, and on the extent to which at each of these points the change of incomes leads first to a change in the cash balances held, before it is passed on in full strength. In the interval money will continue to flow from *A* to *B*; and the total which so moves will correspond exactly to the amounts by which, in the course of the process just described, cash balances have been depleted in the one country and increased in the other.

This part of the description is completely general. But we cannot say how many incomes will have to be changed, how many individual prices will have to be altered upwards or downwards in each of the two countries, in consequence of the initial changes. For this depends entirely on the concrete circumstances of each particular case. In some countries and under some conditions the route will be short because some of the first people whose incomes decrease cut down their expenditure on imported goods, or because the increase of incomes is soon spent on imported goods.[8] In other cases the route may be long and external payments will be made to balance only after extensive price changes have occurred, which induce further people to change the direction of their expenditure.

The important point in all this is that what incomes and what prices will have to be altered in consequence of the initial change will depend

[7]Cf. particularly Frank W. Paish, "Banking Policy and the Balance of International Payments", *Economica, N. S.*, vol. 3, no. 12, November 1936; Karl Friedrich Maier, *Goldwanderungen* (Jena: G. Fischer, 1935); and P. B. Whale, "The Working of the Pre-War Gold Standard", *Economica*, vol. 4, no. 13, February 1937.

[8]On this point, see particularly the article by Frank W. Paish just quoted.

on whether and to what extent the value of a particular factor of service, directly or indirectly, depends on the particular change in demand which has occurred, and not on whether it is inside or outside the same 'currency area'. We can see this more clearly if we picture the series of successive changes of money incomes, which will follow on the initial shift of demand, as single chains, neglecting for the moment the successive ramifications which will occur at every link. Such a chain may either very soon lead to the other country or first run through a great many links at home. But whether any particular individual in the country will be affected will depend on whether he is a link in that particular chain, that is whether he has more or less immediately been serving the individuals whose income has first been affected, and not simply on whether he is in the same country or not. In fact this picture of the chain makes it clear that it is not impossible that most of the people who ultimately suffer a decrease of income in consequence of the initial transfer of demand from *A* to *B* may be in *B* and not in *A*. This is often overlooked because the whole process is presented as if the chain of effects came to an end as soon as payments between the two countries balance. In fact however each of the two chains—that started by the decrease of somebody's income in *A*, and that started by the increase of another person's income in *B*—may continue to run on for a long time after they have passed into the other country, and may have even a greater number of links in that country than in the one where they started. They will come to an end only when they meet, not only in the same country but in the same individual, so finally offsetting each other. This means that the number of reductions of individual incomes and prices (not their aggregate amount) which becomes necessary in consequence of a transfer of money from *A* to *B* may actually be greater in *B* than in *A*.

This picture is of course highly unrealistic because it leaves out of account the infinite ramifications which each of these chains of effects will develop. But even so it should, I think, make it clear how superficial and misleading the kind of argument is which runs in terms of *the* prices and *the* incomes of the country, as if they would necessarily move in unison or even in the same direction. It will be prices and incomes of particular individuals and particular industries which will be affected, and the effects will not be essentially different from those which will follow any shifts of demand between different industries or localities.

This whole question is of course the same as that which I discussed in my first lecture in connection with the problem of what constitutes one monetary system, namely the question of whether there exists a particularly close coherence between prices and incomes, and particularly wages, in any one country which tends to make them move as a whole relatively to the price structure outside. As I indicated then, I shall not be able to deal with it more completely until later on. But there are two points which, I think, will have become clear now and which are important for the understanding of the contrast between the working of the homogeneous international currency we are considering and the mixed system to which I shall presently proceed.

In the first place it already appears very doubtful whether there is any sense in which the terms inflation and deflation can be appropriately applied to these interregional or international transfers of money. If, of course, we *define* inflation and deflation as changes in the quantity of money, or the price level, *within a particular territory*, then the term naturally applies. But it is by no means clear that the consequences which we can show will follow if the quantity of money in a closed system changes will also apply to such redistributions of money between areas. In particular there is no reason why the changes in the quantity of money within an area should bring about those merely temporary changes in relative prices which, in the case of a real inflation, lead to misdirections of production—misdirections because eventually the inherent mechanism of these inflations tends to reverse these changes in relative prices. Nor does there seem to exist any reason why, to use a more modern yet already obsolete terminology, saving and investment should be made to be equal within any particular area which is part of a larger economic system.[9] But all these questions can be really answered only when I come to discuss the two conflicting views about the main significance of inflation and deflation which underlie most of the current disputes about monetary policy.

The second point which I want particularly to stress here is that with a homogeneous international currency there is apparently no reason why an outflow of money from one area and an inflow into another should necessarily cause a rise in the rate of interest in the first area and a fall in the second. So far I have not mentioned the rate of interest, because there seems to be no general ground why we should expect that the causes which lead to the money flows between two countries should affect the rate of interest one way or the other. Whether they will have such an effect and in what direction will depend entirely on the concrete circumstances. If the initial change which reduces the money income of some people in one country leads to an immediate reduction of their expendi-

[9]Cf. J. M. Keynes, *A Treatise on Money* (London: Macmillan, 1930), vol. 1, chapter 4. [Hayek wrote an extended review of this work, which in turn elicited an irritated reply from Keynes. See F. A. Hayek, *Contra Keynes and Cambridge* (1995), Bruce Caldwell, ed., being vol. 9 of the Collected Works of F. A. Hayek, op. cit., Part II. —Ed.]

ture on consumers' goods, and if in addition they use for additional investments the surplus of their cash balances which they no longer regard worth keeping, it is not impossible that the effect may actually be a fall in the rate of interest.[10] It seems that we have been led to regard what happens to be the rule under the existing mixed systems as due to causes much more fundamental than those which actually operate. But this leads me to the most important difference between the cases of a 'purely metallic' and that of a 'mixed' currency. To the latter case, therefore, I now turn.

III

If in the two countries concerned there are two separate banking systems, whether these banking systems are complete with a central bank or not, considerable transfers of money from the one country to the other will be effected by the actual transmission of only a part of the total, the further adjustment being brought about by an expansion or contraction of the credit structure according as circumstances demand. It is commonly believed that nothing fundamentally is changed but something is saved by substituting the extinction of money in one region and the creation of new money in the other for the actual transfer of money from individual to individual. This is however a view which can be held only on the most mechanistic form of the quantity theory and which completely disregards the fact that the incidence of the change will be very different in the two cases. Considering the methods available to the banking system to bring about an expansion or contraction, there is no reason to assume that they can take the money to be extinguished exactly from those persons where it would in the course of time be released if there were no banking system, or that they will place the additional money in the hands of those who would absorb the money if it came to the country by direct transfer from abroad. There are on the contrary strong grounds for believing that the

[10]Although it is even conceivable that a fall in incomes might bring about a temporary rise in investments, because the people who are now poorer feel that they can no longer afford the luxury of the larger cash balances they used to keep before, and proceed to invest part of them, this is neither a very probable effect nor likely to be quantitatively significant. Much more important, however, may be the effect of the fall of incomes on the demand for investment. Particularly if the greater part of the existing capital equipment is of a very durable character, a fall in incomes may for some time almost completely suspend the need for investment and in this way reduce the rate of interest in the country quite considerably. Another case where the same cause which would lead to a flow of money from one country to another would at the same time cause a fall in the rate of interest in the first would be if in one of several countries where population used to increase at the same rate, this rate were considerably decreased.

burden of the change will fall entirely, or to an extent which is in no way justified by the underlying change in the real situation, on investment activity in both countries.

To see why and how this will happen it is necessary to consider in some detail the actual organisation of the banking systems and the nature of their traditional policies. We have seen that where bank deposits are used extensively this means that all those who hold their most liquid assets in this form rely on their banks to provide them whenever needed with the kind of money which is acceptable outside the circle of the clients of the bank. The banks in turn, and largely because they have learnt to rely on the assistance of other (note-issuing) banks, particularly the central bank, have come themselves to keep only very slender cash reserves, that is, reserves which they can use to meet any adverse clearing balance to other banks or to make payments abroad. These are indeed not meant to do more than to tide over any temporary and relatively small difference between payments and receipts. They are altogether insufficient to allow the banks ever to reduce these reserves by the full amount of any considerable reduction of their deposits. The very system of proportional reserves, which so far as deposits are concerned is today universally adopted and even in the case of bank notes applies practically everywhere outside Great Britain, means that the cash required for the conversion of an appreciable part of the deposits has to be raised by compelling people to repay loans.

We shall best see the significance of such a banking structure with respect to international money flows if we consider again the effects which are caused by an initial transfer of demand from country *A* to country *B*. The main point here is that, with a national banking system working on the proportional reserve principle, unless the adverse balance of payments corrects itself very rapidly, the central bank will not be in a position to let the outflow of money go on until it comes to its natural end. It cannot, without endangering its reserve position, freely convert all the bank deposits or banknotes which will be released by individuals into money which can be transferred into the other countries. If it wants to prevent an exhaustion or dangerous depletion of its reserves it has to speed up the process by which payments from *A* to *B* will be decreased or payments from *B* to *A* will be increased. And the only way in which it can do this quickly and effectively is generally and indiscriminately to bring pressure on those who have borrowed from it to repay their loans. In this way it will set up additional chains of successive reductions of outlay, first on the part of those to whom it would have lent and then on the part of all others to whom this money would gradually have passed. So that leaving aside for the moment the effects which a rise in interest rates will have on international movements of short-term capital we can see that the forces which earlier or later will reduce payments abroad and, by reducing prices of home products, stimulate purchases from abroad will be intensified. And if sufficient pressure is exercised in this way, the period during which the outflow of money continues, and thereby the total amount of money that will actually leave the country before payments in and out will balance again, may be reduced to almost any extent.

The important point, however, is that in this case the people who will have to reduce their expenditure in order to produce that result will not necessarily be the same people who would ultimately have to do so under a homogeneous international currency system, and that the equilibrium so reached will of its nature be only temporary. In particular, since bank loans, to any significant extent, are only made for investment purposes, it will mean that the full force of the reduction of the money stream will have to fall on investment activity. This is shown clearly by the method by which this restriction is brought about. We have seen before that under a purely metallic currency an outflow of money need not actually bring about a rise in interest rates. It may, but this is not necessary and it is even conceivable that the opposite will happen. But with a banking structure organised on national lines, that is, under a national reserve system, it is inevitable that it will bring a rise in interest rates, irrespective of whether the underlying real change has affected either the profitability of investment or the rate of savings in such a way as to justify such a change. In other words, to use an expression which has given rise to much dispute in the recent past but which should be readily understood in this connection, the rise of the bank rate under such circumstances means that it has to be deliberately raised above the equilibrium or 'natural' rate of interest.[11] The reason for this is not, or need not be, that the initiating change has affected the relation between the supply of investible funds and the demand for them, but that it tends to disturb the customary proportion between the different parts of the credit structure and that the only way to restore these proportions is to cancel loans made for investment purposes.

To some extent, but only to some extent, the credit contraction will, as I have just said, by lowering prices induce additional payments from

[11]This has been rightly pointed out, but has hardly been sufficiently explained, in an interesting article by J. C. Gilbert, "The Present Position of the Theory of International Trade", *The Review of Economic Studies,* vol. 3, no. 1, October 1935, particularly pp. 23–26. To say that money rates of interest in a particular country may be made to deviate from the equilibrium rate by monetary factors peculiar to that country is, of course, not to say that the equilibrium rate in that country is independent of international conditions.

abroad and in this form offset the outflow of money. But to a considerable extent its effect will be that certain international transfers of money which would have taken the place of a transfer of goods and would in this sense have been a final payment for a temporary excess of imports will be intercepted, so that consequently actual transfers of goods will have to take place. The transfer of only a fraction of the amount of money which would have been transferred under a purely metallic system, and the substitution of a multiple credit contraction for the rest, as it were, deprives the individuals in the country concerned of the possibility of delaying the adaptation by temporarily paying for an excess of imports in cash.

That the rise of the rate of interest in the country that is losing gold, and the corresponding reduction in the bank rate in the country which is receiving gold, need have nothing to do with changes in the demand for or the supply of capital appears also from the fact that, if no further change intervenes, the new rates will have to be kept in force only for a comparatively short period, and that after a while a return to the old rates will be possible. The changes in the rates serve the temporary purpose of speeding up a process which is already under way. But the forces which would have brought the flow of gold to an end earlier or later in any case do not therefore cease to operate. The chain of successive reductions of income in country *A* set up by the initiating changes will continue to operate and ultimately reduce the payments out of the country still further. But since payments in and payments out have in the meantime already been made to balance by the action of the banks, this will actually reverse the flow and bring about a favourable balance of payments. The banks, wanting to replenish their reserves, may let this go on for a while, but once they have restored their reserves, they will be able to resume at least the greater part of their lending activity which they had to curtail.

This picture is admittedly incomplete because I have been deliberately neglecting the part played by short-term capital movements. I shall discuss these in my fourth lecture. At present my task merely is to show how the existence of national banking systems, based on the collective holding of national cash reserves, alters the effects of international flows of money. It seems to me impossible to doubt that there is indeed a very considerable difference between the case where a country, whose inhabitants are induced to decrease their share in the world's stock of money by ten per cent, does so by actually giving up this ten per cent in gold, and the case where, in order to preserve the accustomed reserve proportions, it pays out only one per cent in gold and contracts the credit superstructure in proportion to the reduction of reserves. It is as if all balances of international payments had to be squeezed through a narrow bottleneck as special pressure has to be brought on people, who would otherwise not have been affected by the change, to give up money which they would have invested productively.

Now the changes in productive activity which are made necessary in this way are not of a permanent nature. This means not only that in the first instance many plans will be upset, that equipment which has been created will cease to be useful and that people will be thrown out of employment. It also means that the revised plans which will be made are bound soon to be equally disappointed in the reverse direction and that the readjustment of production which has been enforced will prove to be a misdirection. In other words, it is a disturbance which possesses all the characteristics of a purely monetary disturbance, namely that it is self-reversing in the sense that it induces changes which will have to be reversed because they are not based on any corresponding change in the underlying real facts.[12]

It might perhaps be argued that the contraction of credit in the one country and the expansion in the other brings about exactly the same effects that we should expect from a transfer of a corresponding amount of capital from the one country to the other, and that since the amount of money which would otherwise have to be transferred would represent so much capital, there can be no harm in the changes in the credit structure. But the point is exactly that not every movement of money is in this sense a transfer of capital. If a group of people want to hold more money because the value of their income rises, while another group of people reduce their money holdings because the value of their income falls, there is no reason why in consequence the funds available for investment in the first group should increase and those available in the second group should decrease. It is, on the other hand, quite possible that the demand for such funds in the first group will rise and in the second group will fall. In such a case, as we have seen, there would be more reason to expect that the rate of interest will rise in the country to which the money flows rather than in the country from which the money comes.

The case is of course different when the initiating cause is not a shift in demand from one kind of consumers' goods to another kind of consumers' goods, but when funds which have been invested in one type of producers' goods in one country are transferred to investment in another

[12][The self-reversing character of monetary disturbances which would not reflect real changes in supply and demand conditions were the nub of Hayek's continuing argument against attempts to stabilize currencies. Hayek refers the reader to this passage in F. A. Hayek, *The Pure Theory of Capital* (Chicago: University of Chicago Press, 1941; and London: Routledge & Kegan Paul, 1941), p. 34, note 1. —Ed.]

type of producers' goods in another country. Then indeed we have a true movement of capital and we should be entitled to expect it to affect interest rates in the usual manner. What I am insisting on is merely that this need not be the general rule and that the fact that it is generally the case is not the effect of an inherent necessity but due to purely institutional reasons.

IV

There are one or two further points which I must shortly mention before I can conclude this subject. One is the rather obvious point that the disturbing effects of the organization of the world's monetary system on the national reserve principle are of course considerably increased when the rate of multiple expansion or contraction, which will be caused by a given increase or decrease of gold, is different in different countries. If this is the case, and it has of course always been the case under the gold standard as we knew it, it means that every flow of gold from one country to another will mean either an inflation or a deflation from the world point of view, accordingly as the rate of secondary expansion is greater or smaller in the country receiving gold than in the country losing gold.

The second point is one on which I am particularly anxious not to be misunderstood. The defects of the mixed system which I have pointed out are not defects of a particular kind of policy, or of special rules of central bank practice. They are defects inherent in the system of the collective holding of proportional cash reserves for national areas, whatever the policy adopted by the central bank or the banking system. What I have said provides in particular no justification for the common infringements of the 'rules of the game of the gold standard', except, perhaps, for a certain reluctance to change the discount rate too frequently or too rapidly when gold movements set in. But all the attempts to substitute other measures for changes in the discount rate as a means to 'protect reserves' do not help, because it is the necessity of 'protecting' reserves rather than letting them go (i.e., using the conversion into gold as the proper method of reducing internal circulation), not the methods by which it has to be done, which is the evil. The only real cure would be if the reserves kept were large enough to allow them to vary by the full amount by which the total circulation of the country might possibly change; that is, if the principle of Peel's Act of 1844 could be applied to all forms of money, including in particular bank deposits. I shall come back to this point in my last lecture. What I want to stress, however, is that in the years before the breakdown of the international gold standard the attempts to make the supply of money of individual countries independent of international gold movements had already gone so far that not only had an ouflow or inflow of gold often no effect on the internal circulation but that sometimes the latter moved actually in the opposite direction. To 'offset' gold movements, as was apparently done by the Bank of England,[13] by replacing the gold lost by the central bank by securities bought from the market, is of course not to correct the defects of the mixed system, but to make the international standard altogether ineffective.

One should probably say much more on this subject. But I am afraid I must conclude here. I hope that what I have said today has at least made one point clear which I made yesterday; namely that many objections which are raised against the gold standard as we knew it, are not really objections against the gold standard, or against any international standard as such, but objections against the mixed system which has been in general vogue. It should be clear too that the main defect of this system was that it was not sufficiently international. Whether and how these defects can be remedied I can consider only at the end of this course. But before I can do this I shall yet have to consider the more completely nationalist systems which have been proposed.

Lecture 3. Independent Currencies

I

When the rates of exchange between currencies of different countries are variable, the consequences which will follow from changes which under an international system would lead to flows of money from country to country will depend on the monetary policies adopted by the countries concerned. It is therefore necessary, before we can say anything about those effects, to consider the aims which will presumably guide the monetary policy of countries which have adopted an independent standard. This raises immediately the question whether there is any justification for applying any one of the principles according to which we might think that the circulation in a closed system should be regulated, to a particular country or region which is part of the world economic system.

Now it should be evident that a policy of stabilization, whether it be of the general price level or the general level of money incomes, is one thing if it be applied to the whole of a closed system and quite another if the

[13] Cf. *Minutes of Evidence taken before the Committee on Finance and Industry,* London, 1931, vol. 1, Q. 353. Sir Ernest Harvey: "You will find if you look at a succession of Bank Returns that the amount of Gold we have lost has been almost entirely replaced by an increase in the Bank's securities".

same policy is applied to each of the separate regions into which the total system can be more or less arbitrarily divided. In fact, however, this difficulty is generally ignored by the advocates of Monetary Nationalism, and it is simply assumed that the criteria of a good monetary policy which are applicable to a closed system are equally valid for a single country. We shall have to consider later the theoretical problems here involved. But for the moment we can confine ourselves to an examination of the working of the mechanism which brings about relative changes in the value of the total money holdings of the different nations when each nation follows independently the objective of stabilizing its national price level, or income stream, or whatever it may be, irrespective of its position in the international system.

The case which has figured most prominently in these discussions in recent years, and which is apparently supposed to represent the relative positions of England and the United States, is that of two countries with unequal rates of technological progress, so that, in the one, costs of production will tend to fall more rapidly than in the other. Under a regime of fixed parities this would mean that the fall in the prices of some products produced in both countries could be faster than the fall in their cost in the country where technological progress is slower, and that in consequence it would become necessary to reduce costs there by scaling down money wages, etc. The main advantage of a system of movable parities is supposed to be that in such a case the downward adjustment of wages could be avoided and equilibrium restored by reducing the value of money in the one country relative to the other country.

It is, however, particularly important in this connection not to be misled by the fact that this argument is generally expressed in terms of averages, that is in terms of general levels of prices and wages. A change in the level of prices or of costs in one country relatively to that of another means that, in consequence of changes in relative costs, the competitive position of a particular industry or perhaps group of industries in the one country has deteriorated. In other words the lower prices in the one country will lead to a transfer of demand from the other country to it. The case is therefore essentially similar to that which we have been considering in the last lecture and it will be useful to discuss it in the same terms. We shall therefore in the first instance again consider the effects of a simple shift of demand if rates of exchange are allowed to vary and if the monetary authorities in each country aim either at stability of some national price level, or—what amounts very much to the same thing for our purpose—at a constant volume of the effective money stream within the country. Only occasionally, where significant differences arise, I shall specially refer to the case where the shift of demand has been induced by unequal technological progress.

Now of course no monetary policy can prevent the prices of the product immediately affected from falling relatively to the prices of other goods in the one country, and a corresponding[14] rise taking place in the other. Nor can it prevent the effects of the change of the income of the people affected in the first instance from gradually spreading. All it can do is to prevent this from leading to a change in the *total* money stream in the country; that is, it must see that there will be offsetting changes of other prices so that the price level remains constant. It is on this assumption that we conduct our investigations. For purposes of simplicity, too, I assume that at the outset a state of full employment prevails.

II

It will be convenient to concentrate first on the country from which demand has turned away and from which under an international monetary system there would in consequence occur an outflow of money. But in the present case not only would a real outflow of money be impossible, but it would also be contrary to the intentions of the monetary authorities to sell additional quantities of foreign exchange against national money and to cancel the national money so received. The monetary authorities might hold some reserves of foreign exchange to even out what they regarded as merely temporary fluctuations of exchange rates. But there would be no point in using them in the case of a change which they would have to regard as permanent. We can, therefore, overlook the existence of such reserves and proceed as if only current receipts from abroad were available for outward payments.

On this assumption it is clear that the immediate effect of the adverse balance of payments will be that foreign exchange rates will rise. But the full amount that importers used to spend on buying foreign exchange is not likely to be spent on the reduced supply of foreign exchange; since with the higher price of imported goods some of the money which used to be spent on them will probably be diverted to home substitutes.[15] The foreign exchanges will therefore probably rise less than in proportion to the fall in supply. But via the sale of foreign exchange at the higher rate those who continue to export successfully will receive greater amounts of

[14]Where the shift of demand has been induced by a reduction of cost and a consequent fall of prices in the one country, this will only be a relative rise and will of course only partly counteract this fall in the price of the final product, but may bring about an actual rise in the prices of the factors used in their production.

[15]The assumption that the demand for the commodities in question is elastic, that is, that the total expenditure upon them will be reduced when their prices rise and vice versa, will be maintained throughout this discussion. To take at every step the opposite case into account would unduly lengthen the argument without affecting the conclusion.

the national currency. For those whose sales abroad have not been unfavourably affected by the initial change in question, this will mean a net gain and the price of their products will correspondingly rise in terms of the national currency. And those whose exports have fallen in price will find that this reduced price in terms of the foreign currency will now correspond to a somewhat greater amount in the national currency than what they could obtain before the exchange depreciation, although not as much as they received before the first change took place.

This impact effect of the rise of exchange rates on relative prices in terms of the national currency will however be temporary. The relative costs of the different quantities of the different commodities which are being produced have not changed and it is not likely that they will go on being produced in these quantities if their prices have changed. Moreover all the changes in the direction of the money streams caused by the rise in exchange rates will continue to work. More is being spent on home goods, and this, together with the increased profitability of those export industries which have not been adversely affected by the initial change, will tend to bring about a rise of all prices except those which are affected by the decreased demand from the declining industry and from the people who draw their income from it.

It seems therefore that the argument in favour of depreciation in such cases is based on a too-simplified picture of the working of the price mechanism. In particular it seems to be based on the assumption (underlying much of the classical analysis of these problems) that relative prices within each country are uniquely determined by (constant) relative cost. If this were so, a proportional reduction of all prices in a country relatively to those in the rest of the world would indeed be sufficient to restore equilibrium. In fact, however, there can be little doubt that the changes in the relative quantities of goods to be produced by the different industries which will become necessary in consequence of the initial change can be brought about only by changes in the relative prices and the relative incomes of the different kinds of resources within the country.

Without following the effects in all their complicated detail it must be clear that the ultimate result of depreciation can only be that, instead of prices and incomes in the industry originally affected falling to the full extent, a great many other prices and incomes will have to rise to restore the proportions appropriate to cost conditions and the relative volume of output now required. Even disregarding the absolute height of prices, the final positions will not be the same as that which would have been reached if exchanges had been kept fixed; because in the course of the different process of transition all sorts of individual profits and losses will have been made which will affect that final position. But roughly speaking and disregarding certain minor differences, it can be said that the same change in relative prices which, under fixed exchanges, would have been brought about by a reduction of prices in the industry immediately affected is now being brought about largely by a corresponding rise of all other prices.

Two points, however, need special mention. One is that the decrease of the comparative advantage of the export industry originally affected cannot be changed in this way; and that to this extent a contraction of the output of this industry will remain unavoidable. The other is that at least in certain respects the process which brings about the rise in prices will be of a definitely inflationary character. This will show itself partly by some industries becoming *temporarily* more profitable so that there will be an inducement to expand production there, although this increase will soon be checked and even reversed by a rise in cost; and partly by some of the cash released by importers finding its way, via the repayment of loans, to the banks, who will be able to increase their loans to others and, in order to find lenders, will relax the terms on which they will be ready to lend. But this too will prove a merely temporary effect, since as soon as costs begin generally to rise it will become apparent that there are really no funds available to finance additional investments. In this sense, the effects of this redistribution of money will be of that self-reversing character which is typical of monetary disturbances. This leads, however, already to the difficult question of what constitutes an inflation or deflation within a national area. But before we can go on to this it is necessary to consider what happens in the converse case of the country which has been put in a more favourable condition by the change.

III

Let us first assume that the monetary authorities here as in the other country aim at a constant price level and a constant income stream. The industry which directly benefits from the initial shifts in demand will then find that, because of the fall of foreign exchanges, the increase of their receipts in terms of the national currency will not be as large as would correspond to the increase of their sales in terms of foreign money, while the other export industries will see their receipts actually reduced. Similarly those home industries whose products compete with imports which are now cheaper in terms of the national currency will have to lower their prices and will find their incomes reduced. In short, if the quantity of money in the country, or the price level, is kept constant, the increase of the aggregate value of the products of one industry due to a change in international demand will mean that there has to be a compensating reduction of the prices of the products of other industries. Or, in other words, part of the price reduction which under a regime of stable exchanges would have been necessary in the industry and in the country from which demand has turned away, will under a regime of independent currencies and national stabilization have to take place in the country towards which demand has turned, and in industries which have not been directly affected by the shift in demand.

This at least should be the case if the principle of national stabilization were consistently applied. But it is of course highly unlikely that it ever would be so applied. That in order to counteract the effects of a severe fall of prices in one industry in a country other prices in the country should be allowed to rise appears fairly plausible. But that in order to offset a rise of prices of the products of one industry which is due to an increase in international demand, prices in the other industries should be made to fall sounds far less convincing. I find it difficult to imagine the President of a Central Bank explaining that he has to pursue a policy which means that the prices of many home industries have to be reduced, by pointing out that an increase of international demand has led to an increase of prices in an important export industry, and it seems fairly certain what would happen to him if he tried to do so.

Indeed, if we take a somewhat more realistic point of view, there can be little doubt what will happen. While, in the country where in consequence of the changes in international demand some prices will tend to fall the price level will be kept stable, it will certainly be allowed to rise in the country which has been benefited by the same shift in demand. It is not difficult to see what this implies if all countries in the world act on this principle. It means that prices would be stabilized only in that area where they tend to fall lowest relatively to the rest of the world, and that all further adjustments are brought about by proportionate increases of prices in all other countries. The possibilities of inflation which this offers if the world is split up into a sufficient number of very small separate currency areas seem indeed very considerable. And why, if this principle is once adopted, should it remain confined to average prices in particular national areas? Would it not be equally justified to argue that no price of any single commodity should ever be allowed to fall and that the quantity of money in the world should be so regulated that the price of that commodity which tends to fall lowest relatively to all others should be kept stable, and that the prices of all other commodities would be adjusted upwards in proportion? We only need to remember what happened, for instance, a few years ago to the price of rubber to see how such a policy would surpass the wishes of even the wildest inflationist. Perhaps this may be thought an extreme case. But, once the principle has been adopted, it is difficult to see how it could be confined to 'reasonable' limits, or indeed to say what 'reasonable' limits are.

IV

But let us disregard the practical improbability that a policy of stabilization will be followed in the countries where, with stable exchanges, the price level would rise, as well as in the countries where in this case it would have to fall. Let us assume that, in the countries which benefit from the increase of the demand, the prices of other goods are actually lowered to preserve stability of the national price level and that the opposite action will be taken in the countries from which demand has turned away. What is the justification and significance of such a policy of national stabilization?

Now it is difficult to find the theoretical case for national stabilization anywhere explicitly argued. It is usually just taken for granted that any sort of policy which appears desirable in a closed system must be equally beneficial if applied to a national area. It may therefore be desirable before we go on to examine its analytical justification to trace the historical causes which have brought this view to prominence. There can be little doubt that its ascendancy is closely connected with the peculiar difficulties of English monetary policy between 1925 and 1931. In the comparatively short space of the six years during which Great Britain was on a gold standard in the postwar period, it suffered from what is known as overvaluation of the pound. Against all the teaching of 'orthodox' economics—already a hundred years before Ricardo had expressly stated that he should never advise a government to restore a currency, which was depreciated 30 per cent, to par"[16]—in 1925 the British currency had been brought back to its former gold value. In consequence, to restore equilibrium, it was necessary to reduce *all* prices and costs in proportion as the value of the pound had been raised. This process, particularly because of the notorious difficulty of reducing money wages, proved to be very painful and prolonged. It deprived England of real participation in the boom which led up to the crisis of 1929, and, in the end, its results proved insufficient to secure the maintenance of the restored parity. But all this was not due to an initial shift in the conditions of demand or to any of the causes which may affect the condition of a particular country

[16]In a letter to John Wheatley, dated September 18, 1821, reprinted in *Letters of David Ricardo to Hutches Trower and Others,* edited by James Bonar and Jacob Henry Hollander (Oxford: Clarendon Press, 1899), p. 160. [*The Works and Correspondence of David Ricardo,* ed. Piero Sraffa with the collaboration of M. H. Dobb, vol. 9, *Letters July 1821–1823* (Cambridge: Cambridge University Press, 1952), pp. 71–74. —Ed.]

under stable exchanges. It was an *effect* of the change in the external value of the pound. It was not a case where with given exchange rates the national price or cost structure of a country as a whole had got out of equilibrium with the rest of the world, but rather that the change in the parities had suddenly upset the relations between all prices inside and outside the country.

Nevertheless this experience has created among many British economists a curious prepossession with the relations between national price- and cost- and particularly wage-levels, as if there were any reason to expect that as a rule there would arise a necessity that the price and cost structure of one country as a whole should change relatively to that of other countries. And this tendency has received considerable support from the fashionable pseudo-quantitative economics of averages with its argument running in terms of national 'price levels', 'purchasing power parities', 'terms of trade', the 'multiplier', and what not.

The purely accidental fact that these averages are generally computed for prices in a national area is regarded as evidence that in some sense all prices of a country could be said to move together relatively to prices in other countries.[17] This has strengthened the belief that there is some peculiar difficulty about the case where 'the' price level of a country had to be changed relatively to its given cost level and that such adjustment had better be avoided by manipulations of the rate of exchange.

Now let me add immediately that of course I do not want to deny that there may be cases where some change in conditions might make fairly extensive reductions of money wages necessary in a particular area if exchange rates are to be maintained, and that under present conditions such wage reductions are at best a very painful and long-drawn-out process. At any rate in the case of countries whose exports consist largely of one or a few raw materials, a severe fall in the prices of these products might create such a situation. What I want to suggest, however, is that many of my English colleagues, because of the special experience of their country in recent times, have got the practical significance of this particu-

[17]The fact that the averages of (more or less arbitrarily selected) groups of prices move differently in different countries does of course in no way prove that there is any tendency of the price structure of a country to move as a whole relatively to prices in other countries. It would however be a highly interesting subject for statistical investigation, if a suitable technique could be devised, to see whether, and to what extent, such a tendency existed. Such an investigation would of course involve a comparison not only of some mean value of the price changes in different countries, but of the whole frequency distribution of relative price changes in terms of some common standard. And it should be supplemented by similar investigations of the relative movements of the price structure of different parts of the same country.

lar case altogether out of perspective: that they are mistaken in believing that by altering parities they can overcome many of the chief difficulties created by the rigidity of wages and, in particular, that by their fascination with the relation between 'the' price level and 'the' cost level in a particular area they are apt to overlook the much more important consequences of inflation and deflation.[18]

V

As I have already suggested at an earlier point, the difference of opinion here rests largely on a difference of view on the meaning and consequence of inflation and deflation, or rather in the importance attached to two sorts of effects which spring from changes in the quantity of money. The one view stresses what I have called before the self-reversing character of the effects of monetary changes. It emphasizes the misdirection of production caused by the wrong expectations created by changes in relative prices which are necessarily only temporary, of which the most conspicuous is of course the trade cycle. The other view emphasizes the effects which are due to rigidity of certain money prices, and particularly wages. Now the difficulties which arise when money wages have to be lowered cannot really be called monetary disturbances; the same difficulties would arise if wages were fixed in terms of some commodity. It is only a monetary problem in the sense that this difficulty might to some extent be overcome by monetary means when wages are fixed in terms of money. But the problem left unanswered by the authors who stress this second aspect is whether the difficulty created by the rigidity of money wages can be overcome by monetary adjustments without setting up new disturbances of the first kind. And there are in fact strong reasons to believe that the two aims of avoiding so far as possible downward adjustments of wages and preventing misdirections of production may not always be reconcilable.

This difference in emphasis is so important in connection with the

[18]The propensity of economists in the Anglo-Saxon countries to argue exclusively in terms of national price and wage levels is probably mainly due to the great influence which the writings of Professor Irving Fisher have exercised in these countries. Another typical instance of the dangers of this approach is the well-known controversy about the reparations problem, where it was left to Professor [Bertil] Ohlin to point out against his English opponents that what mainly mattered was not so much effects on total price levels but rather the effects on the position of particular industries. [Ohlin engaged Keynes in an extended debate over the "transfer problem". See *Economic Journal,* March, June, September 1929; also, see the Keynes-Ohlin correspondence in *The Collected Writings of John Maynard Keynes,* vol. 11, *Economic Articles and Correspondence: Academic* (1983), pp. 451–480. —Ed.]

opinions about what are the appropriate principles of national monetary policy because, if one thinks principally in terms of the relation of prices to given wages and particularly if one thinks in terms of national wage 'levels', one is easily led to the conclusion that the quantity of money should be adjusted for each group of people among whom a given system of contracts exists. (To be consistent, of course, the argument should be applied not only to countries but also to particular industries, or at any rate to 'non-competing groups' of workers in each country.) On the other hand, there is no reason why one should expect the self-reversing effects of monetary changes to be connected with the change of the quantity of money in a particular area which is part of a wider monetary system. If a decrease or increase of demand in one area is offset by a corresponding change in demand in another area, there is no reason why the changes in the quantity of money in the two areas should in any sense misguide productive activity. They are simply manifestations of an underlying real change which works itself out through the medium of money.

To illustrate this difference let me take a statement of one of the most ardent advocates of Monetary Nationalism, Roy F. Harrod of Oxford. Harrod is not unfamiliar with what I have called the self-reversing effects of monetary changes. At any rate in an earlier publication he argued that "if industry is stimulated to go forward at a pace which cannot be maintained, you are bound to have periodic crises and depressions".[19] Yet for some reason he seems to think that these misdirections of industry will occur even when the changes in the quantity of money of a particular country take place in the course of the normal redistributions of money between countries. In his *International Economics* there appears the following remarkable passage which seems to express the theoretical basis, or as I think the fallacy, underlying Monetary Nationalism more clearly than any other statement I have yet come across. Harrod is discussing the case of unequal economic progress in different countries with a common standard and concludes that "[t]he less progressive countries would thus be afflicted with the additional inconvenience of a deflatory monetary system. Inflation would occur just where it is most dangerous, namely, in the rapidly advancing countries. This objection appears in one form or

[19]*The International Gold Problem, Collected Papers: A record of the discussions of a study group of members of the Royal Institute of International Affairs, 1929–31* (London: Oxford University Press, Humphrey Milford, 1932), p. 29. Cf. also, in the light of this statement, the remarkable passage in the same author's *International Economics*, Cambridge Economic Handbooks VIII (London: Nisbet, and New York: Harcourt, Brace, 1933), p. 150, where it is argued that "the only way to avoid a slump is to engineer a boom", although only two lines later a boom is still "defined as an increase in the rate of output which cannot be maintained in the long period".

another in all projects for a common world money. . .".[20] And the lesson which Mr. Harrod derives from these considerations is that "the currencies of the more progressive countries must be made to appreciate in terms of the others"[21].

It is interesting to inquire in what sense inflation and deflation are here represented as *additional* inconveniences, superimposed, as it were, on the difficulties created by unequal economic progress. One might think at first that what Mr. Harrod has in mind are the *extra* difficulties caused by the secondary expansions and contractions of credit which are made necessary by the national reserve systems which I have analyzed in an earlier lecture. But this interpretation is excluded by the express assertion that this difficulty appears under *all* forms of a common world money. It seems that the terms inflation and deflation are here used simply as equivalents to increases and decreases of money demand relatively to given costs. In this sense the terms could equally be applied to shifts in demand between different industries and would really mean no more than a change in demand relative to supply. But the objection to this is not only that the terms inflation and deflation are here unnecessarily applied to phenomena which can be described in simpler terms. It is rather whether in this case there is any reason to expect any of the special consequences which we associate with monetary disturbances, that is, whether there really is any "additional inconvenience" by monetary factors proper. We might ask whether in this case there will be any of the peculiar self-reversing effects which are typical of purely monetary causes; in particular whether "inflation" as used here with reference to the increase of money in one country at the expense of another "stimulates industry to go forward at a pace which cannot be maintained"; and whether deflation in the same sense implies a temporary and avoidable contraction of production.

The answer to these questions is not difficult. We know that the really harmful effects of inflation and deflation spring, not so much from the fact that all prices change in the same direction and in the same proportion, but from the fact that the relation between individual prices changes in a direction which cannot be maintained; or in other words that it temporarily brings about a distribution of spending power between individuals which is not stable. We have seen that the international redistributions of money are part of a process which at the same time brings about a redistribution of relative amounts of money held by the different individuals in each country, a redistribution within the nation which would also

[20]Roy F. Harrod, *International Economics*, op. cit., p. 170.
[21]*Ibid.*, p. 174.

have to come about if there were no international money. The difference, however, in the latter case, the case of free currencies, is that here first the relative value of the total amounts of money in each country is changed and that the process of internal redistribution takes place in a manner different from that which would occur with an international monetary standard. We have seen before that the variation of exchange rates will in itself bring about a redistribution of spending power in the country, but a redistribution which is in no way based on a corresponding change in the underlying real position. There will be a temporary stimulus to particular industries to expand, although there are no grounds which would make a lasting increase in output possible. In short, the successive changes in individual expenditure and the corresponding changes of particular prices will not occur in an order which will direct industry from the old to the new equilibrium position. Or, in other words, the effects of keeping the quantity of money in a region or country constant when under an international monetary system it would decrease are essentially inflationary, while to keep it constant if under an international system it would increase at the expense of other countries would have effects similar to an absolute deflation.

I do not want to suggest that the practical importance of the deflationary or inflationary effects of a policy of keeping the quantity of money in a particular area constant is very great. The practical arguments which to me seem to condemn such a policy I have already discussed. The reason why I wanted at least to mention this more abstract consideration is that, if it is correct, it shows particularly clearly the weakness of the theoretical basis of Monetary Nationalism. The proposition that the effects of keeping the quantity of money constant in a territory where with an international currency it would decrease are inflationary and vice versa[22] is of course directly contrary to the position on which Monetary Nationalism is based. Far from admitting that changes in the relative money holdings of different nations which go parallel with changes in their share of

[22]Without giving disproportionate space to what is perhaps a somewhat esoteric theoretical point it is not possible to give here a complete proof of this proposition. A full discussion of the complicated effects would require almost a separate chapter. But a sort of indirect proof may be here suggested. It would probably not be denied that if without any other change the amount of money in one currency area were decreased by a given amount and at the same time the amount of money in another currency area increased by a corresponding amount, this would have deflationary effects in the first area and inflationary effects in the second. And most economists (the more extreme monetary nationalists only excepted) would agree that no such effects would occur if these changes were made simultaneous with corresponding changes in the relative volume of transactions in the two countries. From this it appears to follow that if such a change in the relative volume of transactions in the two countries occurs but the quantity of money in each country is kept constant, this must have the effect of a relative inflation and deflation respectively.

the world's income are harmful, we believe that such redistributions of money are the only way of effecting the change in real income with a minimum of disturbance. And to speak in connection with such changes of national inflation or deflation can only lead to a serious confusion of thought.[23]

Before I leave this subject I should like to supplement these theoretical reflections by a somewhat more practical consideration. While the whole idea of a monetary policy directed to adjust everything to a 'given' wage level appears to me misconceived on purely theoretical grounds, its consequences seem to me to be fantastic if we imagine it applied to the present world where this supposedly given wage level is at the same time the subject of political strife. It would mean that the whole mechanism of collective wage bargaining in the future be used exclusively to raise wages, while any reduction—even if it were necessary only in one particular industry—would have to be brought about by monetary means. I doubt whether such a proposal could ever have been seriously entertained except in a country and in a period where labour has been for long on the defensive.[24] It is difficult to imagine how wage negotiations would be carried on if it became the recognised duty of the monetary authority to offset any unfavourable effect of a rise in wages on the competitive position of national industries on the world market. But of one thing we can probably be pretty certain: that the working class would not be slow to learn that an engineered rise of prices is no less a reduction of wages than a deliberate cut of money wages, and that in consequence the belief that it is easier to reduce by the roundabout method of depreciation the wages of all workers in a country than directly to reduce the money wages of those who are affected by a given change will soon prove illusory.

Lecture 4. International Capital Movements

I

For the purposes of this lecture, by international capital movements I shall mean the acquisition of claims on persons or of rights to property in one country by persons in another country, or the disposal of such claims or property rights in another country to people in that country. This definition is meant to exclude from capital movements the purchase

[23]See on this point also Lionel Robbins, *Economic Planning and International Order,* op. cit., pp. 281 et seq.

[24]It is interesting to note that those countries in Europe where up to 1929 wages had been rising relatively most rapidly were on the whole those most reluctant to experiment with exchange depreciation. The recent experience of France seems also to suggest that a working-class government may never be able to use exchange depreciation as an instrument to lower real wages.

and sale of commodities which pass from one country to the other at the same time as they are paid for and change their owners. But it also excludes any net movement of gold (or other international money) in so far as these movements are payments for commodities or services received (or 'unilateral' payments) and therefore involve a transfer of ownership in that money without creating a new claim from one country to the other. This is of course not the only possible definition of capital movements, and strong arguments could be advanced in favour of a more comprehensive definition, which in effect would treat every transfer of assets from country to country as a capital movement. The reason which leads me to adopt here the former definition is that only on that definition is it possible to distinguish between those items in international transactions which are, and those which are not, capital items.

The first kind of capital item of this sort and the one which will occupy us in this lecture more than any other is the acquisition, or sale, of amounts of the national money of one country by inhabitants of the other.[25] The form which this kind of transaction today predominantly takes is the holding of balances with the banks of one country on the part of banks and individuals in the other country. Such balances will to some extent be held even if there is a safe and stable international standard, since, rather than actually send money, it will as a rule be cheaper for the banks to provide out of such balances those of their customer's requirements which arise out of the normal day-to-day differences between payments and receipts abroad. And if it is possible to hold such balances either in the form of interest-bearing deposits or in the form of bills of exchange, there will be a strong inducement to hold such earning assets as substitutes for the sterile holdings of international money. It was in this way that what is called the gold exchange standard tended more and more to supplant the gold standard proper. In the years immediately preceding 1931 this assumed very great significance.

If there exists a system of fluctuating exchanges, or a system where people are not altogether certain about the maintenance of the existing parities, these balances become even more important. There are two new elements which enter in this case. In the first place it will then no longer be sufficient if banks and others who owe debts in different currencies keep one single liquidity reserve against all their liabilities. It will become

[25]This is not to be interpreted as meaning that I subscribe to the view that all money is in some sense a 'claim'. The statement in the text applies strictly only to credit money and particularly to bank deposits, which will be mainly considered in what follows. But it would not apply to the acquisition of gold by foreigners for export. The gold coins so acquired would thereby cease to be 'national' money in the sense in which this term is here used, that is, they would not be assets belonging to the country where they have been issued.

necessary for them to keep separate liquid assets in each of the different currencies in which they owe debts, and to adjust them to the special circumstances likely to affect liabilities in each currency. We get here new artificial distinctions of liquidity created by the multiplicity of currencies and involving all the consequential possibilities of disturbances following from changes in what is now called 'liquidity preference'. Secondly there will be the chance of a gain or loss on these foreign balances due to changes in the rates of exchange. Thus the anticipation of any impending variation of exchange rates will tend to bring about temporary changes of a speculative nature in the volume of such balances. Whether these two kinds of motives must really be regarded as different, or whether they are better treated as essentially the same, there can be no doubt that variability of exchange rates introduces a new and powerful reason for short-term capital movements, and a reason which is fundamentally different from the reasons which exist under a well-secured international standard.

Foreign bank balances and other holdings of foreign money are of course only part, although probably the most important part, of the volume of short-term foreign investment. It is here that the impact effect of any change in international indebtedness arising out of current transactions will show itself; and it is here that there will be the most ready response to changes in the relative attractiveness of holding assets in the different countries. Once we go beyond this field it becomes rather difficult to say what can properly be called movements of short-term capital. In fact, with the exception of non-funded long-term loans, almost any form of international investment may have to be regarded as short-term investment, including in particular all investments in marketable securities.[26] But for the monetary problems with which we are here concerned it is mainly the short-term credits which are of importance, because it is here that we have to deal with large accumulated funds which are apt to change their location at comparatively slight provocation. Compared with these 'floating' funds, the supply of capital for long-term investment, limited as it will be to a certain part of new savings, will be relatively small.

Now the chief question which we shall have to consider is the question, to what extent under different monetary systems international capital movements are likely to cause monetary disturbances, and to what extent and by what means it may be possible to prevent such disturbances. It

[26]Even the intentions of the lender or investor would hardly provide a sufficient criterion for a distinction between what are short- and what are long-term capital movements, since it may very well be clear in a particular case to the outside observer that circumstances will soon lead the investors to change their intentions.

will again prove useful if we approach this task in three stages, beginning with a consideration of the mechanism and function of international capital movements under a homogeneous standard. Then we shall go on to inquire how this mechanism and the effects are modified if we have 'mixed' currency systems organized on the national reserve principle but with fixed exchange rates. And finally we shall have to see what will be the effects of the existence of variable exchange rates and the way in which fluctuations of the exchange and capital movements mutually influence one another.

II

If exchange rates were regarded as invariably fixed we should expect capital movements to be guided by no other considerations except expected net yield, including of course adjustments which will have to be made for the different degrees of risk inherent in the different sorts of investments. This does not mean that there would not be frequent changes in the flow of capital from country to country. There might of course be a permanent tendency on the part of one country to absorb part of the current savings of another at terms more favourable than those at which these savings could be invested in the country where they are made. Quite apart from these flows of capital for more or less permanent investment, however, there would be periodic or occasional short-term lending to make up for temporary differences between imports and exports of commodities and services.

Now there is of course no reason why exports and imports should move closely parallel from day to day or even from month to month. If in all transactions payment had to be made simultaneously with the delivery of the goods, this would mean, in external trade no less than in internal, a restriction of the possible range of transactions similar in kind to what would occur if all transactions had to take the form of barter. The possibility of credit transactions, the exchange of present goods against future goods, greatly widens the range of advantageous exchanges. In international trade it means in particular that countries may import more than they export in some seasons because they will export more than they import during other seasons. Whether this is made possible by the exporter directly crediting the importer with the price, or whether it takes place by some credit institution in either country providing the money, it will always mean that the indebtedness of the importing country to the exporting increases temporarily, that is, that net short-term lending takes place.

At this point it is necessary especially to be on guard against a form of stating these relations which suggests that short-term lending is made necessary by, or is in any sense a consequence of, a passive balance of trade—that the loans are made so to speak with the purpose of covering a deficit in the balance of trade. We shall get a more correct picture if we think of the great majority of the individual transactions in both ways being credit transactions so that it is the excess lending in one direction during any given period which has made possible a corresponding excess of exports in the same direction. If we look on the whole process in this way we can see how considerable a part of trade is only made possible by short-term capital movements. We can see also how misleading it may be to think of capital movements as exclusively directed by previous changes in the relative rates of interest in the different money markets. What directs the use of the available credit and therefore decides in what direction the balance of indebtedness will shift at a particular moment is in the first instance the relation between prices in different places. It is of course true that where each country habitually finances its exports and borrows its imports any absolute increase of exports will tend to bring about an increase in the demand loans and therefore a rise in the rate of interest in the exporting country. But in such a case the rise in the rate of interest is rather the effect of this country lending more abroad than a cause of a flow of capital to the country. And although this rise in money rates may lead to a flow of funds in the reverse direction, that will be more a sign that the main mechanism for the distribution of funds works imperfectly than a part of this mechanism. There is no more reason to say that the international redistribution of short-term capital is brought about by changes in the rates of interest in the different localities than there would be for saying that the seasonal transfers of funds from, say, agriculture to coal mining are brought about by a fall of the rate of interest in agriculture and rise in coal mining or vice versa.

Changes in short-term international indebtedness must therefore be considered as proceeding largely concurrently with normal fluctuations in international trade; and only certain remaining balances will be settled by a flow of funds, largely of an inter-bank character, induced by differences in interest rates to be earned. It is of course not to be denied that, apart from changes in international indebtedness which are more directly connected with international trade, there may also be somewhat sudden and considerable flows of funds which may be caused either by the sudden appearance of very profitable opportunities for investment, or by some panic which causes an insistent demand for cash. In this last case indeed it is true that the flow of short-term funds may transmit monetary disturbances to parts of the world which have nothing to do with the original cause of the disturbance, as say a war-scare in South America might conceivably lead to a general rise in interest rates in London. But, apart from such special cases, it is difficult to see how under a homogeneous international standard, capital movements, and particularly short-term capital movements, should be a source of instability or lead to any changes in productive activity which are not justified by corresponding changes in the real conditions.

III

This conclusion was, however, to be somewhat modified if, instead of a homogeneous international currency, we consider a world consisting of separate national monetary and banking systems, even if we still leave the possibility of variations in exchange rates out of account. It is of course a well-known fact that one of the main purposes of changes in the discount rate of central banks is to influence the international movements of short-term capital.[27] A central bank which is faced with an outflow of gold will raise its discount rate in the hope that by attracting short-term credits it will offset the gold outflow. To the extent that it succeeds it will postpone the necessity of more drastic credit contraction at home, and—if the cause of the adverse balance of trade is transitory—it may perhaps altogether avoid it. But it is by no means evident that it will attract the funds just from where the gold would tend to flow, and it may well be that it only passes on the necessity of credit contraction to another country. And if for some reason all or the majority of central banks should at a particular moment feel that they ought to become more liquid and for this purpose raise their discount rates, the sole effect will be a kind of general tug-of-war in which all central banks, trying to prevent an outflow of funds and if possible to attract funds, only succeed in bringing about a violent contraction of credit at home. But although the fact that central banks react to all major gold movements with changes in the rate of discount may mean that changes in the volume and direction of short-term credits will be more frequent and violent if we have a number of banking systems organized on national lines, it is again not the fact that the system is international, but rather that it creates impediments to the free international flow of funds which must be regarded as responsible for these disturbances.

Again we must be careful not to ascribe this difficulty to the existence of central banks in particular, although in a sense the growth of the sort

[27]If this effect was disregarded in the discussion of changes in the discount rates in the two preceding lectures, this was done to make the effects discussed there stand out more clearly; but this must not be taken to mean that this effect on capital movements is not, at any rate in the short run, perhaps the most important effect of these changes.

of credit structure to which they are due was only made possible by the existence of some such institutions. The ultimate source of the difficulty is the differentiation between moneys of different degrees of acceptability or liquidity, the existence of a structure consisting of superimposed layers of reserves of different degrees of liquidity, which makes the movement of short-term money rates, and in consequence the movement of short-term funds, much more dependent on the liquidity position of the different financial institutions than on changes in the demand for capital for real investment. It is because with 'mixed' national monetary systems the movements of short-term funds are frequently due, not to changes in the demand for capital for investment, but to changes in the demand for cash as liquidity reserves, that short-term international capital movements have such a bad reputation as causes of monetary disturbances. And this reputation is not altogether undeserved.

But now the question arises whether this defect can be removed not by making the medium of circulation in the different countries more homogeneous, but rather, as the Monetary Nationalists wish, by severing even the remaining tie between the national currencies, the fixed parities between them. This question is of particular importance since the idea that the national monetary authorities should never be forced by an outflow of capital to take any action which might unfavourably affect economic activity at home is probably the main source of the demand for variable exchanges. To this question therefore we must return now.

IV

The chief questions which we shall have to consider here are three: Will the volume of short-term capital movement be larger or smaller when there exists uncertainty about the future of exchange rates? Are the national monetary authorities in a position either to prevent capital movements which they regard as undesirable, or to offset their effects? And, finally, what further measures, if any, are necessary if the aims of such a policy are to be consistently followed?

We have already partly furnished the answer to the first question. Although the contrary has actually been asserted, I am altogether unable to see why under a regime of variable exchanges the volume of short-term capital movements as well as the frequency of changes in their direction should be anything but greater.[28] Every suspicion that exchange rates

[28]The only argument against this view which I find at all intelligible is that, under the gold standard, movements to one of the gold points will create a certain expectation that the movement will soon be reversed and thus provides a special inducement to speculative shifts of funds. But while this is perfectly true, it only shows that the defects of the tradi-

were likely to change in the near future would create an additional powerful motive for shifting funds from the country whose currency was likely to fall or to the country whose currency was likely to rise. I should have thought that the experience of the whole post-war period and particularly of the last few years had so amply confirmed what one might have expected a priori that there could be no reasonable doubt about this.[29] There is only one point which perhaps still deserves to be stressed a little further. Where the possible fluctuations of exchange rates are confined to narrow limits above and below a fixed point, as between the two gold points, the effect of short-term capital movements will be on the whole to reduce the amplitude of the actual fluctuations, since every movement away from the fixed point will as a rule create the expectation that it will soon be reversed. That is, short-term capital movements will on the whole tend to relieve the strain set up by the original cause of a temporarily adverse balance of payments. If exchanges, however, are variable, the capital movements will tend to work in the same direction as the original cause and thereby to intensify it. This means that if this original cause is already a short-term capital movement, the variability of exchanges will tend to multiply its magnitude and may turn what originally might have been a minor inconvenience into a major disturbance.

Much more difficult is the answer to the second question: Can the authorities control these movements; since what the monetary authorities can achieve in a particular direction will largely depend on what other consequences of their action they are willing to put up with. In the particular case the question is mainly whether they would be willing to let exchange rates fluctuate to any degree or whether they would not feel that although moderate fluctuations of exchange rates were not worth the cost

---

tional gold standard were due to the fact that it was not a homogeneous international currency. If the same arrangements applied to international as to infranational payments, the problem would disappear. This would be the case either if within the country as much as between countries the costs of transfers of money were not borne by some institution like the central banks and cconsequently (as in the United States before the establishment of the Federal Reserve System) rates of exchange between the different towns were allowed to fluctuate, and if at the same time gold were freely obtainable near the frontier as well as in the capital, or on the other hand, if the system of par clearance were applied to international as well as national payments. On the last point compare below, lecture 5, p. 93.

[29]Since it is being more and more forgotten that the period before 1931 was, on prewar standards, already one of marked instability—and uncertainty about the future—of exchange rates, it is perhaps worth stressing that in particular the accumulation of foreign balances in London during that period was almost entirely a consequence of the fact that Sterling was regarded as relatively the most safe of the European currencies. Cf. on this T. E. Gregory, *The Gold Standard and its Future,* 3rd edition (New York: Dutton, 1934), pp. 48 et. seq.

of preventing them, yet they must not be allowed to exceed certain limits, since the unsettling effects from large fluctuations would be worse than the measures by which they could be prevented. In practice we must probably assume that even if the authorities are prepared to allow a slow and gradual depreciation of exchanges, they would feel bound to take strong action to counteract it as soon as it threatened to lead to a flight of capital or a strong rise of prices of imported goods.

The theory that by keeping exchange rates flexible a country could prevent dear money abroad from affecting home conditions is of course not a new one. It was for instance argued by the opponents of the introduction of the gold standard in Austria in 1892 that the paper standard insulated and protected Austria from disturbances originating on the world markets. But I doubt whether it has ever been carried quite as far as by some of our contemporary Monetary Nationalists, for instance Mr. Harrod, who declared that he could not accept exchange stabilization "if thereby a country is committed to an interior monetary policy which involves raising the bank rate of interest".[30] The modern idea apparently is that never under any circumstances must an outflow of capital be allowed to raise interest rates at home, and the advocates of this view seem to be satisfied that if the central banks are not committed to maintain a particular parity they will have no difficulty either in preventing an outflow of capital altogether or in offsetting its effect by substituting additional bank credit for the funds which have left the country.

It is not easy to see on what this confidence is founded. So long as the outward flow of capital is not effectively prevented by other means, a persistent effort to keep interest rates low can only have the effect of prolonging this tendency indefinitely and of bringing about a continuous and progressive fall of the exchanges. Whether the outward flow of capital starts with a withdrawal of balances held in the country by foreigners, or with an attempt on the parts of nationals of the country to acquire assets abroad, it will deprive banking institutions at home of funds which they were able to lend, and at the same time lower the exchanges. If the central bank succeeds in keeping interest rates low in the first instance by substituting new credits for the capital which has left the country, it will not only perpetuate the conditions under which the export of capital has been attractive; the effect of capital exports on the rates of exchange will,

[30]Cf. Antwerp Chambre de Commerce, *Compte-rendu des travaux de la réunion d'économistes organisée par la Chambre de commerce d'Anvers les 11, 12, et 13 juillet 1935, [Report of the Proceedings of the Meeting of Economists held at the Antwerp Chamber of Commerce on July 11, 12, and 13, 1935]*, published by the Antwerp Chamber of Commerce (Brecht-Anvers: Typ. Braeckmans, 1935), p. 107.

as we have seen, tend to become self-inflammatory and a 'flight of capital' will set in. At the same time the rise of prices at home will increase the demand for loans because it means an increase in the 'real' rate of profit. And the adverse balance of trade which must necessarily continue while part of the receipts from exports is used to repay loans or to make new loans abroad means that the supply of real capital and therefore the 'natural' or 'equilibrium' rate of interest in the country will rise. It is clear that under such conditions the central bank could not, merely by keeping its discount rate low, prevent a rise of interest rates without at the same time bringing about a major inflation.

V

If this is correct it would be only consistent if the advocates of Monetary Nationalism should demand that monetary policy proper should be supplemented by a strict control of the export of capital. If the main purpose of monetary management is to prevent exports of capital from disturbing conditions of the money market at home, this clearly is a necessary complement of central banking policy. But those who favour such a course seem hardly to be conscious of what it involves. It would certainly not be sufficient in the long run merely to prohibit the more conspicuous forms of sending money abroad. It is of course true that if there are no impediments to the export of capital the most convenient and therefore perhaps the quantitatively most important form which the export of capital will take is the actual transfer of money from country to country. And it is conceivable that this might be pretty effectively prevented by mere prohibition and control. To make even this really effective would of course involve not only a prohibition of foreign lending and of the import of securities of any description, but could hardly stop short of a full-fledged system of foreign exchange control. But exchange control designed to prevent effectively the outflow of capital would really have to involve a complete control of foreign trade, since of course any variation in the terms of credit on exports or imports means an international capital movement.

To anyone who doubts the importance of this factor, I strongly recommend the very interesting memorandum on International Short Term Indebtedness which has recently been published by Mr. F. G. Conolly of the staff of the Bank for International Settlements in the recent joint publication of the Carnegie Endowment and the International Chamber of Commerce.[31] I will quote only one paragraph. "It has been the experi-

[31] Frederick George Conolly, "Memorandum on the International Short-term Indebtedness", in *The Improvement of Commercial Relations Between Nations. The Problem of Monetary Stabilization:* Separate Memoranda from the Economists consulted by the Joint Committee of the

ence of every country whose currency has come under pressure", writes Mr. Conolly, "that importers tend not only to refuse to utilise the normal period of credit but to cover their requirements for months in advance: they prefer to utilise the home currency while it retains its international value rather than run the risk of being forced to pay extra for the foreign currency necessary for their purchases. Exporters, on the other hand, tend to allow foreign currencies, the proceeds of exports already made, to lie abroad and to finance their current operations as far as possible by borrowing at home. Thus a double strain falls on the exchange market: the normal supply of foreign currencies from exports dries up while the demands from importers greatly increase. For a country with a large foreign trade the strain on the exchange market due to the effects of this change over in trade financing may be very considerable".[32] What Mr. Conolly here describes amounts, of course, to an export of capital which could only be prevented by controlling the terms of every individual transaction of the country's foreign trade, an export of capital which may be equally formidable whether the country carries on its foreign trade 'actively' or 'passively',[33] that is whether it normally provides the capital to finance the trade herself or borrows it. Indeed to anyone who has had any experience of foreign exchange control there should be no doubt possible that an export of capital can only be prevented by controlling not only the volume of exports and imports so that they will always balance, but also the terms of credit of all these transactions.

At first indeed, and so long as discrepancies between national rates of interest are not too big and people have not yet fully learnt to adapt themselves to fluctuating exchanges, much less thoroughgoing measures may be quite effective. I can already hear some of my English friends point out to me the marvellous discipline of the City of London, which on a slight hint from the Bank that capital exports would be undesirable will refrain from acting against the general interest. But we need only visualize how big the discrepancies between national interest rates would become if capital movements were for a time effectively stopped in order to realize how illusionary must be the hopes that anything but the strictest control will be able to prevent them.

Carnegie Endowment for International Peace and the International Chamber of Commerce on the improvement of commercial relations between nations and the problems of monetary stabilization, followed by the practical conclusions of a Committee of Experts (Paris: International Chamber of Commerce, June, 1936), pp. 352 et seq.

[32] *Ibid.*, p. 360.

[33] Cf. Nikolaas G. Pierson, "The Problem of Value in the Socialist Society, in *Collectivist Economic Planning: Critical Studies on the Possibilities of Socialism* by N. G. Pierson, Ludwig von Mises, Georg Halm and Enrico Barone. Edited, with an Introduction and a concluding essay, by F. A. Hayek (London: Routledge & Kegan Paul, 1935).

But let us disregard for the moment the technical difficulties inherent in any effective control of international capital movements. Let us assume that the monetary authorities are willing to go any distance in creating new impediments to international trade and that they actually succeed in preventing any unwanted change in international indebtedness. Will this successfully insulate a country against the shocks which may result from changes in the rates of interest abroad? Or will these not still transmit themselves via the effect such a change of interest rates will have on the relative prices of the internationally traded securities and commodities? It is probably obvious that so long as there is a fairly free international movement of securities no great divergence in the movement of rates of interest in the different countries can persist for any length of time. But Monetary Nationalists would probably not hesitate at any rate to attempt to inhibit these movements. It is not so generally recognised however that commodity movements will have a similar effect, and perhaps this needs a few more words of explanation.

It will probably not be denied that a considerable rise in the rate of interest will lead to a fall in the prices of some commodities relative to those of others, particularly of those which are largely used for the production of capital goods and of those of which large stocks are held, compared with those which are destined for more or less immediate consumption. And surely, in the absence of immediate adjustments in tariffs or quotas, such a fall will transmit itself to the prices of similar commodities in the country in which interest rates at first are not allowed to rise. But if the prices of the goods which are largely used for investment fall relative to the prices of other goods, this means an increased profitability of investment compared with current production, consequently an increased demand for loans at the existing rates of interest, and, unless the central bank is willing to allow an indefinite expansion of credit, it will be compelled by the rise of interest rates abroad to raise its own rate of interest, even if any outflow of capital has been effectively prevented. Although the supply of capital may not change, the kind of goods which under the changed circumstances it will be most profitable to import and export will still alter the demand for capital with the same effects.[34]

The truth of the whole matter is that for a country which is sharing in the advantages of the international division of labour it is not possible to escape from the effects of disturbances in these international trade relations by means short of severing all the trade ties which connect it with the rest of the world. It is of course true that the less the points of contact with the rest of the world, the less will be the extent to which disturbances originating outside the country will affect its internal conditions. But it

[34]Cf. on this Lionel Robbins, *The Great Depression* (London: Macmillan, 1934), p. 175.

is an illusion that it would be possible, while remaining a member of the international commercial community, to prevent disturbances from the outside world from reaching the country by following a national monetary policy such as would be indicated if the country were a closed community. It is for this reason that the ideology of Monetary Nationalism has proved, and if it remains influential will prove to an even greater extent in the future, to be one of the main forces destroying what remnants of an international economic system we still have.

There are two more points which I should like specially to emphasize before I conclude for today. One is that up to this point I have, following the practice of the Monetary Nationalists, considered mainly the disturbing effects on a country of changes in the demand for capital originating abroad. But there is of course another side to this picture. What from the point of view of the country to which the effects are transmitted from abroad is a disturbance is from the point of view of the country where the original change takes place a stabilising effect. To have to give up capital because somewhere a sudden more urgent demand has arisen is certainly unsettling. But to be able to obtain capital at short notice if a sudden unforeseen need arises at home will certainly tend to stabilise conditions at home. It is more than unlikely that fluctuations on the national capital market would be smaller if the world were cut up into watertight compartments. The probability is rather that in this case fluctuations within each national territory would be much more violent and disturbing than they are now.

Closely connected with this is the second point, on which I can touch only even more briefly. I have already mentioned the probability that the restrictions on capital movements involved in a policyof Monetary Nationalism would tend to increase the differences between national interest rates. This would of course be due to the fact that while instability of exchange rates would tend to increase the volume and frequency of irregular flows of short-term funds, it would to an even greater degree decrease the volume of international long-term investment. Although by some this is regarded as a good thing, I doubt whether they fully appreciate what it would mean. The purely economic effects, the restriction of international division of labour which it implies, and the reduction in the total volume of investment to which it would almost certainly lead, are bad enough. But even more serious seem to me the political effects of the intensification of the differences in the standard of life between different countries to which it would lead. It does not need much imagination to visualize the new sources of international friction which such a situation would create.[35] But this leads me beyond the proper scope of these lec-

[35]Cf. in this Lionel Robbins, *Economic Planning and International Order*, op. cit., pp. 68 et seq.

tures and I must confine myself to drawing your attention to it without attempting to elaborate it any further.

Lecture 5. The Problems of a Really International Standard

I

I have now concluded the negative part of my argument, the case against independent national currencies. While I cannot hope in the space of these few lectures completely to have refuted the theoretical basis of Monetary Nationalism, I hope at least to have shown three things: that there is no rational basis for the separate regulation of the quantity of money in a national area which remains a part of a wider economic system; that the belief that by maintaining an independent national currency we can insulate a country against financial shocks originating abroad is largely illusory; and that a system of fluctuating exchanges would on the contrary introduce new and very serious disturbances of international stability. I do not want now further to add to this, except that I might perhaps remind you that my argument throughout assumed that such a system would be run as intelligently as is humanly possible. I have refrained from supporting my case by pointing to the abuses to which such a system would almost certainly lend itself, to the practical impossibility of different countries agreeing on what degree of depreciation is justified, to the consequent danger of competitive depreciation, and the general return to mercantilist policies of restriction which now, as in earlier centuries, are the inevitable reaction to debasement in other countries.[36]

We must recognize, therefore, that independent regulation of the various national currencies cannot be regarded as in any sense a substitute for a rationally regulated world monetary system. Such a system may today seem an unattainable ideal. But this does not mean that the question of what we can do to get as near the ideal as may be practicable does not present a number of important problems. Of course some 'international' systems would be far from ideal. I hope I have made it clear in particular that I do not regard the sort of international system which we have had in the past as by any means completely satisfactory. The Monetary Nationalists condemn it because it is international; I, on the other hand, ascribe its shortcomings to the fact that it is not international enough. But

[36]I feel I must remind the reader here that limitations of time made it impossible for me to dwell in these lectures on the tremendously important practical effects of a policy of Monetary Nationalism on commercial policy as long as I should have wished. Although this is well-trodden ground, it cannot be too often reiterated that without stability of exchange rates it is vain to hope for any reduction of trade barriers.

the question how we can make it more satisfactory, that is, more genuinely international, I have not yet touched upon. It is a question which raises exceedingly difficult problems; I can survey them only rapidly in this final lecture.

The first, but by no means the most important or most interesting question which I must consider, is the question whether the international standard need be gold. On purely economic grounds it must be said that there are hardly any arguments which can be advanced for, and many serious objections which can be raised against, the use of gold as the international money. In a securely established world State with a government immune against the temptations of inflation, it might be absurd to spend enormous effort in extracting gold out of the earth if cheap tokens would render the same service as gold with equal or greater efficiency. Yet in a world consisting of sovereign national States there seem to me to exist compelling political reasons why gold (or the precious metals) alone and no kind of artificial international currency, issued by some international authority, could be used successfully as the international money. It is essential for the working of an international standard that each country's holdings of the international money should represent for it a reserve of exchange medium which in all eventualities will remain universally acceptable in international transactions. And so long as there are separate sovereign States, there will always loom large among these eventualities the danger of war or of the breakdown of the international monetary arrangements for some other reason. And since people will always feel that against these emergencies they will have to hold some reserve of the one thing which by age-long custom civilized as well as uncivilized people are ready to accept—that is, since gold alone will serve one of the purposes for which stocks of money are held—and since to some extent gold will always be held for this purpose, there can be little doubt that it is the only sort of international standard which in the present world has any chance of surviving. But, to repeat, while an international standard is desirable on purely economic grounds, the choice of gold with all its undeniable defects is made necessary entirely by political considerations.

What should be done if the well-known defects of gold should make themselves too strongly felt, if violent changes in the condition of its production or the appearance of a large new demand for it should threaten sudden changes in its value, is of course a problem of major importance. But it is neither the most interesting nor the most important problem and I do not propose to discuss it here. The difficulties which I want to consider are rather those which were inherent in the international gold standard, even before 1914, and to a still greater degree during its short postwar existence. They are the problems which arise out of the fact that the so-called gold currencies are connected with gold only through the comparatively small national reserves which form the basis of a multiple superstructure of credit money which itself consists of many different layers of different degrees of liquidity or acceptability. It is, as we have seen, this fact which makes the effects of changes in the international flow of money different from merely interlocal shifts, to which is due the existence of separate national monetary systems which to some extent have a life of their own. The homogeneity of the circulating medium of different countries has been destroyed by the growth of separate banking systems organized on national lines. Can anything be done to restore it?

II

It is important here first to distinguish between the need for some 'lender of last resort' and the organization of banking on the 'national reserve' principle. That an extensive use of bank deposits as money would not be possible, that deposit banking of the modern type could not exist, unless somebody were in a position to provide the cash if the public should suddenly want to convert a considerable part of its holdings of bank deposits into more liquid forms of money, is probably beyond doubt. It is far less obvious why all the banking institutions in a particular area or country should rely on a single national reserve. This is certainly not a system which anybody would have deliberately devised on rational grounds and it grew up as an accidental by-product of a policy concerned with different problems.[37] The rational choice would seem to lie between either a system of 'free banking', which not only gives all banks the right of note issue and at the same time makes it necessary for them to rely on their own reserves, but also leaves them free to choose their field of operation and their correspondents without regard to national boundaries,[38] and on the other hand, an international central bank. I need not add that both of these ideals seem utterly impracticable in the world as we know it. But I am not certain whether the compromise we have chosen, that of national central banks which have no direct power over the bulk of the national circulation but which hold as the sole ultimate reserve a comparatively small amount of gold, is not one of the most unstable arrangements imaginable.

Let us recall for a moment the essential features of the so-called gold standard systems as they have existed in modern times. The most widely

[37]Cf. W. Bagehot, *Lombard Street* (London: P. S. King, 1873) and Vera C. Smith, *The Rationale of Central Banking* (London: P. S. King, 1936; reprinted, Indianapolis, Ind.: Liberty-Press, 1990).

[38]Cf. Ludwig von Mises, *Geldwertstabilisierung und Konjunkturpolitik* (Jena: G. Fischer, 1928).

used medium of exchange, bank deposits, is not fixed in quantity. Additional deposits may at any time spontaneously spring up (be 'created' by the banks) or part of the total may similarly disappear. But while they are predominantly used in actual payments, they are by no means the only forms in which balances can be held to meet such payments. In this function deposits on current account are only one item—a very liquid one, although by no means the most liquid of all—in a long range of assets of varying degrees of liquidity.[39] Overdraft facilities, saving deposits, and many types of very marketable securities on the one hand, and bank notes and coin on the other, will at different times and to different degrees compete with bank deposits in this function. And the amounts which will be held on current account to meet expected demands need not therefore fluctuate with the expected magnitude of these payments; they may also change with any change in the views about the ease with which it will be possible to convert these other assets into bank deposits. The supply of bank deposits on the other hand will depend on similar considerations. How much the banks will be willing to owe in this form in excess of the ready cash they hold will depend on their view as to how easy it will be to convert other assets into cash. It is when general confidence is high, so that comparatively small amounts of bank deposits will be needed for a given volume of payments, that the banks will be more ready to increase the amount of bank deposits. On the other hand, any increase of uncertainty about the future will lead to an increased demand for all the more liquid forms of assets, that is, in particular, for bank deposits and cash, and to a decrease in the supply of bank deposits.

Where there is a central bank the responsibility for the provision of cash for the conversion of deposits is divided between the banks and the central bank, or one should probably better say shifted from the banks to the central bank, since it is now the recognized duty of the central banks to supply in an emergency—at a price—all the cash that may be needed to repay deposits. Yet while the ultimate responsibility to provide the cash when needed is thus placed on the central bank, until this demand actually arises, the latter has little power to prevent the expansion leading to an increased demand for cash.

But with an international standard, a national central bank is itself not a free agent. Up to this point the cash about which I have been speaking is the money created by the central bank which within the country is

[39]Refer particularly to John R. Hicks, *A Suggestion for Simplifying the Theory of Money* (*Economica, N. S.*, vol. 2, no. 5, February 1935; reprinted in Hicks, *Critical Essays in Monetary Theory* (Oxford: Oxford University Press, 1967), and Frederick Lavington, *The English Capital Market* (London: Methuen, 1921), p. 30.

generally acceptable and is the only means of payment outside the circle of the customers of a particular bank. The central bank, however, has not only to provide the required amounts of the medium generally accepted within the country; it has also to provide the even more liquid, internationally acceptable, money. This means that in a situation where there is a general tendency towards greater liquidity there will be at the same time a greater demand for central bank money and for the international money. But the only way in which the central bank can restrict the demand for and increase the supply of the international money is to curtail the supply of central bank money. In consequence, in this stage as in the preceding one, any increase in the demand for the more liquid type of money will lead to a much greater decrease in the supply of the somewhat less liquid kinds of money.

This differentiation between the different kinds of money into those which can be used only among the customers of a particular bank and those which can be used only within a particular country and finally those which can be used internationally—these artificial distinctions of liquidity (as I have previously called them)—have the effect, therefore, that any change in the relative demand for the different kinds of money will lead to a cumulative change in the total quantity of the circulating medium. Any demand on the banks for conversion of part of their deposits into cash will have the effect of compelling them to reduce their deposits by more than the amount paid out and to obtain more cash from the central bank, which in turn will be forced to take countermeasures and so to transmit the tendency towards contraction to the other banks. And the same applies, of course, *mutatis mutandis* to a decrease in the demand for the more liquid type of assets, which will bring about a considerable increase in the supply of money.

All this is of course only the familiar phenomenon which Ralph Hawtrey has so well described as the "inherent instability of credit". But there are two points about it which deserve special emphasis in this connection. One is that, in consequence of the particular organisation of our credit structure, changes in liquidity preference as between different kinds of money are probably a much more potent cause of disturbances than the changes in the preference for holding money *in general* and holding goods *in general* which have played such a great role in recent refinements of theory. The other is that this source of disturbance is likely to be much more serious when there is only a single bank for a whole region or when all the banks of a country have to rely on a single central bank; since the effect of any change in liquidity preference will generally be confined to the group of people who directly or indirectly rely on the same reserve of more liquid assets.

It seems to follow from all this that the problem with which we are concerned is not so much a problem of currency reform in the narrower sense as a problem of banking reform in general. The seat of the trouble is what has been very appropriately called the perverse elasticity of bank deposits[40] as a medium of circulation, and the cause of this is that deposits, like other forms of 'credit money', are claims for another, more generally acceptable sort of money, that a proportional reserve of that other money must be held against them, and that their supply is therefore inversely affected by the demand for the more liquid type of money.

III

By far the most interesting suggestion on Banking Reform which has been advanced in recent years, not because in its present form it seems to be practicable or even theoretically right, but because it goes to the heart of the problem, is the so-called Chicago or 100 per cent plan.[41] This proposal amounts in effect to an extension of the principles of Peel's Act of 1844 to bank deposits. The most practicable suggestion yet made for its execution is to give the banks a sufficient quantity of paper money to increase the reserves held against demand deposits to 100 per cent and henceforth to require them to maintain permanently such a 100 per cent reserve.

In this form the plan is conceived as an instrument of Monetary Nationalism. But there is no reason why it should not equally be used to create a homogeneous international currency.[42] A possible, although perhaps somewhat fantastic, solution would seem to be to reduce proportionately the gold equivalents of all the different national monetary units to such an extent that all the money in all countries could be covered 100 per cent by gold, and from that date onwards to allow variations in the national circulations only in proportion to changes in the quantity of gold in the country.[43] Such a plan would clearly require as an essential complement an international control of the production of gold, since the increase in the value of gold would otherwise bring about an enormous

[40] Lauchlin Currie, *The Supply and Control of Money in the United States,* Harvard Economic Studies, vol. 47 (Cambridge, Mass.: Harvard University Press, 1934), pp. 130 et seq.

[41] On the significance of the "Chicago Plan" compare particularly the interesting and stimulating article by H. C. Simons, "Rule versus Authority in Monetary Policy", *Journal of Political Economy,* vol. 44, no. 1, February 1936, and Friedrich August Lutz, *Das Grundproblem der Geldverfassung* (Stuttgart and Berlin: W. Kohlhammer, 1936), where references to the further literature on the proposal will be found.

[42] See H. C. Simons, *op. cit.,* p. 5, note 3.

[43] A perhaps somewhat less impracticable alternative might be international bimetallism at a suitable ratio.

increase in the supply of gold. But this would only provide a safety valve probably necessary in any case to prevent the system from becoming all too rigid.[44]

The undeniable attractiveness of this proposal lies exactly in the feature which makes it appear somewhat impracticable, in the fact that in effect it amounts, as is fully realized by at least one of its sponsors, to an abolition of deposit banking as we know it.[45] It does provide instead of the variety of media of circulation which today range according to their degree of acceptability from bank deposits to gold, one single kind of money. And it would do away effectively with that most pernicious feature of our present system: namely that a movement towards more liquid types of money causes an actual decrease in the total supply of money and vice versa. The most serious question which it raises, however, is whether by abolishing deposit banking as we know it we would effectively prevent the principle on which it rests from manifesting itself in other forms. It has been well remarked by the most critical among the originators of the scheme that banking is a pervasive phenomenon[46] and the question is whether, when we prevent it from appearing in its traditional form, we will not just drive it into other and less easily controllable forms. Historical precedent rather suggests that we must be wary in this respect. The Act of 1844 was designed to control what then seemed to be the only important substitute for gold as a widely used medium of exchange and yet failed completely in its intention because of the rapid growth of bank deposits. Is it not possible that if similar restrictions to those placed on bank notes were now placed on the expansion of bank deposits, new forms of money substitutes would rapidly spring up or existing ones would assume increasing importance? And can we even today draw a sharp line between what is money and what is not? Are there not already all sorts of 'near-moneys'[47] like savings deposits, overdraft facilities, bills of exchange, etc., which satisfy at any rate the demand for liquid reserves nearly as well as money?

[44][This proposal was not as infeasible as it now might seem. In 1934, after the United States devalued the dollar from $25 per ounce of gold to $34 and continued alone among nations to purchase all gold offered at that price, the supply of monetary gold increased dramatically, drawn from Asian hordes and newly profitable mines in South Africa. Frank Graham wrote at the time, "There is enough gold in the monetary reserves of the world to replace all ordinary currency of the entire world 100 per cent with gold coins. Never until the present decade was such a situation as this even approached". Frank D. Graham and Charles R. Whittlesey, *Golden Avalanche* (Princeton: Princeton University Press, 1939), p. 15.—Ed.]

[45]See H. C. Simons, op. cit., p. 16.

[46]*Ibid.*, p. 17.

[47]Op. cit., p. 17.

I am afraid all must be admitted, and it considerably detracts from the alluring simplicity of the 100 per cent banking scheme. It appears that for this reason it has now also been abandoned by at least one of its original sponsors.[48] The problem is evidently a much wider one, and I agree with Henry C. Simons that "it cannot be dealt with merely by legislation directed at what we call banks".[49] Yet in one respect at least the 100 per cent proposal seems to me to point in the right direction. Even if, as is probably the case, it is impossible to draw a sharp line between what is to be treated as money and what is not, and if consequently any attempt to fix rigidly the quantity of what is more or less arbitrarily segregated as 'money' would create serious difficulties, it yet remains true that, within the field of instruments which are undoubtedly generally used as money, there are unnecessary and purely institutional distinctions of liquidity which are the sources of serious disturbances and which should as far as possible be eliminated. If this cannot be done for the time being by a general return to the common use of the same international medium in the great majority of transactions, it should at least be possible to approach this goal by reducing the distinctions of liquidity between the different kinds of money actually used, and offsetting as far as possible the effects of changes in the demand for liquid assets on the total quantity of circulating medium.

IV

This brings me to the more practical question of what can be done to diminish the instability of the credit structure if the general framework of the present monetary system is to be maintained. The aim, as we have just seen, must be to increase the certainty that one form of money will always be readily exchangeable against other forms of money at a known rate, and that such changes should not lead to changes in the total quantity of money. In so far as the relations between different national currencies are concerned, this leads, of course, to a demand for reforms in exactly the opposite direction from those advocated by Monetary Nationalists. Instead of flexible parities or a widening of the 'gold points', absolute fixity of the exchange rates should be secured by a system of international par clearance. If all the central banks undertook to buy and sell foreign exchange freely at the same fixed rates, and in this way prevented even fluctuations with the 'gold points', the remaining differences in denomination of the national currencies would really be no more significant

[48]*Ibid.*, p. 17.
[49]*Ibid.*

than the fact that the same quantity of cloth can be stated in yards and in meters. With an international gold settlement fund on the lines of that operated by the Federal Reserve System, which would make it possible to dispense with the greater part of the actual gold movements which used to take place in the past, invariable rates of exchange could be maintained without placing any excessive burden on the central banks.[50] The main aim here would of course be rather to remove one of the main causes of international movements of short-term funds than to prevent such movements or to offset their effects by means which will only increase the inducement to such movements.[51]

But invariability of the exchange rates is only one precondition of a successful policy directed to minimize monetary disturbances. It eliminates one of the institutional differentiations of liquidity which are likely to give rise to sudden changes in favour of holding one sort of money instead of another. But there remains the further distinction between the different sorts of money which constitute the national monetary systems; and, so long as the general framework of our present banking systems is retained, the dangers to stability which arise here can hardly be combatted otherwise than by a deliberate policy of the national central banks.

The most important change which seems to be necessary here is that the gold reserves of all the central banks should be made large enough to relieve them of the necessity of bringing about a change in the total national circulation *in proportion* to the changes in their reserves; that is, that any change in the relative amounts of money in different countries should be brought about by the actual transfer of corresponding amounts from country to country without any 'secondary' contractions and expansions of the credit superstructure of the countries concerned. This would be the case only if individual central banks held gold reserves large enough to be used freely without resort to any special measures for their 'protection'.

[50]The founders of the Bank for International Settlements definitely contemplated that the Bank might establish such a fund, and article 24 of its Statutes specifically states that the bank may enter into special agreements with central banks to facilitate the settlement of international transactions between them: "For this purpose it may arrange with central banks to have gold earmarked for their account and transferable on their order, to open accounts through which central banks can transfer their assets from one currency to another and to take such other measures as the Board may think advisable within the limits of the powers granted by these Statutes".

[51]In a book which has appeared since these lectures were delivered (Charles R. Whittlesey, *International Monetary Issues* (New York: McGraw-Hill, 1937)) the author, after pointing out that a widening of the gold points would have the effects of increasing the volume of short-term capital movements of this sort (p. 116) concludes that "the only way of overcoming this factor would be to eliminate the gold points" (p. 117). But the only way of eliminating the gold points of which he can think is to abolish the gold standard!

Now the present abundance of gold offers an exceptional opportunity for such a reform. But to achieve the desired result not only the absolute supply of gold but also its distribution is of importance. In this respect it must appear unfortunate that those countries which command already abundant gold reserves and would therefore be in a position to work the gold standard on these lines should use that position to keep the price artificially high. The policy on the part of those countries which are already in a strong gold position, if it aims at the restoration of an international gold standard, should have been, while maintaining constant rates of exchange with all countries in a similar position, to reduce the price of gold in order to direct the stream of gold to those countries which are not yet in a position to resume gold payments. Only when the price of gold had fallen sufficiently to enable those countries to acquire sufficient reserves should a general and simultaneous return to a free gold standard be attempted.

It may seem at first that even if one could start with an appropriate distribution of gold between countries which at first would put each country in a position where it could allow its stock of gold to vary by the absolute amounts by which its circulation would have to increase or decrease, some countries would soon again find their gold stocks so depleted that they would be compelled to take traditional measures for their protection. And it cannot be denied that so long as the stock of gold of any country is anything less than 100 per cent of its total circulation, it is at least conceivable that it may be reduced to a point where, in order to protect the remainder, the monetary authorities might have to have recourse to a policy of credit contraction. But a short reflection will show that this is extraordinarily unlikely to happen if a country starts out with a fairly large stock of gold and if its monetary authorities adhere to the main principle not only with regard to decreases but equally with regard to increases in the total circulation.

If we assume the different countries to start with a gold reserve amounting to only a third of the total monetary circulation[52] this would probably provide a margin amply sufficient for any reduction of the country's share in the world's stock of money which is likely to become necessary. That a country's share in the world's income, and therefore its rela-

[52]At the present value of gold, the world's stock of monetary gold (at the end of 1936) amounts to 73.5 per cent of all sight liabilities of the central banks *plus* the circulation of Government paper money. The percentage would of course be considerably lower if, as would be necessary for this purpose, the comparison were made with the total of sight deposits with commercial banks *plus* bank notes, etc., in the hands of the public. But there can be no doubt that even if the price of gold should be somewhat lowered (say by one-seventh, i.e., from 140 to 120 shillings or from $35 to $30 per ounce) there would still be ample gold available to provide sufficient reserves.

tive demand for money, should fall off by more than this would at any rate be an exceptional case requiring exceptional treatment.[53] If history seems to suggest that such considerable losses of gold are not at all infrequent, this is due to the operation of a different cause which should be absent if the principle suggested were really applied. If under the traditional gold standard any one country expanded credit out of step with the rest of the world, this did usually bring about an outflow of gold only after a considerable time lag. This in itself would mean that, before equilibrium would be restored by the direct operations of the gold flows, an amount of gold approximately equal to the credit created in excess would have to flow out of the country. If, however, as has often been the case, the country should be tardy in decreasing its circulation by the amount of gold it has lost, that is, if it should try to 'offset' the losses of gold by new creations of credit, there would be no limits to the amount of gold which may leave the country except the size of the reserves. Or in other words, if the principle of changing the total circulation by the full amount of gold imported or exported were strictly applied, gold movements would be much smaller than has been the case in the past, and the size of the gold movements experienced in the past create therefore no presumption that they would be equally large in the future.

V

These considerations will already have made it clear that the principle of central banking policy here proposed by no means implies that the central banks should be relieved from all necessity of shaping their credit policy according to the state of their reserves. Quite the contrary. It only means that they should not be compelled to adhere to the mechanical rule of changing their notes and deposits *in proportion* to the change in their reserves. Instead of this, they would have to undertake the much more difficult task of influencing the total volume of money in their countries in such a way that this total would change by the same absolute amounts as their reserves. And since the central bank has no direct power over the greater part of the circulating medium of the country, it would have to try to control its volume indirectly. This means that it would have to use its power to change the volume of its notes and deposits so as to

[53] If in spite of this in an individual case the gold reserves of a country should be nearly exhausted, the necessary remedy would be to acquire the necessary amount of gold through an external loan and to give this amount to the central bank in repayment of part of the state debt which presumably will constitute at least part of its non-gold assets (or in payments of any other assets which the bank would have to sell to the Government). The main point here is that the acquisition of this gold must be paid for out of taxation and not by the creation of additional credit by the central bank.

make the superstructure of credit built on those move in conformity with its reserves. But as the amount of ordinary bank deposits and other forms of common means of exchange based on a given volume of central bank money will be different at different times, this means that the central bank, in order to make the total amount of money move with its reserves, would frequently have to change the amount of central bank money independently of changes in its reserves and occasionally even in a direction opposite to that in which its reserves may change.

It should perhaps always have been evident that, with a banking system which has grown up to rely on the assistance of a central bank for the supply of cash when needed, no sort of control of the circulating medium can be achieved unless the central bank has power and uses this power to control the volume of bank deposits in ordinary times. And the policy to make this control effective will have to be very different from the policy of a bank which is concerned merely with its own liquidity. It will have to act persistently against the trend of the movement of credit in the country, to contract the credit basis when the superstructure tends to expand and to expand the former when the latter tends to contract.

It is today almost a commonplace that, with a developed banking structure, the policy of the central bank can in no way be automatic. It would indeed require the greatest art and discernment for a central bank to succeed in making the credit money provided by the private banks behave as a purely metallic circulation would behave under similar circumstances. But while it may appear very doubtful whether this ideal will ever be fully achieved, there can be no doubt that we are still so far from it that very considerable changes from traditional policy would be required before we shall be able to say that even what is possible has been achieved.

In any case it should be obvious that the existence of a central bank which does nothing to counteract the expansions of banking credit made possible by its existence only adds another link in the chain through which the cumulative expansions and contractions of credit operate. So long as central banks are regarded, and regard themselves, only as "lenders of last resort" which have to provide the cash which becomes necessary in consequence of a previous credit expansion with which, until this point arrives, they are not concerned, so long as central banks wait until "the market is in the Bank" before they feel bound to check expansion, we cannot hope that wide fluctuations in the volume of credit will be avoided. Certainly Mr. Hawtrey was right with his now-celebrated statement that "so long as the credit is regulated with reference to reserve proportions, the trade cycle is bound to recur".[54] But I am afraid only

[54]Ralph George Hawtrey, *Monetary Reconstruction* (London and New York: Longmans, Green, 1923), p. 144.

one and that not the more important of the essential corollaries of this proposition is usually derived from this statement. What is usually emphasized is the fact that concern with reserve proportions will ultimately compel central banks to stop a process of credit expansion and actually to bring about a process of credit contraction. What seems to me much more important is that sole regard to their own reserve proportions will not lead central banks to counteract the increase of bank deposits, even if it means an increase of the credit circulation of the country relative to the gold reserve, and although it is an increase largely made possible by the certain expectation on the part of the other banks that the central bank will in the end supply the cash needed.

On the question how far central banks are in practice likely to succeed in this difficult task, different opinions are clearly possible. The optimist will be convinced that they will be able to do much more than merely offset the dangers which their existence creates. The pessimist will be sceptical whether on balance they will not do more harm than good. The difficulty of the task, the impossibility of prescribing any fixed rule, and the extent to which the action of the central banks will always be exposed to the pressure of public opinion and political influence certainly justify grave doubts. And though the alternative solution is today probably outside of the realm of practical politics, it is sufficiently important to deserve at least a passing consideration before we leave this subject.

As I have pointed out before, the "national reserve principle" is not insolubly bound up with the centralization of the note issue. While we must probably take it for granted that the issue of notes will remain reserved to one or a few privileged institutions, these institutions need not necessarily be the keepers of the national reserve. There is no reason why the Banks of Issue should not be entirely confined to the functions of the issue department of the Bank of England, that is to the conversion of gold into notes and notes into gold, while the duty of holding appropriate reserves is left to individual banks. There could still be in the background—for the case of a run on the banks—the power of a temporary "suspension" of the limitations of the note issue and of the issue of an emergency currency at a penalizing rate of interest.

The advantage of such a plan would be that one tier in the pyramid of credit would be eliminated and the cumulative effects of changes in liquidity preference accordingly reduced. The disadvantage would be that the remaining competing institutions would inevitably have to act on the proportional reserve principle and that nobody would be in a position, by a deliberate policy, to offset the tendency to cumulative changes. This might not be so serious if there were numerous small banks whose spheres of operation freely overlapped over the whole world. But it can hardly be recommended where we have to deal with the existing banking systems which consist of a few large institutions covering the same field of a single nation. It is probably one of the ideals which might be practical in a liberal world federation but which is impracticable where national frontiers also mean boundaries to the normal activities of banking institutions. The practical problem remains that of the appropriate policy of national central banks.

VI

It is unfortunately impossible to say more here about the principles which a rational central banking policy would have to follow without going into some of the most controversial problems of the theory of the trade cycle which clearly fall outside the scope of these lectures. I must therefore confine myself to pointing out that what I have said so far is altogether independent of the particular views on this subject for which I have been accused, I think unjustly, of being a deflationist. Whether we think that the ideal would be a more or less constant volume of the monetary circulation, or whether we think that this volume should gradually increase at a fairly constant rate as productivity increases, the problem of how to prevent the credit structure in any country from running away in either direction remains the same.

Here my aim has merely been to show that whatever our views about the desirable behaviour of the total quantity of money, they can never legitimately be applied to the situation of a single country which is part of an international economic system, and that any attempt to do so is likely in the long run and for the world as a whole to be an additional source of instability. This means of course that a really rational monetary policy could be carried out only by an international monetary authority, or at any rate by the closest cooperation of the national authorities and with the common aim of making the circulation of each country behave as nearly as possible as if it were part of an intelligently regulated international system.

But I think it also means that so long as an effective international monetary authority remains an utopian dream, any mechanical principle (such as the gold standard) which at least secures some conformity of monetary changes in the national area to what would happen under a truly international monetary system is far preferable to numerous independent and independently regulated national currencies. If it does not provide a really rational regulation of the quantity of money, it at any rate tends to make it behave on roughly foreseeable lines, which is of the greatest importance. And since there is no means, short of complete autarchy, of protecting a country against the folly or perversity of the monetary policy of other countries, the only hope of avoiding serious disturbances is to submit to some common rules, even if they are by no means ideal, in order to induce other countries to follow a similarly reasonable policy. That there is much scope for an improvement of the rules of the game which were supposed to exist in the past, nobody will deny. The most important step in this direction is that the *rationale* of an international standard and the true sources of the instability of our present system should be properly appreciated. It was for this reason that I felt that my most urgent task was to restate the broader theoretical considerations which bear on the practical problem before us. I hope that by confining myself largely to these theoretical problems I have not too much disappointed the expectations to which the title of these lectures may have given rise. But, as I said at the beginning of these lectures, I do believe that in the long run human affairs are guided by intellectual forces. It is this belief which for me gives abstract considerations of this sort their importance, however slight may be their bearing on what is practicable in the immediate future.

Addendum: Correspondence between Hayek and John Hicks[55]

Hicks to Hayek, November 27, 1967

Dear Fritz,

Now for the main letter.

We have (a) full employment, (b) static expectations, (c) 'equilibrium' at every stage, so that demand = supply in every market, prices being determined by current demand and supply. Add to these the Wicksell assumption, of a pure credit economy, and we clearly find that if there are no lags, the market rate of interest cannot be reduced below the natural rate in an equilibrium position;

[55][In 1966, John Hicks wrote to Hayek to say that he was preparing a book of essays which would include a new essay about Hayek's economic theories, specifically *Prices and Production*. What prompted this unusual (for that time) reappraisal of Hayek's ideas appears to have been an essay on Henry Thornton which Hicks had just completed, which both relied on Hayek's introduction to Thornton's *Paper Credit* and differed from it in ways that Hicks realized might not be entirely congenial to Hayek. When it came to Hayek's own work, Hicks did not want to give offense, but he did have a new interpretation to offer. As he wrote in the published essay, "There was some inner mystery to which we failed to penetrate. . . . [T]here was something central that was missing". What emerges from the correspondence is that the "mystery" stemmed from Hayek's view of how money affects prices. At bottom, it is how money must serve as the link between saving and credit as well as provide a common measure for prices that was somehow mysterious, and Hicks and

though it may indeed be so reduced in the disequilibrium position, while the economy is passing from one equilibrium to another. If we describe the process as a sequence of equilibria, then in each equilibrium the rate of interest is the same (apart from non-monetary disturbances); if the monetary authority tries to reduce the rate of interest, the result will just be that prices (all prices) rise. *Relative prices will continue to be determined by real causes.*

Even if one introduces a 'hard' money, I doubt if there is much difference. In the disequilibrium position, the public is induced to hold the additional money supply by the fall in the rate of interest; but this is a disequilibrium position. For if the other assumptions are retained, demands will be increased by the lower rate of interest; prices will therefore rise and at the higher prices (and incomes) more money will be required to finance transactions. The additional money is thus absorbed into transactions balances and is not available in *equilibrium* to bring the rate of interest down. (See the diagram on p. 149 of *Critical Essays*.)

All this of course is pedantic; but I think that some pedantry is required to make sure we are keeping on the track of an argument. I insist that the position in which the rate of interest is *really* lowered is a disequilibrium position, because I want to make sure, when dealing with such positions, that we know in what sense they are disequilibria. I hold that one can only analyze such positions by dropping one or [an]other of the assumptions with which I began. We can drop the Full Employment assumption (Keynes or Robertson); we can drop the static expectation assumption (Lindahl); but I was convinced by you that neither of these would fit your argument. One is left with the possibility of modifying the 'current' demand and supply assumption, so as to allow for lags.

There can of course be many sorts of lags. Even apart from the wage-lag (which means dropping the Full Employment assumption), there may be lags in reaction on the producers' as well as on the consumers' side. I did not consider producers' lags (though I think they would be realistic) because it did not seem to me that in this case they are any help. It may well be that producers take time to remake their decisions in the light of a lower rate of interest; but while they are delaying, the structure of production will not be distorted, and as soon as they do react, consumption prices will rise as well as producers' prices, if there is no consumption lag. It is only the consumption lag (of consumption behind wages) which can be a real help. If there is such a lag, there will be a disequilibrium position in which wages (and other producers' good prices) will have risen, but in which

Hayek were both right in seeing that Thornton offered some crucial insights. In his response to Hicks's queries, Hayek provides his most concise statement of how changes in the supply of money affect prices.

Most of the Hicks-Hayek correspondence is preserved in the Hayek archive of the Hoover Institution, Stanford University. John Hicks's "Thornton's *Paper Credit* (1802)" and "The Hayek Story" are published in John Hicks, *Critical Essays in Monetary Theory*, op. cit. Hayek's Introduction [1939] to Henry Thornton, *An Enquiry into the Nature and Effects of the Paper Credit of Great Britain* [1802] is published in F. A. Hayek, *The Trend of Economic Thinking* (1991), W. W. Bartley, III, and Stephen Kresge, eds, being vol. 3 of *The Collected Works of F. A. Hayek*, op. cit.—Ed.]

consumption has not yet responded, so that consumption prices will not have risen, or not risen so much. This would give the *relative* price-movement which is implied in your argument.

But surely this is a very weak effect. Suppose that consumption is lagged one period (whatever that is), so that when the wage-level is that appropriate for time t, consumption is at the level appropriate to time t − 1. One can then construct a sequence in which the rate of interest is kept at natural rate δ; but wages (and consumption prices) will then have to rise at δ per period, if the disequilibrium is to be maintained. If the lag is one fortnight and δ is 0.5%, prices will have to rise at 0.5% per fortnight, or nearly 15% per annum. This seems to me a big rise for so small an interest discrepancy.

Of course if we allow the producers to anticipate the rise in prices, the effect will be much bigger. But then it is the optimism of producers which is the *causa causans,* a rise in the marginal efficiency of capital a la Keynes (or Pigou). I see no reason why we should assume that an [excess] of optimism should be so nicely arranged as to produce the particular distortion you had in mind. It will tend to increase investment relatively to consumption (as soon as one allows almost any sort of lag) but that is all.

I should be interested to know what you think of my note on the *Treatise* which has some bearing on these matters. It was written last of all, after our last year's correspondence.

Yours ever,
John Hicks
All Souls College, Oxford

Hayek to Hicks, December 2, 1967

It is the first paragraph of your letter (of Nov. 27) where the basic difference between us arises. I suppose that if the last sentence ("Relative prices will continue to be determined by real causes [only]") were true, all the rest would necessarily follow. But this cannot be true.

I accept assumption (a), full employment. I am not sure that I quite know what (b) "static expectations" means, but if it means that at each stage of the process everybody acts in the expectation that future prices will be the same as present prices, I accept that too—though we shall see that these expectations must be disappointed. Of (c) I can accept that at each stage in every separate market demand = supply in the sense that at the ruling price all buyers and sellers buy and sell as much as they want to buy at that market, but not in the sense that any change in the supply which a change in price will bring about in the course of time has already taken place or that prices correspond to the marginal costs at which producers now begin to produce. Nor need there [be] at any but the initial stage an overall equilibrium between the different markets, because a change of price necessary to secure equality between demand and supply in any one market will make at the next stage a change of other prices inevitable as a result of the changed receipts in the first market being spent.

Let us now start with a system in full stationary equilibrium: constant prices and no net saving or investment and no changes in the supply of factors or tastes and a constant flow of money (which may be a token or partly credit money). The only change which we will assume then to occur is that the bank begins to offer additional money in the form of loans to investors at a rate of interest below that prevailing before, and that it continues to add by this method to the current money stream × per cent per period. This can, and I shall assume will, continue for an indefinite period.

This money will be borrowed by investors only if it is offered at a rate of interest lower than the pre-existing one and this we describe by saying that the market rate is lowered below the 'natural' rate. This is the initial change which starts the stream of additional money entering the system through the purchase of investment goods which (under full employment) will have to be produced instead of formerly produced consumers' goods.

Now, surely, such a change is as much [a] change in the *data* determining the structure of relative prices as any 'real' change, and as long as this new datum exists (i.e., as long as the influx of money financing new real net investment amounting to a certain percentage of aggregate real income continues) the 'equilibrium' price structure will be different from what it would have been if this new datum had not appeared.

The concept of a 'lag' applies here only to the question how long it would take for a single 'dose' of additional money injected into the system at a particular moment to affect any particular other price after that of the good on which it is first spent—or, perhaps, until it had spread all over so evenly that this chain of effects had spent itself. But this theoretical lag (or infinite number of conceivable lags) is almost wholly uninteresting for my purposes and relevant only when we compare the speed with which the effect of any single act of additional expenditure [spreads] with the speed at which successive injections (at a rate growing with the growth of the total money stream) follow each other.

In analyzing such a process we have necessarily to deal with a succession of changes in the money prices of the different goods, and however quickly these effects spread, so long as the process continues, those prices which have been affected earliest will all the time keep ahead of those which have been affected only in the second or later stage of the process, since we must assume that the repercussions of the initial change will ultimately also increase the demand for the goods on which the extra money has been spent first and the continued influx of money at this point must keep the demand for these goods all the time a step ahead of that for the others.

In other words, we have necessarily to deal with a succession of changes in the money prices of the different goods, and however quickly the effects spread, so long as the process of an influx of additional money at a particular point continues those prices which have been affected earlier will throughout the process preserve a lead over the others.

This may also be accounted for in a different manner: As we start out from a condition of full employment and zero net investment, those using the additional funds offered by the banks for new net investment must outbid others for some of the factors and thereby drive up the prices of those factors relatively to others. They will be able to continue net investment to the same real amount only if the money they can spend on it increases *pari passu* with the increase in the demand by others consequent upon the progressive increase in the total money stream.

I have always found it difficult, as you probably know, to attach a clear meaning to the concept of a structure of prices which is determined *only* by the 'real' factors but, like everybody else, have found it necessary to use the conception. But I find it impossible to apply it to situations [in which] I know that other lasting causes operate, such as a prolonged inflow (or outflow) of money into (or out of) the system, if not compensated for by independent changes which alter the demand for cash balances in the same direction. In such a situation the continued influx of new money ('new' in the sense that it is not received for previous sales) seems to me one of the factors necessarily determining the price structure. And since this factor may act as a constant datum for quite a prolonged period, I find it necessary to think of a fluid equilibrium which is different from that determined by the real factors only.

To put it still differently: it seems to me altogether impossible that all prices rise (or fall) at the same time and in the same proportion. But if they change in a certain order of succession, however rapidly the individual changes may follow upon each other, but each as a consequence of another having changed before, it must be true that so long as the process of change lasts the relations between the prices will be different from what it has been before the process of change in the quantity of money has started or will be after it has ceased.

This is what already Cantillon and Hume objected [to in] the crude Lockean quantity theory and what seems to me equally to apply to any argument assuming that during a process of inflation or deflation relative prices will continue to be determined by real causes only. They cannot be but different from what they would be if there were no inflation or deflation, and this seems to me much more important than all the effects on debtor-creditor relations or any simple relation between the 'level' of costs and the 'level' of product prices.

The essence of what you call the disequilibrium position is precisely that the lower rate of interest will not yet induce those into whose hands the additional money has yet got to hold it, but that they will still spend it. But here may be the source of another difference between us: Do you assume that if the rate of interest is lowered additional money will be borrowed chiefly or entirely by people who, at this lower rate of interest, want to hold more money? There may be some such, but this additional money will for the time being have no effect on prices. I am interested here only in the additional money borrowed by people who intend to invest it,[56] or received by [the] people to whom they [have paid it] and the increase of whose cash balances will in no way be related to the amount by which they

[56]The money which, at the lower rate of interest, people will borrow for liquidity reasons, does not count here, since it will according to this assumption not be spent and therefore have no influence on prices. The additional money that alone counts is the money that is borrowed to be spent, or, at the next stage, is received as additional income and (if prices are expected to remain at the new level) is likely to be spent again (except for a small part

may want to increase them because of the lower rate of interest, and who are in consequence likely to spend it. Indeed I believe that the kind of persons to whom the extra money will be [paid] as a result of increased investment are not likely to increase their cash holdings because the rate of interest has fallen but only in proportion as their expected incomes rise (transaction motive). This seems to me to mean, however, that so long as the influx of money continues, the whole price structure must be distorted by an imposed gradient corresponding to the temporal order in which particular commodities are reached by the stream of new money, and that in consequence the prices cannot all rise simultaneously or in the same proportion.

The position I am considering *is*, of course, a disequilibrium position in the sense that the relations which will prevail will continue to prevail only so long as the change (the influx of money) continues, and will disappear some time after that change ceases. (Although one might of course treat such a continuous increase in the supply of money, once it comes to be expected, also as a sort of constant datum.) But if we treat it as a continuous change it clearly is a change which may continue to proceed for a long time. A fuller analysis would have to distinguish three phases in its effect (even if we assume that while it proceeds the change in the income stream caused by the investment fed from additional money proceeds at a constant [percentage] rate. During the first stage, prices will be affected successively and there will be continuous changes in the structure of relative prices. This we can describe by as many 'lags' as we care to introduce. After a considerable time, a position may be reached when all prices will continue to rise proportionally, but retain the new relations caused by the path the stream of new money takes. When, finally, the influx of money stops, we enter phase three in the course of which phase one will be repeated approximately but in reverse order and something like the initial price structure will be restored.

Only in phases 1 and 3 is it meaningful to speak of 'lags' in the sense of definite intervals between the change of one particular price and that of another. During phase 2 there will be no lags properly speaking, but merely a persisting adaptation of the whole price structure, which we may or may not describe as a sort of equilibrium but which must certainly be characterized by a structure of relative prices different from that which would exist if no additional money were coming into and progressively distributing itself throughout the system. And this seems to me to be a simple consequence of the fact that those who create money (or use money so created) can exercise a demand pull in a direction which would not operate if no new money were currently created.

F.A.H.

---

to adapt cash balances to the larger income expected) and will go on adding to the incomes of successive individuals until it all has been retained for fractional increases of cash balances.

TWO

A COMMODITY RESERVE CURRENCY[1]

I

The gold standard as we knew it undoubtedly had some grave defects. But there is some danger that the sweeping condemnation of it which is now the fashion may obscure the fact that it also had some important virtues which most of the alternatives lack. A wisely and impartially controlled system of managed currency for the whole world might, indeed, be superior to it in all respects. But this is not a practical proposition for a long while yet. Compared, however, with the various schemes for monetary management on a national scale, the gold standard had three very important advantages: It created in effect an international currency without submitting national monetary policy to the decisions of an international authority; it made monetary policy in a great measure automatic and thereby predictable; and the changes in the supply of basic money which its mechanism secured were on the whole in the right direction.

II

The importance of these advantages should not be lightly underestimated. The difficulties of a deliberate coordination of national policies are enormous, because our present knowledge gives us unambiguous guidance in only a few situations, and decisions in which nearly always some interests must be sacrificed to others will have to rest on subjective judgements. Uncoordinated national policies, however, directed solely by the immediate interests of the individual countries, may in their aggregate effect on every country well be worse than the most imperfect international standard. Similarly, though the automatic operation of the gold standard is far from perfect, the mere fact that under the gold standard policy is guided by known rules, and that, in consequence, the action of the authorities can be foreseen, may well make the imperfect gold stan-

[1][First published in the *Economic Journal*, vol. 53, no. 210, June–September, 1943, pp. 176–184. —Ed.]

dard less disturbing than a more rational but less comprehensible policy. The general principle that the production of gold is stimulated when its value begins to rise and discouraged when its value falls is right at least in the direction, if not in the way in which it operates in practice.

It will be noticed that none of these points claimed in favour of the standard is directly connected with any property inherent to gold. Any internationally accepted standard based on a commodity whose value is regulated by its cost of production would possess essentially the same advantages. What in the past made gold the only substance on which in practice an international standard could be based was mainly the irrational, but no less real, factor of its prestige—or, if you will, of the ruling superstitious prejudice in favour of gold, which made it universally more acceptable than anything else. So long as this belief prevailed, it was possible to maintain an international currency based on gold without much design or deliberate organization to support it. But if it was prejudice which made the international gold standard possible, the existence of such a prejudice at least made an international money possible at a time when any international system based on explicit agreement and systematic cooperation was out of the question.

III

The decisive change which has occurred in recent times, and which has fundamentally altered our prospects and opportunities in this field, is the psychological one that the unreasoning prejudice in favour of gold, which gave gold what special advantage it possessed, has been gravely shaken—though perhaps not so much as many people imagine; that in many quarters it has even been replaced by an equally strong and unreasoned prejudice against gold; and that people generally are much more ready to consider rational alternatives. It is therefore important that we should seriously reconsider alternative systems which preserve the advantages of an automatic international standard with freedom from the special defects of gold. One such alternative in particular, which has recently been worked out in its practical detail by competent students of monetary problems, is of a kind which makes it appeal to many who in the past have defended the gold standard—not because they regarded it as ideal, but because it seemed to them superior to anything else which was practical politics.

Before describing this new proposal, it is necessary briefly to consider the real faults of the gold standard which we want to avoid. They are not mainly those which are most generally recognized. The much-discussed 'vagaries' in the production of gold can easily be exaggerated. The great increases in the supply of gold in the past have in fact occurred when a prolonged scarcity had created a real need for them. The really serious objection against gold is rather the slowness with which its supply adjusts itself to genuine changes in demand. A temporary increase in the general demand for highly liquid assets, or the adoption of the gold standard by a new country, was bound to cause great changes in the value of gold while the supply adjusted itself only slowly. By a sort of delay action the increased supplies often became available only when they were no longer needed. Not only did these new supplies thus tend to become an embarrassment rather than a relief, but the increase of the stock of gold in response to a temporary increase in demand remained permanent and provided the basis for an excessive expansion of credit as soon as the demand again fell.

This last point is closely connected with the one really paradoxical feature of the gold standard: Namely, the fact that the striving of all individuals to become more liquid did not put society into a more liquid position at all. Yet there are times when the desire of the individuals to put themselves in a more liquid position expresses a real social need. There will always be periods in which increased uncertainty about the future will make it desirable that a larger portion of our assets should be given forms in which they can be readily converted to the needs of what are still unpredictable circumstances. A rational arrangement of our affairs would require that at such times production is in some measure switched from things of more restricted usefulness to the kind of things which will be needed in all conditions, such as the most widely used raw materials. The true irony of the gold standard is that under its rule a general increase in the desire for liquidity leads to the increase in the production of the one thing which can be used for practically no other purpose than to provide a liquidity reserve to individuals; and of a thing, moreover, which not only has few other uses but which can be supplied in increased quantity only so slowly that an increase in the demand for it will act much more on its value than on its quantity or, in other words, will cause a general fall in prices; while once the supply has increased and the demand again falls, the excess supply can be worked off only by a fall in its value or by a general rise of prices.

IV

More rational schemes relying on the use of commodities other than gold have often been proposed, but so long as the universal prejudice was in favour of gold they were scarcely of practical interest. In the present situation, however, at least one of these proposals, recently elaborated in detail by two American scholars, deserves close attention for its successful combination of great theoretical and practical merits. Benjamin Graham, of New York, and Frank D. Graham, of Princeton, who had, unknown to each other, arrived at very similar ideas, have in recent years fully elaborated their proposal in a series of important publications.[2] Though at first their plan may appear strange and complicated, it is in fact very simple and eminently practical.

The basic idea is that currency should be issued solely in exchange against a fixed combination of warehouse warrants for a number of storable commodities and be redeemable in the same 'commodity unit'. For example, £100, instead of being defined as so-and-so many ounces of gold, would be defined as so much wheat, *plus* so much sugar, *plus* so much copper, *plus* so much rubber, etc. Since money would be issued only against the complete collection of all the raw commodities in their proper physical quantities (twenty-four different commodities in Benjamin Graham's plan), and since money would also be redeemable in the same manner, the aggregate price of this collection of commodities would be fixed, but only the aggregate price and not the price of any one of them. In this respect the different commodities would be connected with money not in the way in which gold and silver were connected with it under bimetallism, so that a unit of money was obtainable *either* for a fixed quantity of gold *or* for a fixed quantity of silver; but rather as if (according to the plan suggested by Alfred Marshall under the name of "symmetallism")[3] only the price of a certain weight of gold and a certain weight of silver together were fixed, but the price of each metal by itself was allowed to fluctuate.

With this system in operation an increase in the demand for liquid assets would lead to the accumulation of stocks of raw commodities of the most general usefulness. The hoarding of money, instead of causing resources to run to waste, would act as if it were an order to keep raw commodities for the hoarder's account. As the hoarded money was again returned to circulation, and demand for commodities increased, these

[2]See particularly Benjamin Graham, *Storage and Stability* (New York: McGraw-Hill, 1937), and Frank D. Graham, *Social Goals and Economic Institutions* (Princeton: Princeton University Press, 1942). An almost identical proposal had been made earlier by the Dutch economist, Professor J. Goudriaan, in a pamphlet, *How To Stop Deflation* (London: The Search Publishing Co., 1932), which I had not seen at the time of writing [this] article. Benjamin Graham has since further elaborated his proposals in a book, *World Commodities and World Currency* (New York: McGraw-Hill, 1945).

[3][See Alfred Marshall, "Remedies for Fluctuations of General Prices" [1887], reprinted in *Memorials of Alfred Marshall*, ed. A. C. Pigou (London: Macmillan, 1925), pp. 188–211. —Ed.]

stocks would be released to satisfy the new demand. Since the collection of commodities could always be exchanged against a fixed sum of money, its aggregate price could never fall below that figure; and, since money would be redeemable at the same (or an only slightly different) rate, their aggregate price could never rise above that figure. In this respect the aim of the proposal is similar to that of the 'tabular standard' or the 'index currencies', which were at one time much discussed. But it differs from them in its direct and automatic operation. It is at least doubtful whether the price level of any selection of commodities could be effectively kept constant by deliberate adjustments of the quantity of money. But there can be no doubt that the aggregate price of the selected raw commodities could not vary so long as the monetary authority stood ready to sell and buy the commodity unit at a fixed price.

As proposed by its American protagonists, the plan is designed primarily for adoption on a national scale by the United States. The arguments in its favour apply, however, no less to other countries. As the adoption of the plan by several countries, who based it, however, on different collections of commodities, would produce a new cause of serious instability, it would appear that the plan not only could but, to achieve its ends, ought to be adopted internationally—or, what comes in practice to the same thing, that it ought to be operated on the same principle by all the major countries. The particular collection of raw commodities on which Benjamin Graham's scheme is based (five grains, four fats and oilseeds, three other foodstuffs, four metals, three textile fibers, tobacco, hides, rubber, and petroleum) and certain other details would have to be modified; but the principle raises no serious difficulties to international application. In the following outline of the way in which the scheme would operate it will be assumed that commodity units of the same composition are adopted as the basis of currency at least in the British Empire and the United States.

V

For reasons which will presently appear, the plan is most easily put into operation when a fall of demand threatens. It can be made automatically to come into effect at such a time by fixing beforehand a buying price for the commodity unit slightly below the ruling market value. Once the demand for raw commodities then begins to slacken and their prices to fall, the monetary authorities of the participating countries will be offered any commodity units which cannot be disposed in the market at the fixed price. Their purchases will make up for the fall of the industrial demand—and for every amount of money that is being accumulated in private hands a corresponding amount of raw commodities is accumulated in the warehouses. The demand for raw commodities in general is thus maintained—but only the demand for the group as a whole and not that for any particular commodity, the output of which may well be excessive and in need of curtailment.

It will be readily seen how the operation of the scheme would tend to stabilize the demand for raw commodities. As in the past gold-mining used to be the only industry that regularly prospered during periods of depression, so the producers of raw commodities might under this plan enjoy in the same circumstances even a moderate increase in prosperity through being able to exchange their products at more favourable terms against manufactures. But while gold-mining is far too small an industry for its prosperity to have significant effects outside it, the secure income of the producers of raw commodities would also go far to stabilize the demand for manufactures and to prevent the depression from becoming serious. The benefit would indeed not be confined to the producers of the commodities included in the commodity unit. Even a country in which none of these commodities was produced would gain from its operation hardly less than the others. So long as it stood ready to buy commodity units at a fixed price in its national currency, any money thus issued to the producers of raw commodities would be of no use to them except for buying the products of the country to which they had sold their raw produce.

VI

At first it may appear as if the operation of the plan might create the danger of serious inflationary expansion. But on examination it proves that its effect could not be really inflationary in any significant sense of that word; whatever monetary expansion it would permit could hardly lead either to a general rise of prices or to that shortage of consumers' goods through which the most harmful effects of inflation operate. It is, in fact, one of the great merits of the scheme that it provides an automatic check to any expansion before it can become dangerous. We have considered its operation during a depression first, because its effectiveness during a boom depends on the previous accumulation of commodity stocks such as would take place during a period of slackening activity. The manner in which the scheme would operate while an improvement in the general outlook leads to a mobilization of the idle cash reserves is, however, no less important.

The aggregate price of the raw commodities making up the commodity unit could not rise so long as the monetary authorities are able to sell from their stocks at the fixed figure. Instead of a rise in prices and a consequent increase in output as demand increased, and *pari passu* with the return into circulation of the accumulated money hoards, raw commodities would be released from the stocks and the money received for them impounded. The savings made by individuals in the form of cash during the slack period would not have run to waste but would be waiting in the form of raw commodities ready to be used. In consequence, the revival of activity will not lead to an extra stimulus to the production of raw commodities which would continue on an even keel. There is reason to regard the temporary stimulus to an excessive expansion of the production to raw commodities, which used to be given by the sharp rise of their prices in boom periods, as one of the most serious causes of general instability. This would be entirely avoided under the proposed scheme—at least so long as the monetary authority had any stocks from which to sell. But since it would necessarily possess sufficient reserves to redeem all the extra cash accumulated during the period of slackness (and considerably more if the commodity stocks held by governments at the initiation of the scheme were brought in), the boom would almost certainly be damped down by the contraction of the circulation before the reserves are exhausted.

VII

As has been remarked before, the scheme *sounds* complicated, but is, in fact, exceedingly simple to operate. There would, in particular, be no need for the monetary authorities or the government in any way directly to handle the many commodities of which the commodity unit is composed. Both the bringing-together of the required assortment of warrants and the actual storing of the commodities could be safely left to private initiative. Specialist brokers would soon take care of the collecting and tendering of warrants as soon as their aggregate market price fell ever so little below the standard figure and of withdrawing and redistributing the warrants to their various markets if their aggregate price rose above that figure. In this respect the business of the monetary authority would be as mechanical as the buying and selling of gold under the gold standard.

This is not to say that the proposal does not raise numerous problems, which cannot be fully discussed in this short outline. At least the more important of these problems have been considered and practicable solutions suggested in the publications already referred to. To mention only a few of these points: The cost of the physical storage of the commodities could be defrayed out of the difference between the prices at which the monetary authority buys and sells commodity units. (It should be noticed that the cost of storage would not include any interest charge, because the loss of interest would be voluntarily borne by the holders of the money issued against the commodities.) The problems raised by the composition of the commodity unit and the periodical changes in it which will become necessary can also be solved by the adoption of an objective principle which would lift it out of the sphere of political wrangle. Similarly the problems of the differences of quality and distinctions according to the place of storage and the like do not raise insuperable difficulties. It should be remembered in this connection that for the purposes of the plan the inclusion of the most important variety of any commodity would have nearly the same effect on the prices of its close substitutes as if they were themselves included.

Two special points must, however, be mentioned even in so brief a survey. The first is the important feature of the plan that the monetary authority shall be empowered in precisely defined circumstances to accept in place of (or substitute for) warrants for stored commodities contracts for future delivery of any commodity. This meets the difficulties which would otherwise be caused by a temporary shortage of any one commodity included in the unit and makes it possible to use the reserves for some measure of stabilization even of individual commodity prices. This would be achieved, for example, by substituting 'futures' for present commodities whenever the current price rose by more than a fixed percentage over the 'future' price.

The second point is that, if it were wished to preserve the value of gold or to prevent a too rapid decline of it, it would not be difficult to link up the value of gold in such a way with the commodity scheme that, though gold would have no significant effect on the value of money, the value of gold would be stabilized at the same time with the value of money. Whether this is desirable in view of the interest whole nations have in the preservation of the value of gold, and whether it ought to be used to maintain the production of gold indefinitely near its present level or rather to bring about a gradual but predictable decline of the resources devoted to it, is a political problem we need not consider here. The important point is merely that there are many ways in which gold could be linked with the new scheme if desired without thereby impairing the advantages of the scheme.

It is probably true to say that all the rational arguments which can be advanced in favour of the gold standard apply even more strongly to this proposal, which is at the same time free from most of the defects of the former. In judging the feasibility of the plan, it must, however, not be regarded solely as a scheme for currency reform. It must be borne in mind that the accumulation of commodity reserves is certain to remain part of national policy and that political considerations render it unlikely that the markets for raw commodities will in any future for which we can now plan be left entirely to themselves. All plans aiming at the direct control of the prices of particular commodities are, however, open to the most serious objections and certain to cause grave economic and political difficulties. Even apart from monetary consideration, the great need is for a system under which these controls are taken from the separate bodies which can but act in what is essentially an arbitrary and unpredictable manner and to make the controls instead subject to a mechanical and predictable rule. If this can be combined with the reconstruction of an international monetary system which would once more secure to the world stable international currency relations and a greater freedom in the movement of raw commodities, a great step would have been taken in the direction towards a more prosperous and stable world economy.

THREE

CHOICE IN CURRENCY[1]

I

The chief root of our present monetary troubles is, of course, the sanction of scientific authority which Lord Keynes and his disciples have given to the age-old superstition that by increasing the aggregate of money expenditure we can lastingly ensure prosperity and full employment. It is a superstition against which economists before Keynes had struggled with some success for at least two centuries.[2] It had governed most of earlier history. This history, indeed, has been largely a history of inflation; significantly, it was only during the rise of the prosperous modern industrial systems and during the rule of the gold standard that over a period of about two hundred years (in Britain from about 1714 to 1914, and in the United States from about 1749 to 1939) prices were at the end about where they had been at the beginning. During this unique period of monetary stability, the gold standard had imposed upon monetary authorities a discipline which prevented them from abusing their powers, as they have done at nearly all other times. Experience in other parts of the world does not seem to have been very different: I have been told that a Chinese law attempted to prohibit paper money for all time (of course, ineffectively), long before the Europeans ever invented it!

It was John Maynard Keynes, a man of great intellect but limited knowledge of economic theory, who ultimately succeeded in rehabilitating a view long the preserve of cranks with whom he openly sympathized. He had attempted by a succession of new theories to justify the same, superficially persuasive, intuitive belief that had been held by many practical men before, but that will not withstand rigorous analysis of the price

[1][First published in its present form in *New Studies in Philosophy, Politics, Economics and the History of Ideas* (Chicago: University of Chicago Press, and London: Routledge, 1978). Based on an address entitled "International Money" delivered to the Geneva Gold and Monetary Conference on September 25, 1975, at Lausanne, Switzerland, and published as a brochure with this title by the Institute of Economic Affairs, London, 1976. —Ed.]

[2]See Addendum to this chapter.

mechanism: Just as there cannot be a uniform price for all kinds of labour, an equality of demand and supply for labour in general cannot be secured by managing *aggregate* demand. The volume of employment depends on the correspondence of demand and supply *in each sector* of the economy, and therefore on the wage structure and the distribution of demand between the sectors. The consequence is that over a longer period the Keynesian remedy does not cure unemployment but makes it worse.

The claim of an eminent public figure and brilliant polemicist to provide a cheap and easy means of permanently preventing serious unemployment conquered public opinion and, after his death, professional opinion too. Sir John Hicks has even proposed that we call the third quarter of this century, 1950 to 1975, the age of Keynes, as the second quarter was the age of Hitler.[3] I do not feel that the harm Keynes did is really so great as to justify *that* description. But it is true that, so long as his prescriptions seemed to work, they operated as an orthodoxy which it appeared useless to oppose.

I have often blamed myself for having given up the struggle after I had spent much time and energy criticizing the first version of Keynes's theoretical framework. Only after the second part of my critique had appeared did he tell me that he had changed his mind and no longer believed what he had said in the *Treatise on Money*[4] of 1930 (somewhat unjustly towards himself, as it seems to me, since I still believe that volume 2 of the *Treatise* contains some of the best work he ever did). At any rate, I felt it then to be useless to return to the charge, because he seemed so likely to change his views again. When it proved that this new version—the *General Theory* of 1936[5]—conquered most of the professional opinion, and when in the end even some of the colleagues I most respected supported the wholly Keynesian Bretton Woods agreement, I largely withdrew from the debate, since to proclaim my dissent from the near-unanimous views of the orthodox phalanx would merely have deprived me of a hearing on other matters about which I was more concerned at the time. (I believe, however, that, so far as some of the best British economists were concerned, their support of Bretton Woods was determined more by a misguided patriotism—the hope that it would benefit Britain

[3]John Hicks, *The Crisis in Keynesian Economics* (Oxford: Basil Blackwell, 1974), p. 1.

[4]J. M. Keynes, *A Treatise on Money,* 2 vols (London: Macmillan, 1930). [Reprinted as volumes 5 (subtitled *The Pure Theory of Money*) and 6 (subtitled *The Applied Theory of Money*) (1971) of *The Collected Writings of John Maynard Keynes,* Austin Robinson and Donald Moggridge, eds (London: Macmillan (for the Royal Economic Society), 1971–89). —Ed.]

[5][J. M. Keynes, *The General Theory of Employment, Interest, and Money* [1936], reprinted as vol. 7 of *The Collected Writings of J. M. Keynes* (1973), op. cit. —Ed.]

in her post-war difficulties—than a belief that it would provide a satisfactory international monetary order.)

II

I wrote 36 years ago on the crucial point of difference:

> It may perhaps be pointed out that it has, of course, never been denied that employment can be rapidly increased, and a position of "full employment" achieved in the shortest possible time by means of monetary expansion—least of all by those economists whose outlook has been influenced by the experience of a major inflation. All that has been contended is that the kind of full employment which can be created in this way is inherently unstable, and that to create employment by these means is to perpetuate fluctuations. There may be desperate situations in which it may indeed be necessary to increase employment at all costs, even if it be only for a short period—perhaps the situation in which Dr. Brüning found himself in Germany in 1932 was such a situation in which desperate means would have been justified. But the economist should not conceal the fact that to aim at the maximum of employment which can be achieved in the short run by means of monetary policy is essentially the policy of the desperado who has nothing to lose and everything to gain from a short breathing space.[6]

To this I would now like to add, in reply to the constant deliberate misrepresentation of my views by politicans, who like to picture me as a sort of bogey whose influence makes conservative parties dangerous, what I regularly emphasize and stated nine months ago in my Nobel Memorial Prize Lecture at Stockholm in the following words:

> The truth is that by a mistaken theoretical view we have been led into a precarious position in which we cannot prevent substantial unemployment from reappearing: not because, as my view is sometimes misrepresented, this unemployment is deliberately brought about as a means to combat inflation, but because it is now bound to appear as a deeply regrettable but *inescapable* consequence of the mistaken policies of the past as soon as inflation ceases to accelerate.[7]

This manufacture of unemployment by what are called 'full employment policies' is a complex process. In essence it operates by temporary

[6] F. A. Hayek, *Profits, Interest and Investment* (London: Routledge, 1939), p. 63n.

[7] F. A. Hayek, "The Pretence of Knowledge", Nobel Memorial Prize Lecture 1974, in *New Studies in Philosophy, Politics, Economics and the History of Ideas*, op. cit., pp. 23–34.

changes in the distribution of demand, drawing both unemployed and already employed workers into jobs which will disappear with the end of inflation. In the periodically recurrent crises of the pre-1914 years, the expansion of credit during the preceding boom served largely to finance industrial investment, and the over-development and subsequent unemployment occurred mainly in the industries producing capital equipment. In the engineered inflation of the last decades, things were more complex.

What will happen during a major inflation is illustrated by an observation from the early 1920s which many of my Viennese contemporaries will confirm: In the city many of the famous coffeehouses were driven from the best corner sites by new bank offices and returned after the 'stabilization crisis', when the banks had contracted or collapsed and thousands of bank clerks swelled the ranks of the unemployed.

The whole theory underlying the full employment policies has by now of course been thoroughly discredited by the experience of the last few years. In consequence the economists are also beginning to discover its fatal intellectual defects which they ought to have seen all along. Yet I fear the theory will still give us a lot of trouble: It has left us with a lost generation of economists who have learnt nothing else. One of our chief problems will be to protect our money against those economists who will continue to offer their quack remedies, the short-term effectiveness of which will continue to ensure them popularity. It will survive among blind doctrinaires who have always been convinced that they have the key to salvation.

In consequence, though the rapid descent of Keynesian doctrine from intellectual respectability can be denied no longer, it still gravely threatens the chances of a sensible monetary policy. Nor have people yet fully realized how much irreparable damage it has already done, particularly in Britain, the country of its origin. The sense of financial respectability which once guided British monetary policy has rapidly disappeared. From a model to be imitated, Britain has in a few years descended to be a warning example for the rest of the world. This decay was recently brought home to me by a curious incident: I found in a drawer of my desk a British penny dated 1863 which, a short 12 years ago—that is, when it was exactly a hundred years old—I had received as change from a London bus conductor and had taken back to Germany to show to my students what long-run monetary stability meant. I believe they were duly impressed. But they would laugh in my face if I now mentioned Britain as an instance of monetary stability.

III

A wise man should perhaps have foreseen that less than 30 years after the nationalization of the Bank of England the purchasing power of the pound sterling would have been reduced to less than one-quarter of what it had been at that date. As has sooner or later happened everywhere, government control of the quantity of money has once again proved fatal. I do not want to question that a very intelligent and wholly independent national or international monetary authority *might* do better than an international gold standard, or any other sort of automatic system. But I see not the slightest hope that any government, or any institution subject to political pressure, will ever be able to act in such a manner.

I never had much illusion in this respect, but I must confess that in the course of a long life my opinion of governments has steadily worsened: The more intelligently they try to act (as distinguished from simply following an established rule), the more harm they seem to do—because once they are known to aim at particular goals (rather than merely maintaining a self-correcting spontaneous order) the less they can avoid serving sectional interests. And the demands of all organized group interests are almost invariably harmful—except when they protest against restrictions imposed upon them for the benefit of other group interests. I am by no means reassured by the fact that, at least in some countries, the civil servants who run affairs are mostly intelligent, well-meaning, and honest men. The point is that, if governments are to remain in office in the prevailing political order, they have no choice but to use their powers for the benefit of particular groups—and one strong interest is always to get additional money for extra expenditure. However harmful inflation is in general seen to be, there are always substantial groups of people, including some for whose support collectivist-inclined governments primarily look, which in the short run greatly gain by it—even if only by staving off for some time the loss of an income which it is human nature to believe will be only temporary if they can tide over the emergency.

The pressure for more and cheaper money is an ever-present political force which monetary authorities have never been able to resist, unless they were in a position credibly to point to an absolute obstacle which made it impossible for them to meet such demands. And it will become even more irresistible when these interests can appeal to an increasingly unrecognizable image of St. Maynard. There will be no more urgent need than to erect new defences against the onslaughts of popular forms of Keynesianism, that is, to replace or restore those restraints which, under the influence of his theory, have been systematically dismantled. It was the main function of the gold standard, of balanced budgets, and of the limitation of the supply of 'international liquidity', to make it impossible for the monetary authorities to capitulate to the pressure for more money. And it was exactly for that reason that all these safeguards against inflation, which had made it possible for representative governments to resist the demands of powerful pressure groups for more money, have been removed at the instigation of economists who imagined that, if governments were released from the shackles of mechanical rules, they would be able to act wisely for the general benefit.

I do not believe we can now remedy this position by *constructing* some new international monetary order, whether a new international monetary authority or institution, or even an international agreement to adopt a particular mechanism or system of policy, such as the classical gold standard. I am fairly convinced that any attempt now to reinstate the gold standard by international agreement would break down within a short time and merely discredit the ideal of an international gold standard for even longer. Without the conviction of the public at large that certain immediately painful measures are occasionally necessary to preserve reasonable stability, we cannot hope that any authority which has power to determine the quantity of money will long resist the pressure for, or the seduction of, cheap money.

The politician, acting on a modified Keynesian maxim that in the long run we are all out of office, does not care if his successful cure of unemployment is bound to produce more unemployment in the future. The politicians who will be blamed for it will not be those who created the inflation but those who stopped it. No worse trap could have been set for a democratic system in which the government is forced to act on the beliefs that the people think to be true. Our only hope for a stable money is indeed now to find a way to protect money from politics.

With the exception only of the 200-year period of the gold standard, practically all governments of history have used their exclusive power to issue money in order to defraud and plunder the people. There is less ground than ever for hoping that, so long as the people have no choice but to use the money their government provides, governments will become more trustworthy. Under the prevailing systems of government, which are supposed to be guided by the opinion of the majority but under which in practice any sizeable group may create a 'political necessity' for the government by threatening to withhold the votes it needs to claim majority support, we cannot entrust dangerous instruments to it. Fortunately we need not yet fear, I hope, that governments will start a war to please some indispensable group of supporters, but money is certainly too dangerous an instrument to leave to the fortuitous expediency of politicians—or, it seems, economists.

What is so dangerous and ought to be done away with is not governments' right to issue money but the *exclusive* right to do so and their power to force people to use it and to accept it at a particular price. This monopoly of government, like the postal monopoly, has its origin not in any benefit it secures for the people but solely in the desire to enhance the coercive powers of government. I doubt whether it has ever done any good except to the rulers and their favourites. All history contradicts the belief that governments have given us a safer money than we would have had without their claiming an exclusive right to issue it.

IV

But why should we not let people choose freely what money they want to use? By 'people' I mean the individuals who ought to have the right to decide whether they want to buy or sell for francs, pounds, dollars, D-marks, or ounces of gold. I have no objection to governments issuing money, but I believe their claim to a *monopoly*, or their power to *limit* the kinds of money in which contracts may be concluded within their territory, or to determine the *rates* at which monies can be exchanged, to be wholly harmful.

At this moment it seems that the best thing we could wish governments to do is for, say, all the members of the European Economic Community, or, better still, all the governments of the Atlantic Community, to bind themselves mutually not to place any restrictions on the free use within their territories of one another's—or any other—currencies, including their purchase and sale at any price the parties decide upon, or on their use as accounting units in which to keep books. This, and not a Utopian European Monetary Unit, seems to me now both the practicable and the desirable arrangement to aim at. To make the scheme effective it would be important, for reasons I shall state later, also to provide that banks in one country be free to establish branches in any of the others.

This suggestion may at first seem absurd to all brought up on the concept of 'legal tender'. Is it not essential that the law designate one kind of money as the legal money? This is, however, true only to the extent that, *if* the government does issue money, it must also say what must be accepted in discharge of debts incurred in that money. And it must also determine in what manner certain noncontractual legal obligations, such as taxes or liabilities for damage or torts, are to be discharged. But there is no reason whatever why people should not be free to make contracts, including ordinary purchases and sales, in any kind of money they choose, or why they should be obliged to sell against any particular kind of money.

There could be no more effective check against the abuse of money by the government than if people were free to refuse any money they distrusted and to prefer money in which they had confidence. Nor could there be a stronger inducement to governments to ensure the stability of their money than the knowledge that, so long as they kept the supply below the demand for it, that demand would tend to grow. Therefore, let us deprive governments (or their monetary authorities) of all power to protect their money against competition: If they can no longer conceal that their money is becoming bad, they will have to restrict the issue.

The first reaction of many readers may be to ask whether the effect of such a system would not according to an old rule be that the bad money would drive out the good. But this would be a misunderstanding of what is called Gresham's Law. This indeed is one of the oldest insights into the mechanism of money, so old that 2,400 years ago Aristophanes, in one of his comedies, could say that it was with politicians as it is with coins, because the bad ones drive out the good.[8] But the truth which apparently even today is not generally understood is that Gresham's Law operates *only* if the two kinds of money have to be accepted at a prescribed rate of exchange. Exactly the opposite will happen when people are free to exchange the different kinds of money at whatever rate they can agree upon. This was observed many times during the great inflations when even the most severe penalties threatened by governments could not prevent people from using other kinds of money—even like cigarettes and bottles of brandy rather than the government money—which clearly meant that the good money was driving out the bad.[9]

Make it merely legal and people will be very quick indeed to refuse to use the national currency once it depreciates noticeably, and they will make their dealings in a currency they trust. Employers, in particular, would find it in their interest to offer, in collective agreements, not wages

[8]Aristophanes, *The Frogs,* trans. J. H. Frere (London: W. Nicol, 1939), 891–898, in Frere's translation:

> Oftentimes we have reflected on a similar abuse
> In the choice of men for office, and of coins for common use,
> For our old and standard pieces, valued and approved and tried,
> Here among the Grecian nations, and in all the world besides,
> Recognized in every realm for trusty stamp and pure assay,
> Are rejected and abandoned for the trash of yesterday,
> For a vile adulterated issue, drossy, counterfeit and base,
> Which the traffic of the city passes current in their place.

About the same time, the philosopher Diogenes called money "the legislators' game of dice"!

[9]During the German inflation after the First World War, when people began to use dollars and other solid currencies in the place of marks, a Dutch financier (if I rightly remember, Mr. Vissering) asserted that Gresham's Law was false and the opposite true.

anticipating a foreseen rise of prices but wages in a currency they trusted and could make the basis of rational calculation. This would deprive government of the power to counteract excessive wage increases, and the unemployment they would cause, by depreciating their currency. It would also prevent employers from conceding such wages in the expectation that the national monetary authority would bail them out if they promised more than they could pay.

There is no reason to be concerned about the effects of such an arrangement on ordinary men who know neither how to handle nor how to obtain strange kinds of money. So long as the shopkeepers knew that they could turn it instantly at the current rate of exchange into whatever money they preferred, they would be only too ready to sell their wares at an appropriate price for any currency. But the malpractices of government would show themselves much more rapidly if prices rose only in terms of the money issued by it, and people would soon learn to hold the government responsible for the value of the money in which they were paid. Electronic calculators, which in seconds would give the equivalent of any price in any currency at the current rate, would soon be used everywhere. But, unless the national government all too badly mismanaged the currency it issued, it would probably continue to be used in everyday retail transactions. What would be affected mostly would be not so much the use of money in daily payments as the willingness to *hold* different kinds of money. It would mainly be the tendency of all business and capital transactions rapidly to switch to a more reliable standard (and to base calculations and accounting on it) which would keep national monetary policy on the right path.

V

The upshot would probably be that the currencies of those countries trusted to pursue a responsible monetary policy would tend to displace gradually those of a less reliable character. The reputation of financial righteousness would become a jealously guarded asset of all issuers of money, since they would know that even the slightest deviation from the path of honesty would reduce the demand for their product.

I do not believe there is any reason to fear that in such a competition for the most general acceptance of a currency there would arise a tendency to deflation or an increasing value of money. People will be quite as reluctant to borrow or incur debts in a currency expected to appreciate as they will hesitate to lend in a currency expected to depreciate. The convenience of use is decidedly in favour of a currency which can be expected to retain an approximately stable value. If governments and other issuers of money have to compete in inducing people to *hold* their money, and make long-term contracts in it, they will have to create confidence in its long-run stability.

Where I am not sure is whether in such a competition for reliability any government-issued currency would prevail, or whether the predominant preference would not be in favour of some such units as ounces of gold. It seems not unlikely that gold would ultimately re-assert its place as "the universal prize in all countries, in all cultures, in all ages", as Jacob Bronowski has recently called it in his brilliant book on *The Ascent of Man*,[10] if people were given complete freedom to decide what to use as their standard and general medium of exchange—more likely, at any rate, than as the result of any organized attempt to restore the gold standard.

The reason why, in order to be fully effective, the free international market in currencies should extend also to the services of banks is, of course, that bank deposits subject to cheque represent today much the largest part of the liquid assets of most people. Even during the last hundred years or so of the gold standard, this curcumstance increasingly prevented it from operating as a fully international currency, because any flow in or out of a country required a proportionate expansion or contraction of the much larger superstructure of the national credit money, the effect of which falls indiscriminately on the whole economy instead of merely increasing or decreasing the demand for the particular goods which was required to bring about a new balance between imports and exports. With a truly international banking system, money could be transferred directly without producing the harmful process of secondary contracts or expansions of the credit structure.

It would probably also impose the most effective discipline on governments if they felt immediately the effects of their policies on the attractiveness of investment in their country. I have just read in an English Whig tract more than 250 years old: "Who would establish a Bank in an arbitrary country, or trust his money constantly there"?[11] The tract, incidentally, tells us that yet another 50 years earlier a great French banker, Jean Baptiste Tavernier, invested all the riches he had amassed in his long rambles over the world in what the authors described as "the barren rocks of Switzerland"; when asked why by Louis XIV, he had the courage to tell him that "he was willing to have something which he could call his own"! Switzerland, apparently, laid the foundations of her prosperity earlier than most people realize.

I prefer the freeing of all dealings in money to any sort of monetary

[10]Jacob Bronowski, *The Ascent of Man* (London: British Broadcasting Corporation, 1973).

[11]John Trenchard and Thomas Gordon, eds, *Cato's Letters*, letters dated May 12, 1722, and February 3, 1721, respectively, published in collected editions (London: printed for W. Wilkins, T. Woodward, J. Walthoe and J. Pelle, 1723–1724), and later.

union also because the latter would demand an international monetary authority which I believe is neither practicable nor even desirable—and hardly to be more trusted than a national authority. It seems to me that there is a very sound element in the widespread disinclination to confer sovereign powers, or at least powers to command, on any international authority. What we need are not international authorities possessing powers of direction, but merely international bodies (or, rather, international treaties which are effectively enforced) which can prohibit certain actions of governments that will harm other people. Effectively to prohibit all restrictions on dealings in (and the possession of) different kinds of money (or claims for money) would at last make it possible that the absence of tariffs, or other obstacles to the movement of goods and men, will secure a genuine free trade area or common market—and do more than anything else to create confidence in the countries committing themselves to it. It is now urgently needed to counter that monetary nationalism which I first criticized almost 40 years ago[12] and which is becoming even more dangerous when, as a consequence of the close kinship between the two views, it is turning into monetary socialism. I hope it will not be too long before complete freedom to deal in any money one likes will be regarded as the essential mark of a free country.[13]

You may feel that my proposal amounts to no less than the abolition of monetary policy; and you would not be quite wrong. As in other connections, I have come to the conclusion that the best the state can do with respect to money is to provide a framework of legal rules within which the people can develop the monetary institutions that best suit them. It seems to me that if we could prevent governments from meddling with money, we would do more good than any government has ever done in this regard. And private enterprise would probably have done better than the best they have ever done.

Addendum: The Age-Old Superstition

Lord Keynes has always appeared to me a kind of new John Law. Law, like Keynes, had been a financial genius who made some real contributions to the theory of money. (Apart from an interesting and original discussion of the factors

[12] *Monetary Nationalism and International Stability* (1937). [This volume, chapter 1. —Ed.]

[13] It may at first seem as if this suggestion were in conflict with my general support of fixed exchange rates under the present system. But this is not so. Fixed exchange rates seem to me to be necessary so long as national governments have a monopoly of issuing money in their territory in order to place them under a very necessary discipline. But this is of course no longer necessary when they have to submit to the discipline of competition with other issuers of money equally current within their territory.

determining the value of money, Law gave the first satisfactory account of the cumulative growth of acceptability once a commodity was widely used as a medium of exchange.) And, like Law, Keynes could never free himself from the false popular belief that, as Law expressed it, "as this addition to the money will employ the people that are now idle, and those now employed to more advantage, so the product will be increased, and manufacture advanced".[14]

It was against the sort of view represented by Law that Richard Cantillon and David Hume began the development of modern monetary theory. Hume in particular put the central point at issue by saying that, in the process of inflation, "it is only in this interval or intermediate situation between the acquisition of money and the rise of prices that the increasing quantity of gold and silver is favourable to industry".[15] It is this work we shall have to do again after the Keynesian flood.

In one sense, however, it would be somewhat unfair to blame Lord Keynes too much for the developments after his death. I am certain he would have been—whatever he had said earlier—a leader in the fight against inflation. But developments, at least in Britain, were also mainly determined by the version of Keynesianism published under the name of Lord Beveridge for which (since he himself understood no economics whatever) his scientific advisers must bear the responsibility. Perhaps, so far as the influence on British policy is concerned, I ought to have spoken of the Kaldorian rather than the Keynesian inflation.[16]

Since I have been censured for charging Keynes in an earlier version of this with a limited knowledge of economic theory, I must become more specific. I believe that his inadequate knowledge of the theory of international trade or of the theory of capital is fairly widely recognized. His deficiencies in the theory of money which I had in mind were by no means his unfamiliarity with the discussion of the relation between money and interest by Swedish and Austrian scholars—that would until the 1930s have been true of most English and US economists—though it was rather a misfortune that the chief works of Wicksell and Mises in this field were reviewed in the *Economic Journal* by Pigou and Keynes, neither of whom understood enough German really to be able to follow the argument. What I had in mind concerning Keynes were the surprising gaps in his knowledge of nineteenth-century English economic theory (and economic history). I had to tell him of the passage by Ricardo [in which he would never advise

[14]John Law, *Money and Trade Considered with a Proposal for Supplying the Nations with Money* (Edinburgh: A. Anderson, 1705; reprinted New York: Augustus M. Kelley, 1966). [Hayek wrote a full account of John Law and his 'system'; in F. A. Hayek, *The Trend of Economic Thinking,* W. W. Bartley III and Stephen Kresge, eds, being vol. 3 of *The Collected Works of F. A. Hayek,* op. cit., chapter 10. —Ed.]

[15]David Hume, "On Money", *Essays Moral, Political, and Literary,* vol. 3, T. H. Green and T. H. Grose, eds (London: Longmans, Green, 1875). [David Hume, *Essays Moral, Political, and Literary,* ed. Eugene F. Miller (Indianapolis, Ind.: Liberty*Classics,* 1985), pp. 286–288. —Ed.]

[16][Hayek's personal recollection of the production of the Beveridge Report may be found in *Hayek on Hayek,* Stephen Kresge and Leif Wenar, eds (Chicago: University of Chicago Press, and London: Routledge, 1994), pp. 85–87. —Ed.]

a government to restore a currency which had been depreciated 30 per cent to par[17]] which, if he had known it, might well have helped him to win the battle against the return to gold at the old parity, and of John Stuart Mill's claim to have regarded in his youth "full employment at high wages" as the chief goal of economic policy[18]. Apart from the Bullion Report and Ricardo's essays provoked by it, so far as I could discover Keynes was wholly unaware of the extensive discussions of that period and particularly of the great work of Henry Thornton,[19] as well as of those later decisive contributions by English writers to the theory of the value of money such as Nassau W. Senior[20] and J. E. Cairnes[21]. Nor did he appear to have ever heard of the long row of English inflationist writers of the last century who might possibly have inspired but more likely would have deterred him: I believe he would have rapidly spotted in their writings the elementary fallacy of believing that employment was a simple function of aggregate demand, and would not have wasted his energies on refinements of the explanation of the mechanism through which changes in the quantity of money would affect aggregate demand.

I hope somebody will some day write a history of inflationism from John Law to John Keynes. It would show how the uncritical acceptance of the belief of such a simple relation between aggregate demand and employment has throughout the last 150 years again and again caused much waste of ingenious intellectual effort.

[17]In a letter to John Wheatley, dated September 18, 1821, reprinted in *Letters of David Ricardo to Hutches Trower and Others,* edited by James Bonar and Jacob Henry Hollander (Oxford: Clarendon Press, 1899), p. 160. [*The Works and Correspondence of David Ricardo,* ed. Piero Sraffa with the collaboration of M. H. Dobb, vol. 9, *Letters July 1821–1823* (Cambridge: Cambridge University Press, 1952), pp. 71–74. –Ed.]

[18]John Stuart Mill, *Autobiography and Other Writings* (London: Longmans, Green, Reader, and Dyer; and New York: Henry Holt, 1873); reprinted, ed. Jack Stillinger (Boston: Houghton, Mifflin, 1969).

[19][On Henry Thornton (1760–1815), see Hayek's essay in F. A. Hayek, *The Trend of Economic Thinking,* op. cit., chapter 14. —Ed.]

[20][About Senior, Hayek wrote, "We must not forget to mention here an absolutely first-rate contribution to monetary science dating from this period. . . . We have in mind a series of lectures on monetary theory held by Nassau William Senior in 1828–29. Senior had just been appointed to Oxford University's first professorship for political economy, and his lectures—which were published only in bits and pieces, in small editions, some of them after years of delay—must be ranked among the most impressive and brilliant achievements, worthy of mention along with the writings of Cantillon and Hume, Thornton, and Ricardo." *The Trend of Economic Thinking,* op. cit., p. 223. —Ed.]

[21][John Elliott Cairnes (1823–1875), often described as 'the last of the classical economists'. —Ed.]

FOUR

THE DENATIONALIZATION OF MONEY: AN ANALYSIS OF THE THEORY AND PRACTICE OF CONCURRENT CURRENCIES[1]

Diseases desperate grown,
By desperate appliances are reli'ved,
Or not at all.

William Shakespeare
(*Hamlet*, Act iv, Scene iii)

Introduction

> For in every country of the world, I believe, the avarice and injustice of princes and sovereign states abusing the confidence of their subjects, have by degrees diminished the real quality of the metal, which had been originally contained in their coins.
>
> Adam Smith[2]

In my despair about the hopelessness of finding a politically feasible solution to what is technically the simplest possible problem, namely to stop inflation, I threw out in a lecture delivered about a year ago[3] a somewhat startling suggestion, the further pursuit of which has opened quite unexpected new horizons. I could not resist pursuing the idea further, since the task of preventing inflation has always seemed to me to be of the greatest importance, not only because of the harm and suffering major inflations cause, but also because I have long been convinced that even mild inflations ultimately produce the recurring depressions and unemployment which have been a justified grievance against the free enterprise system and must be prevented if a free society is to survive.

The further pursuit of the suggestion that government should be deprived of its monopoly of the issue of money opened the most fascinating theoretical vistas and showed the possibility of arrangements which have never been considered. As soon as one succeeds in freeing oneself of the

[1][First published by the Institute of Economic Affairs, London, 1978. —Ed.]

[2]Adam Smith, *An Inquiry into the Nature and Causes of the Wealth of Nations* [1776], Glasgow edition (Oxford: Oxford University Press at the Clarendon Press, 1976), vol. 1, no. 4, p. 43.

[3][See this volume, chapter 3. —Ed.]

universally but tacitly accepted creed that a country must be supplied by its government with its own distinctive and exclusive currency, all sorts of interesting questions arise which have never been examined. The result was a foray into a wholly unexplored field. In this short work I can present no more than some discoveries made in the course of a first survey of the terrain. I am of course very much aware that I have only scratched the surface of the complex of new questions and that I am still very far from having solved all the problems which the existence of multiple concurrent currencies would raise. Indeed, I shall have to ask a number of questions to which I do not know the answer; nor can I discuss all the theoretical problems which the explanation of the new situation raises. Much more work will yet have to be done on the subject; but there are already signs that the basic idea has stirred the imagination of others and that there are indeed some younger brains at work on the problem.[4]

The main result at this stage is that the chief blemish of the market order which has been the cause of well-justified reproaches, its susceptibility to recurrent periods of depression and unemployment, is a consequence of the age-old government monopoly of the issue of money. I have now no doubt whatever that private enterprise, if it had not been prevented by government, could and would long ago have provided the public with a choice of currencies, and those that prevailed in the competition would have been essentially stable in value and would have prevented both excessive stimulation of investment and the consequent periods of contraction.

The demand for the freedom of the issue of money will at first, with good reason, appear suspect to many, since in the past such demands have been raised again and again by a long series of cranks with strong inflationist inclinations. From most of the advocates of 'Free Banking' in the early nineteenth century (and even a substantial section of the advocates of the 'banking principle') to the agitators for a "Free Money" (*Freigeld*)—Silvio Gesell[5] and the plans of Major C. H. Douglas,[6] H. Ritters-

[4]See Benjamin Klein, "The Competitive Supply of Money", *Journal of Money, Credit and Banking,* November 1974; Gordon Tullock, "Paper Money—A Cycle in Cathay", *Economic History Review,* April 1957, pp. 393–407; and Gordon Tullock, "Competing Monies", *Money Credit and Banking,* November 1976, pp. 521–525. [See also George A. Selgin and Lawrence H. White, "How Would the Invisible Hand Handle Money?", *Journal of Economic Literature,* vol. 32, December 1994, pp. 1718–1749; and Milton Friedman and Anna J. Schwartz, "Has Government Any Role in Money?", *Journal of Monetary Economics,* vol. 17, 1986, pp. 37–62. —Ed.]

[5]Silvio Gesell, *The Natural Economic Order* [1916], revised edition (London: Peter Owen, 1958).

[6]Clifford Hugh Douglas, *Social Credit* [1924] (Hawthorne, Calif.: Omni Publications, 4th edition, 1966).

hausen,[7] and Henry Meulen[8]—in the twentieth, they all agitated for free issue because they wanted *more* money. Often a suspicion that the government monopoly was inconsistent with the general principle of freedom of enterprise underlay their argument, but without exception they all believed that the monopoly had led to an undue restriction rather than to an excessive supply of money. They certainly did not recognise that government more often than any private enterprise had provided us with the *Schwundgeld* (shrinking money) that Silvio Gesell had recommended.

I will here merely add that, to keep to the main subject, I will not allow myself to be drawn into a discussion of the interesting methodological question of how it is possible to say something of significance about circumstances with which we have practically no experience, although this fact throws interesting light on the method of economic theory in general.

In conclusion I will merely say that this task has seemed to me important and urgent enough to interrupt for a few weeks the major undertaking to which all my efforts have been devoted for the last few years and the completion of which still demands its concluding third volume.[9] The reader will, I hope, understand that in these circumstances, and against all my habits, after completing a first draft of the text of the present paper, I left most of the exacting and time-consuming task of polishing the exposition and getting it ready for publication to the sympathetic endeavours of Arthur Seldon, the Editorial Director of the Institute of Economic Affairs, whose beneficial care has already made much more readable some of my shorter essays published by that Institute, and who has been willing to assume this burden. His are in particular all the helpful headings of the sub-sections. And the much improved title of what I had intended to call *Concurrent Currencies* was suggested by the General Director of the Institute, Mr. Ralph Harris. I am profoundly grateful to them for thus making possible the publication of this sketch. It would otherwise probably not have appeared for a long time, since I owe it to the readers of *Law, Legislation and Liberty* that I should not allow myself to be diverted from completing it by this rather special concern for longer than was necessary to get a somewhat rough outline of my argument on paper.

A special apology is due to those of my many friends to whom it will be obvious that, in the course of the last few years when I was occupied

[7] H. Rittershausen, *Der Neubau des deutschen Kredit-Systems* (Berlin: G. Stilke, 1932).

[8] Henry Meulen, *Free Banking*, 2nd edition (London: Macmillan, 1934).

[9] Now published as F. A. Hayek, *Law, Legislation and Liberty*, vol. 1 [1973], vol. II [1976], and vol. III [1979] (Chicago: University of Chicago Press, and London: Routledge and Kegan Paul).

with wholly different problems, I have not read their publications closely related to the subject of this *Paper* which would probably have taught me much from which I could have profited in writing it.

Salzburg
June 30, 1976

A Note to the Second Edition

It is just thirteen months after I commenced writing this study and only a little more than six months since its first publication. It is therefore perhaps not very surprising that the additions I found desirable to make in this second edition are due more to further thinking about the questions raised than to any criticisms I have so far received. The comments so far, indeed, have expressed incredulous surprise more often than any objections to my argument.

Most of the additions therefore concern rather obvious points which perhaps I ought to have made more clearly in the first edition. Only one of them, that on page 224 concerns a point on which further thought has led me to expect a somewhat different development from what I had suggested if the reform I propose were adopted. Indeed the clear distinction between two different kinds of competition, the first of which is likely to lead to the general acceptance of one widely used standard (or perhaps a very few such standards), while the second refers to the competition for the confidence of the public in the currency of a particular denomination, seems to me of ever greater importance. I have now sketched, in a somewhat longer insertion to section XXIV, one of the most significant probable consequences, not originally foreseen by me.

I have made only minor stylistic changes to bring out more clearly what I meant to say. I have even let stand the difference between the more tentative tone at the beginning which, as will not have escaped the reader, gradually changes to a more confident tone as the argument proceeds. Further thought has so far only still more increased my confidence both in the desirability and the practicability of the fundamental change suggested.

Some important contributions to the problems considered here which were made at a Mont Pelerin Society conference held after the material for this second edition was prepared could not be used since I had immediately after to start on prolonged travels. I hope that particularly the papers presented then by W. Engels, D. L. Kemmerer, W. Stützel, and R. Vaubel will soon be available in print. I have, however, inserted at a late stage a reply to a comment by Milton Friedman which seemed to me to demand a prompt response.

I should perhaps have added above to my reference to my preoccupation with other problems which have prevented me from giving the present argument all the attention which it deserves, that in fact my despair of ever again getting a tolerable money system under the present institutional structure is as much a result of the many years of study I have now devoted to the prevailing political order, and especially to the effects of government by a democratic assembly with unlimited powers, as to my earlier work when monetary theory was still one of my central interests.

I ought, perhaps, also to add, what I have often had occasion to explain but may never have stated in writing, that I strongly feel that the chief task of the economic theorist or political philosopher should be to operate on public opinion to make politically possible what today may be politically impossible, and that in consequence the objection that my proposals are at present impracticable does not in the least deter me from developing them.

Finally, after reading over once more the text of this Second Edition I feel I ought to tell the reader at the outset that in the field of money I do not want to prohibit government from doing anything except preventing others from doing things they might do better.

Freiburg im Breisgau
[1977]

I. The Practical Proposal

The concrete proposal for the near future, and the occasion for the examination of a much more far-reaching scheme, is that *the countries of the Common Market, preferably with the neutral countries of Europe (and possibly later the countries of North America) mutually bind themselves by formal treaty not to place any obstacles in the way of the free dealing throughout their territories in one another's currencies (including gold coins) or of a similar free exercise of the banking business by any institution legally established in any of their territories.* This would mean in the first instance the abolition of any kind of exchange control or regulation of the movement of money between these countries, as well as the full freedom to use any of the currencies for contracts and accounting. Further, it would mean the opportunity for any bank located in these countries to open branches in any other on the same terms as established banks.

Free Trade in Money

The purpose of this scheme is to impose upon existing monetary and financial agencies a very much needed discipline by making it impossible for any of them, or for any length of time, to issue a kind of money substantially less reliable and useful than the money of any other. As soon as the public became familiar with the new possibilities, any deviations from the straight path of providing an honest money would at once lead to the rapid displacement of the offending currency by others. And the individual countries, being deprived of the various dodges by which they are now able temporarily to conceal the effects of their actions by 'protecting' their currency, would be constrained to keep the value of their currencies tolerably stable.

Proposal More Practicable than Utopian European Currency

This seems to me both preferable and more practicable than the utopian scheme of introducing a new European currency, which would ultimately only have the effect of more deeply entrenching the source and root of all monetary evil, the government monopoly of the issue and control of money. It would also seem that, if the countries were not prepared to adopt the more limited proposal advanced here, they would be even less willing to accept a common European currency. The idea of depriving government altogether of its age-old prerogative of monopolising money is still too unfamiliar and even alarming to most people to have any chance of being adopted in the near future. But people might learn to see the advantages if, at first at least, the currencies of the governments were allowed to compete for the favour of the public.

Though I strongly sympathize with the desire to complete the economic unification of Western Europe by completely freeing the flow of money between them, I have grave doubts about the desirability of doing so by creating a new European currency managed by any sort of supranational authority. Quite apart from the extreme unlikelihood that the member countries would agree on the policy to be pursued in practice by a common monetary authority (and the practical inevitability of some countries getting a worse currency than they have now), it seems highly unlikely, even in the most favourable circumstances, that it would be administered better than the present national currencies. Moreover, in many respects a single international currency is not better but worse than a national currency if it is not better run. It would leave a country with a financially more sophisticated public not even the chance of escaping from the consequences of the crude prejudices governing the decisions of the others. The advantage of an international authority should be mainly to protect a member state from the harmful measures of others, not to force it to join in their follies.

Free Trade in Banking

The suggested extension of the free trade in money to free trade in banking is an absolutely essential part of the scheme if it is to achieve what is intended. First, bank deposits subject to cheque, and thus a sort of privately issued money, are today of course a part, and in most countries much the largest part, of the aggregate amount of generally accepted media of exchange. Secondly, the expansion and contraction of the separate national superstructures of bank credit are at present the chief excuse for national management of the basic money.

On the effects of the adoption of the proposal all I will add at this point is that it is of course intended to prevent national monetary and financial authorities from doing many things politically impossible to avoid so long as they have the power to do them. These are without exception harmful and against the long-run interest of the country doing them but politically inevitable as a temporary escape from acute difficulties. They include measures by which governments can most easily and quickly remove the causes of discontent of particular groups or sections but bound in the long run to disorganize and ultimately to destroy the market order.

Preventing Government from Concealing Depreciation

The main advantage of the proposed scheme, in other words, is that it would prevent governments from 'protecting' the currencies they issue against the harmful consequences of their own measures, and therefore prevent them from further employing these harmful tools. They would become unable to conceal the depreciation of the money they issue, to prevent an outflow of money, capital, and other resources as a result of making their home use unfavourable, or to control prices—all measures which would, of course, tend to destroy the Common Market. The scheme would indeed seem to satisfy all the requirements of a common market better than a common currency without the need to establish a new international agency or to confer new powers on a supra-national authority.

The scheme would, to all intents and purposes, amount to a displacement of the national circulations only if the national monetary authorities misbehaved. Even then they could still ward off a complete displacement of the national currency by rapidly changing their ways. It is possible that in some very small countries with a good deal of international trade and tourism, the currency of one of the bigger countries might come to predominate, but assuming a sensible policy, there is no reason why most of the existing currencies should not continue to be used for a long time. (It would, of course, be important that the parties did not enter into a tacit agreement not to supply so good a money that the citizens of the other nations would prefer it! And the presumption of guilt would of course always have to lie against the government whose money the public did not like!)

I do not think the scheme would prevent governments from doing anything they ought to do in the interest of a well-functioning economy, or which in the long run would benefit any substantial group. But this raises complex issues better discussed within the framework of the full development of the underlying principle.

II. The Generalization of the Underlying Principle

If the use of several concurrent currencies is to be seriously considered for immediate application in a limited area, it is evidently desirable to investigate the consequences of a general application of the principle on which this proposal is based. If we are to contemplate abolishing the exclusive use within each national territory of a single national currency issued by the government, and to admit on equal footing the currencies issued by other governments, the question at once arises whether it should not be equally desirable to do away altogether with the monopoly of government supplying money and to allow private enterprise to supply the public with other media of exchange it may prefer.

The questions this reform raises are at present much more theoretical than the practical proposal because the more far-reaching suggestion is clearly not only much too strange and alien to the general public to be considered for present application. The problems it raises are evidently also still much too little understood even by the experts for anyone to make a confident prediction about the precise consequences of such a scheme. Yet it is clearly possible that there is no necessity or even advantage in the now unquestioned and universally accepted government prerogative of producing money. It may indeed prove to be harmful and its abolition a great gain, opening the way for very beneficial developments. Discussion therefore cannot begin early enough. Though its realization may be wholly impracticable so long as the public is mentally unprepared for it and uncritically accepts the dogma of the necessary government prerogative, this should no longer be allowed to act as a bar to the intellectual exploration of the fascinating theoretical problems the scheme raises.

Competition in Currency Not Discussed by Economists

It is an extraordinary truth that competing currencies have until quite recently never been seriously examined.[10] There is no answer in the available literature to the question why a government monopoly of the provision of money is universally regarded as indispensable, or whether the belief is simply derived from the unexplained postulate that there must be within any given territory one single kind of money in circulation which, so long as only gold and silver were seriously considered as possible kinds of money, might have appeared a definite convenience. Nor can we find an answer to the question of what would happen if that monopoly were abolished and the provision of money were thrown open to the competition of private concerns supplying different currencies. Most people seem to imagine that any proposal for private agencies to be allowed to issue money means that they should be allowed to issue the *same* money as anybody else (in token money this would, of course, simply amount to forgery) rather than *different* kinds of money clearly distinguishable by different denominations among which the public could choose freely.

Initial Advantages of Government Monopoly in Money

Perhaps when the money economy was only slowly spreading into the remoter regions, and one of the main problems was to teach large numbers the art of calculating in money (and that was not so very long ago), a single easily recognizable kind of money may have been of considerable assistance. And it may be argued that the exclusive use of such a single uniform sort of money greatly assisted comparison of prices and therefore the growth of competition and the market. Also, when the genuineness of metallic money could be ascertained only by a difficult process of assaying, for which the ordinary person had neither the skill nor the equipment, a strong case could be made for guaranteeing the fineness of the coins by the stamp of some generally recognized authority which, outside the great commercial centres, could be only the government. But today these initial advantages, which might have served as an excuse for governments to appropriate the exclusive right of issuing metallic money, certainly do not outweigh the disadvantages of this system. It has the defects of all monopolies: One must use their product even if it is unsatis-

[10]But, though I had independently arrived at the realisation of the advantages possessed by independent competing currencies, I must now concede intellectual priority to Professor Benjamin Klein, who, in a paper written in 1970 and published in 1974 (Klein, "The Competitive Supply of Money", op. cit.), until recently unknown to me, had clearly explained the chief advantage of competition among currencies.

factory, and, above all, it prevents the discovery of better methods of satisfying a need for which a monopolist has no incentive.

If the public understood what price in periodic inflation and instability it pays for the convenience of having to deal with only one kind of money in ordinary transactions, and not occasionally to have to contemplate the advantage of using other money than the familiar kind, it would probably find it very excessive. For this convenience is much less important than the opportunity to use a reliable money that will not periodically upset the smooth flow of the economy—an opportunity of which the public has been deprived by the government monopoly. But the people have never been given the opportunity to discover this advantage. Governments have at all times had a strong interest in persuading the public that the right to issue money belongs exclusively to them. And so long as, for all practical purposes, this meant the issue of gold, silver, and copper coins, it did not matter so much as it does today, when we know that there are all kinds of other possible sorts of money, not least paper, which government is even less competent to handle and even more prone to abuse than metallic money.

III. The Origin of the Government Prerogative of Making Money

For more than 2,000 years the government prerogative or exclusive right of supplying money amounted in practice merely to the monopoly of minting coins of gold, silver or copper. It was during this period that this prerogative came to be accepted without question as an essential attribute of sovereignty—clothes with all the mystery which the sacred powers of the prince used to inspire. Perhaps this conception goes back to even before King Croesus of Lydia struck the first coins in the sixth century BC, to the time when it was usual merely to punch marks on the bars of metal to certify its fineness.

At any rate, the minting prerogative of the ruler was firmly established under the Roman emperors.[11] When, at the beginning of the modern era, Jean Bodin developed the concept of sovereignty, he treated the right of coinage as one of the most important and essential parts of it.[12] The *regalia*, as these royal prerogatives were called in Latin, of which coinage,

[11]Wilhelm Endemann, *Studien in der Romanisch-kanonistischen Wirthschafts-und Rechtslehre* (Berlin: J. Gutentag, 1874–1883), vol. 2, p. 171.

[12]J. Bodin, *The Six Books of a Commonweale* [1576], trans. Richard Knolles (London: Impensis G. Bishop, 1606), p. 176. Bodin, who understood more about money than most of his contemporaries, may well have hoped that the governments of large states would be more responsible than the thousands of minor princelings and cities who, during the later part of the Middle Ages, had acquired the minting privilege and sometimes abused it even more than the richer princes of large territories.

mining, and custom duties were the most important, were during the Middle Ages the chief sources of revenue of the princes and were viewed solely from this angle. It is evident that, as coinage spread, governments everywhere soon discovered that the exclusive right of coinage was a most important instrument of power as well as an attractive source of gain. From the beginning the prerogative was neither claimed nor conceded on the ground that it was for the general good but simply as an essential element of governmental power.[13] The coins served, indeed, largely as the symbols of might, like the flag, through which the ruler asserted his sovereignty, and told his people who their master was whose image the coins carried to the remotest parts of his realm.

Government Certificate of Metal Weight and Purity

The task the government was understood to assume was of course initially not so much to make money as to certify the weight and fineness of the materials that universally served as money,[14] which after the earliest times were only the three metals, gold, silver, and copper. It was supposed to be a task rather like that of establishing and certifying uniform weights and measures.

The pieces of metal were regarded as proper money only if they carried the stamp of the appropriate authority, whose duty was thought to be to assure that the coins had the proper weight and purity to give them their value.

During the Middle Ages, however, the superstition arose that it was the act of government that conferred the value upon the money. Although experience always proved otherwise, this doctrine of the *valor impositus*[15] was largely taken over by legal doctrine and served to some extent as justification of the constant vain attempts of the princes to impose the same value on coins containing a smaller amount of the precious metal. (In the early years of this century the medieval doctrine was revived by

[13]The same applies to the postal monopoly which everywhere appears to provide a steadily deteriorating service and of which in Great Britain (according to *The Times,* May 25, 1976) the General Secretary of the Union of Post Office Workers (!) said recently that "Governments of both political complexions have reduced a once great public service to the level of a music-hall joke". *Politically* the broadcasting monopoly may be even more dangerous, but *economically* I doubt whether any other monopoly has done as much damage as that of issuing money.

[14]Cf. Adam Smith, *An Inquiry into the Nature and Causes of the Wealth of Nations,* op. cit., p. 40: ". . . those public offices called mints: institutions exactly of the same nature with those of the aulnagers and stampmasters of woollen and linen cloth".

[15]Endemann, op. cit., p. 172.

the German Professor G. F. Knapp; his *State Theory of Money* still seems to exercise some influence on contemporary legal theory.[16])

There is no reason to doubt that private enterprise would, if permitted, have been capable of providing as good and at least as trustworthy coins. Indeed occasionally it did, or was commissioned by government to do so. Yet so long as the technical task of providing uniform and recognisable coins still presented major difficulties, it was at least a useful task which government performed. Unfortunately, governments soon discovered that it was not only useful but could also be made very profitable, at least so long as people had no alternative but to use the money they provided. That seignorage, the fee charged to cover the cost of minting, proved a very attractive source of revenue, and was soon increased far beyond the cost of manufacturing the coin. And from retaining an excessive part of the metal brought to the government mint to be struck into new coins, it was only a step to the practice, increasingly common during the Middle Ages, of recalling the circulating coins in order to recoin the various denominations with a lower gold or silver content. We shall consider the effect of these debasements in the next section. But since the function of government in issuing money is no longer one of merely certifying the weight and fineness of a certain piece of metal, but involves a deliberate determination of the quantity of money to be issued, governments have become wholly inadequate for the task and, it can be said without qualifications, have incessantly and everywhere abused their trust to defraud the people.

The Appearance of Paper Money

The government prerogative, which had originally referred only to the issue of coins because they were the only kind of money then used, was promptly extended to other kinds of money when they appeared on the scene. They arose originally when governments wanted money which they tried to raise by compulsory loans, for which they gave receipts that they ordered people to accept as money. The significance of the gradual appearance of government paper money, and soon of bank notes, is for our purposes complicated because for a long time the problem was not the appearance of new kinds of money with a different denomination, but the use as money of paper claims on the established kind of metallic money issued by government monopoly.

It is probably impossible for pieces of paper or other tokens of a material itself of no significant market value to come to be gradually accepted

[16]Georg F. Knapp, *The State Theory of Money* [1905] (London: Macmillan, 1924), and compare Frederic Alexander Mann, *The Legal Aspect of Money,* 3rd edition (Oxford: Oxford University Press, 1971).

and held as money unless they represent a claim on some valuable object. To be accepted as money they must at first derive their value from another source, such as their convertibility into another kind of money. In consequence, gold and silver, or claims for them, remained for a long time the only kinds of money between which there could be any competition; and, since the sharp fall in its value in the nineteenth century, even silver ceased to be a serious competitor to gold. (The possibilities of bimetallism are irrelevant for our present problems.)

Political and Technical Possibilities of Controlling Paper Money

The position has become very different, however, since paper money established itself everywhere. The government monopoly of the issue of money was bad enough so long as metallic money predominated. But it became an unrelieved calamity since paper money (or other token money), which can provide the best and the worst money, came under political control. A money deliberately controlled in supply by an agency whose self-interest forced it to satisfy the wishes of the *users* might be best. A money regulated to satisfy the demands of group interests is bound to be the worst possible (Section XVIII).

The value of paper money obviously can be regulated according to a variety of principles even if it is more than doubtful that any democratic government with unlimited powers can ever manage it satisfactorily. Though historical experience would at first seem to justify the belief that only gold can provide a stable currency, and that all paper money is bound to depreciate sooner or later, all our insight into the processes determining the value of money tells us that this prejudice, though understandable, is unfounded. The *political* impossibility that governments will achieve it does not mean there is reason to doubt that it is *technically* possible to control the quantity of any kind of token money so that its value will behave in a desired manner, and that it will for this reason retain its acceptability and its value. It would therefore now be possible, if it were permitted, to have a variety of essentially different monies. They could represent not merely different quantities of the same metal but also different abstract units fluctuating in their value relatively to one another. In the same way, we could have currencies circulating concurrently throughout many countries and offering the people a choice. This possibility appears, until recently, never to have been contemplated seriously. Even the most radical advocates of free enterprise, such as the philosopher Herbert Spencer[17] or the French economist Joseph Garnier,[18] seem

[17] Herbert Spencer, *Social Statics* [1851], rev. ed. (London and Oxford: Williams & Norgate, 1902).

[18] Joseph Garnier, *Traité théorique et pratique du change et des operation de banque* (Paris, 1841).

to have advocated only private coinage, while the free banking movement of the mid-nineteenth century agitated merely for the right to issue notes in terms of the standard currency.[19]

Monopoly of Money Has Buttressed Government Power

While, as we shall see presently, government's exclusive right to issue and regulate money has certainly not helped to give us a better money than we would otherwise have had, and probably a very much worse one, it has of course become a chief instrument for prevailing governmental policies and profoundly assisted the general growth of governmental power. Much of contemporary politics is based on the assumption that government has the power to create and make people accept any amount of additional money it wishes. Governments will for this reason strongly defend their traditional rights. But for the same reason it is also most important that they should be taken from them.

A government ought not, any more than a private person, to be able (at least in peacetime) to take whatever it wants, but be limited strictly to the use of the means placed at its disposal by the representatives of the people, and to be unable to extend its resources beyond what the people have agreed to let it have. The modern expansion of government was largely assisted by the possibility of covering deficits by issuing money—usually on the pretence that it was thereby creating employment. It is perhaps significant, however, that Adam Smith does not mention the control of the issue of money among the "only three duties [which] according to the system of natural liberty, the sovereign has to attend to".[20]

IV. The Persistent Abuse of the Government Prerogative

When one studies the history of money one cannot help wondering why people should have put up for so long with governments exercising an exclusive power over 2,000 years that was regularly used to exploit and defraud them. This can be explained only by the myth (that the government prerogative was necessary) becoming so firmly established that it did not occur even to the professional student of these matters (for a long time including the present writer[21]) ever to question it. But once the validity of the established doctrine is doubted its foundation is rapidly seen to be fragile.

[19] Vera C. Smith, *Rationale of Central Banking* (London: P. S. King, 1936; reprinted, Indianapolis, Ind.: Liberty*Press*, 1990).

[20] Adam Smith, *The Wealth of Nations*, op. cit., p. 687.

[21] F. A. Hayek, *The Constitution of Liberty* (Chicago: University of London Press, and London: Routledge & Kegan Paul, 1960), pp. 324 *et seq.*

We cannot trace the details of the nefarious activities of rulers in monopolising money beyond the time of the Greek philosopher Diogenes who is reported, as early as the fourth century BC, to have called money the politicians' game of dice. But from Roman times to the seventeenth century, when paper money in various forms begins to be significant, the history of coinage is an almost uninterrupted story of debasements or the continuous reduction of the metallic content of the coins and a corresponding increase in all commodity prices.

History Is Largely Inflation Engineered by Government

Nobody has yet written a full history of these developments. It would indeed be all too monotonous and depressing a story, but I do not think it an exaggeration to say that history is largely a history of inflation, and usually of inflations engineered by governments and for the gain of governments—though the gold and silver discoveries in the sixteenth century had a similar effect. Historians have again and again attempted to justify inflation by claiming that it made possible the great periods of rapid economic progress. They have even produced a series of inflationist theories of history[22] which have, however, been clearly refuted by the evidence: Prices in England and the United States were at the end of the period of their most rapid development almost exactly at the same level as two hundred years earlier. But their recurring rediscoverers are usually ignorant of the earlier discussions.

Early Middle Ages' Deflation Local or Temporary

The early Middle Ages may have been a period of deflation that contributed to the economic decline of the whole of Europe. But even this is not certain. It would seem that on the whole the shrinking of trade led to the reduction of the amount of money in circulation, not the other way round. We find too many complaints about the dearness of commodities and the deterioration of the coin to accept deflation as more than a local phenomenon in regions where wars and migrations had destroyed the market and the money economy shrank as people buried their treasure.

[22]Especially Werner Sombart in *Der moderne Kapitalismus* [1902], vol. 2, 2nd edition (Munich and Leipzig: Duncker & Humblot, 1917), and before him Sir Archibald Alison, *The History of Europe from the Commencement of the French Revolution in 1789 to the Restoration of the Bourbons in 1815* (Edinburgh and London: Blackwood and Sons, 1835), vol. 1, and others. Cf. Paul Barth, who has a whole chapter on "History as a function of the value of money" in *Die Philosophie der Geschichte als Soziologie*, 2nd edition (Leipzig: Reisland, 1915), and Marianne Herzfeld, "Die Geschichte als Funktion der Geldwertbewegung", *Archiv für Sozialwissenschaft und Sozialpolitik*, vol. 56, no. 3, 1926, pp. 654–686.

But where, as in Northern Italy, trade revived early, we find at once all the little princes vying with one another in diminishing the coin—a process which, in spite of some unsuccessful attempts of private merchants to provide a better medium of exchange, lasted throughout the following centuries until Italy came to be described as the country with the worst money and the best writers on money.

But though theologians and jurists joined in condemning these practices, they never ceased until the introduction of paper money provided governments with an even cheaper method of defrauding the people. Governments could not, of course, pursue the practices by which they forced bad money upon the people without the cruellest measures. As one legal treatise on the law of money sums up the history of punishment for merely refusing to accept the legal money:

> From Marco Polo we learn that, in the thirteenth century, Chinese law made the rejection of imperial paper money punishable by death, and twenty years in chains or, in some cases death, was the penalty provided for the refusal to accept French *assignats*. Early English law punished repudiation as *lese-majesty*. At the time of the American revolution, non-acceptance of Continental notes was treated as an enemy act and sometimes worked a forfeiture of the debt.[23]

Absolutism Suppressed Merchants' Attempts to Create Stable Money

Some of the early foundations of banks at Amsterdam and elsewhere arose from attempts by merchants to secure for themselves a stable money, but rising absolutism soon suppressed all such efforts to create a non-governmental currency. Instead, it protected the rise of banks issuing notes in terms of the official government money. Even less than in the history of metallic money can we here sketch how this development opened the doors to new abuses of policy.

It is said that the Chinese had been driven by their experience with paper money to try to prohibit it for all time (of course unsuccessfully) before the Europeans ever invented it.[24] Certainly European governments, once they knew about this possibility, began to exploit it ruthlessly, not to provide people with good money, but to gain as much as possible from it for their revenue. Ever since the British Government in 1694 sold

[23] A. Nussbaum, *Money in the Law, National and International* [1939] (Brooklyn: Foundation Press, 1950), p. 53.

[24] On the Chinese events, see Willem Vissering, *On Chinese Currency. Coin and Paper Money* (Leiden: E. J. Brill, 1877), and Gordon Tullock, "Paper Money—A Cycle in Cathay", *Economic History Review*, April 1957, pp. 393–407, who does not, however, allude to the often recounted story of the "final prohibition".

the Bank of England a limited monopoly of the issue of bank notes, the chief concern of governments has been not to let slip from their hand the power over money, formerly based on the prerogative of coinage, to really independent banks. For a time the ascendancy of the gold standard and the consequent belief that to maintain it was an important matter of prestige, and to be driven off it a national disgrace, put an effective restraint on this power. It gave the world the one long period—200 years or more—of relative stability during which modern industrialism could develop, albeit suffering from periodic crises. But as soon as it was widely understood some fifty years ago that the convertibility into gold was merely a method of controlling the *amount* of a currency, which was the real factor determining its value, governments became only too anxious to escape that discipline, and money became more than ever before the plaything of politics. Only a few of the great powers preserved for a time tolerable monetary stability, and they brought it also to their colonial empires. But Eastern Europe and South America never knew a prolonged period of monetary stability.

But, while governments have never used their power to provide a decent money for any length of time, and have refrained from grossly abusing it only when they were under such a discipline as the gold standard imposed, the reason that should make us refuse any longer to tolerate this irresponsibility of government is that we know today that it is possible to control the quantity of a currency so as to prevent significant fluctuations in its purchasing power. Moreover, though there is every reason to mistrust government if not tied to the gold standard or the like, there is no reason to doubt that private enterprise whose business depended on succeeding in the attempt could keep stable the value of a money it issued.

Before we can proceed to show how such a system would work we must clear out of the way two prejudices that will probably give rise to unfounded objections against the proposal.

V. The Mystique of Legal Tender

The first misconception concerns the concept of 'legal tender'. It is not of much significance for our purposes, but is widely believed to explain or justify government monopoly in the issue of money. The first shocked response to the proposal here discussed is usually "But there must be a legal tender", as if this notion proved the necessity for a single government-issued money believed indispensable for the daily conduct of business.

In its strictly legal meaning, 'legal tender' signifies no more than a kind of money a creditor cannot refuse in discharge of a debt due to him in the money issued by government.[25] Even so, it is significant that the term has no authoritative definition in English statute law.[26] Elsewhere it simply refers to the means of discharging a debt contracted in terms of the money issued by government or due under an order of a court. In so far as government possesses the monopoly of issuing money and uses it to establish one kind of money, it must probably also have power to say by what kind of objects debts expressed in its currency can be discharged. But that means neither that all money need be legal tender, nor even that all objects given by the law the attribute of legal tender need to be money. (There are historical instances in which creditors have been compelled by courts to accept commodities such as tobacco, which could hardly be called money, in discharge of their claims for money.)[27]

The Superstition Disproved by Spontaneous Money

The term 'legal tender' has, however, in popular imagination come to be surrounded by a penumbra of vague ideas about the supposed necessity for the state to provide money. This is a survival of the medieval idea that it is the state which somehow confers value on money it otherwise would not possess. And this, in turn, is true only to the very limited extent that government can force us to accept whatever it wishes in place of what we have contracted for; in this sense it can give the substitute the same value for the debtor as the original object of the contract. But the superstition that it is necessary for government (usually called the 'state' to make it sound better) to declare what is to be money, as if it had created the money which could not exist without it, probably originated in the naive belief that such a tool as money must have been 'invented' and given to us by some original inventor. This belief has been wholly displaced by our understanding of the spontaneous generation of such undesigned institutions by a process of social evolution of which money has since become the prime paradigm (law, language, and morals being the other main instances). When the medieval doctrine of the *valor impositus* was in

[25] Arthur Nussbaum, op. cit., Frederic Alexander Mann, op. cit., and S. P. Breckinridge, *Legal Tender* (Chicago: University of Chicago Press, 1903).

[26] Frederic Alexander Mann, op. cit., p. 38. On the other hand, the refusal until recently of English Courts to give judgement for paying in any other currency than the pound sterling has made this aspect of legal tender particularly influential in England. But this is likely to change after a recent decision (Miliangos v. George Frank Textiles Ltd., 1975) established that an English Court can give judgement in a foreign currency on a money claim in a foreign currency, so that, for instance, it is now possible in England to enforce a claim from a sale in Swiss francs. (*Financial Times*, November 6, 1975).

[27] Nussbaum, op. cit., pp. 54f.

this century revived by the much admired German Professor Knapp it prepared the way for a policy which in 1923 carried the German Mark down to 1/1,000,000,000,000 of its former value!

Private Money Preferred

There certainly can be and has been money, even very satisfactory money, without government doing anything about it, though it has rarely been allowed to exist for long.[28] But a lesson is to be learned from the report of a Dutch author about China a hundred years ago who observed of the paper money then current in that part of the world that "*because it is not legal tender* and because it is no concern of the State it is generally accepted as money".[29] We owe it to governments that within given national territories today in general only one kind of money is universally accepted. But whether this is desirable, or whether people could not, if they understood the advantage, get a much better kind of money without all the to-do about legal lender, is an open question. Moreover, a "legal means of payment" (*gesetzliches Zahlungsmittel*) need not be specifically designated by a law. It is sufficient if the law enables the judge to decide in what sort of money a particular debt can be discharged.

The commonsense of the matter was put very clearly 80 years ago by a distinguished defender of a liberal economic policy, the lawyer, statistician, and high civil servant Lord Farrer. In a paper written in 1895[30] he contended that if nations

> make nothing else but the standard unit [of value they have adopted] legal tender, there is no need and no room for the operation of any special law of legal tender. The ordinary law of contract does all that is necessary without any law giving special function to particular forms of currency. We have adopted a gold sovereign as our unit, or standard of value. If I promised to pay 100 sovereigns, it needs no special currency

[28]Occasional attempts by the authorities of commercial cities to provide a money of at least a constant metallic content, such as the establishment of the Bank of Amsterdam, were for long periods fairly successful and their money used far beyond the national boundaries. But even in these cases the authorities sooner or later abused their quasi-monopoly positions. The Bank of Amsterdam was a state agency which people had to use for certain purposes and its money even as exclusive legal tender for payments above a certain amount. Nor was it available for ordinary small transactions or local business beyond the city limits. The same is roughly true of the similar experiments of Venice, Genoa, Hamburg, and Nuremberg.

[29]Willem Vissering, *On Chinese Currency. Coin and Paper Money,* op. cit.

[30]Thomas Henry, Lord Farrer, *Studies in Currency, or Inquiries into certain monetary problems connected with the standard of value and the media of exchange* (London and New York: Macmillan, 1898), p. 43.

> law of legal tender to say that I am bound to pay 100 sovereigns, and that, if required to pay the 100 sovereigns, I cannot discharge the obligation by anything else.

And he concludes, after examining typical applications of the legal tender conception, that

> Looking to the above cases of the use or abuse of the law of legal tender other than the last [i.e., that of subsidiary coins] we see that they possess one character in common—viz. that the law in all of them enables a debtor to pay and requires a creditor to receive something different from that which their contract contemplated. In fact it is a forced and unnatural construction put upon the dealings of men by arbitrary power.[31]

To this he adds a few lines later that "any law of legal tender is in its own nature 'suspect'".[32]

Legal Tender Creates Uncertainty

The truth is indeed that legal tender is simply a legal device to force people to accept in fulfilment of a contract something they never intended when they made the contract. It becomes thus, in certain circumstances, a factor that intensifies the uncertainty of dealings and consists, as Lord Farrer also remarked in the same context,

[31] *Ibid.*, p. 45. The *locus classicus* on this subject from which I undoubtedly derived my views on it, though I had forgotten this when I wrote the First Edition of this essay, is Carl Menger's discussion in 1892 of legal tender under the even more appropriate equivalent German term *Zwangskurs* ("Geld" in *The Collected Works of Carl Menger* (London: London School of Economics, 1934)). See pp. 98–106, especially p. 101, where the *Zwangskurs* is described as "eine Massregel, die in der überwiegenden Zahl der Fälle den Zweck hat, gegen den Willen der Bevölkerung, zumindest durch einen Missbrauch der Münzhoheit oder des Notenregals entstandene pathologische (also exceptionelle) Formen von Umlaufsmitteln, durch einen Missbrauch der Justizhoheit dem Verkehr aufzudrängen oder in demselben zu erhalten"; and p. 104 where Menger describes it as "ein auf die Forderungsberechtigten geübter gesetzlicher Zwang, bei Summenschulden (bisweilen auch bei Schulden anderer Art) solche Geldvereinbarten Inhalte der Forderungen nicht entsprechen, oder dieselben sich zu einem Wert aufdrangen zu lassen, der ihrem Wert im freien Verkehr nicht entspricht". Especially interesting also is the first footnote on p. 102 in which Menger points out that there had been fairly general agreement on this among the liberal economists of the first half of the nineteenth century, while during the second half of that century, through the influence of the (presumably German) lawyers, the economists were led erroneously to regard legal tender as an attribute of perfect money.

[32] *Ibid.*, p. 47.

> in substituting for the free operation of voluntary contract, and a law which simply enforces the performance of such contracts, an artificial construction of contracts such as would never occur to the parties unless forced upon them by an arbitrary law.

All this is well illustrated by the historical occasion when the expression 'legal tender' became widely known and treated as a definition of money. In the notorious 'legal tender cases', fought before the Supreme Court of the United States after the Civil War, the issue was whether creditors must accept at par current dollars in settlement of their claims for money they had lent when the dollar had a much higher value.[33] The same problem arose even more acutely at the end of the great European inflations after the First World War when, even in the extreme case of the German Mark, the principle "Mark is Mark" was enforced until the end—although later some efforts were made to offer limited compensation to the worst sufferers.[34]

Taxes and Contracts

A government must of course be free to determine in what currency taxes are to be paid and to make contracts in any currency it chooses (in this way it can support a currency it issues or wants to favour), but there is no reason why it should not accept other units of accounting as the basis of the assessment of taxes. In non-contractual payments such as damages or compensations for torts, the courts would have to decide the currency in which they have to be paid, and might for this purpose have to develop new rules; but there should be no need for special legislation. There is a real difficulty if a government-issued currency is replaced by another because the government has disappeared as a result of conquest, revolution, or the break-up of a nation. In that event the government taking over will usually make legal provisions about the treatment of private contracts expressed in terms of the vanished currency. If a private issuing bank ceased to operate and was unable to redeem its issue, this currency would presumably become valueless and the holders would have no enforceable claim for compensation. But the courts may decide that in such a case contracts between third parties in terms of that currency, concluded when

[33]Cf. Nussbaum, op. cit., pp. 586–592.

[34]In Austria after 1922 the name "Schumpeter" had become almost a curse word among ordinary people, referring to the principle that "Krone is Krone", because the economist J. A. Schumpeter, during his short tenure as Minister of Finance, had put his name to an order of council, merely spelling out what was undoubtedly valid law, namely that debts incurred in crowns when they had a higher value could be repaid in depreciated crowns, ultimately worth only a 15,000th part of their original value.

there was reason to expect it to be stable, would have to be fulfilled in some other currency that came to the nearest presumed intention of the parties to the contract.

VI. The Confusion about Gresham's Law

It is a misunderstanding of what is called Gresham's law to believe that the tendency for bad money to drive out good money makes a government monopoly necessary. The distinguished economist W. S. Jevons emphatically stated the law in the form that better money cannot drive out worse precisely to prove this. It is true he argued then against a proposal of the philosopher Herbert Spencer to throw the coinage of gold open to free competition, at a time when the only different currencies contemplated were coins of gold and silver. Perhaps Jevons, who had been led to economics by his experience as assayer at a mint, even more than his contemporaries in general, did not seriously contemplate the possibility of any other kind of currency. Nevertheless his indignation about what he described as Spencer's proposal

> that, as we trust the grocer to furnish us with pounds of tea, and the baker to send us loaves of bread, so we might trust Heaton and Sons, or some of the other enterprising firms of Birmingham, to supply us with sovereigns and shillings at their own risk and profit,[35]

led him to the categorical declaration that generally, in his opinion, "there is nothing less fit to be left to the action of competition than money".[36]

What Jevons, as so many others, seems to have overlooked, or regarded

[35] W. S. Jevons, *Money and the Mechanism of Exchange* (London: P. S. King, 1875), International scientific series, vol. 17, p. 64, as against Herbert Spencer, op. cit.

[36] Jevons, *ibid.*, p. 65. An earlier characteristic attempt to justify making banking and note issue an exception from a general advocacy of free competition is to be found in 1837 in the writings of S. J. Loyd (later Lord Overstone), *Further Reflections on the State of the Currency and the Action of the Bank of England* (London: P. Richardson, 1837), p. 49: "The ordinary advantages to the community arising from competition are that it tends to excite the ingenuity and exertion of the producers, and thus to secure to the public the best supply and quantity of the commodity at the lowest price, while all the evils arising from errors or miscalculations on the part of the producers will fall on themselves, and not on the public. With respect to a paper currency, however, the interest of the public is of a very different kind; a steady and equable regulation of its amount by fixed law is the end to be sought and the evil consequence of any error or miscalculation upon this point falls in a much greater proportion upon the public than upon the issuer". It is obvious that Loyd thought only of the possibility of different agencies issuing the *same* currency, not of currencies of *different* denominations competing with one another.

as irrelevant, is that Gresham's law will apply *only* to different kinds of money between which a fixed rate of exchange is enforced *by law.*[37] If the law makes two kinds of money perfect substitutes for the payment of debts and forces creditors to accept a coin of a smaller content of gold in the place of one with a larger content, debtors will, of course, pay only in the former and find a more profitable use for the substance of the latter.

With variable exchange rates, however, the inferior quality money would be valued at a lower rate and, particularly if it threatened to fall further in value, people would try to get rid of it as quickly as possible. The selection process would go on towards whatever they regarded as the best sort of money among those issued by the various agencies, and it would rapidly drive out money found inconvenient or worthless.[38] Indeed, whenever inflation got really rapid, all sorts of objects of a more stable value, from potatoes to cigarettes and bottles of brandy to eggs and foreign currencies like dollar bills, have come to be increasingly used as money,[39] so that at the end of the great German inflation it was contended that Gresham's law was false and the opposite true. It is not false, but it applies only if a *fixed rate of exchange* between the different forms of money is enforced.

VII. The Limited Experience with Parallel Currencies and Trade Coins

So long as coins of the precious metals were the only practicable and generally acceptable kinds of money, with all close substitutes at least redeemable in them (copper having been reduced comparatively early to subsidiary token money), the only different kinds of money which appeared side by side were coins of gold and silver.

The multiplicity of coins with which the old money-changers had to deal consisted ultimately only of these two kinds, and their respective value within each group was determined by their content of either metal

[37]Cf. F. A. Hayek, *Studies in Philosophy, Politics and Economics* (Chicago: University of Chicago Press, and London: Routledge & Kegan Paul, 1967), and Frank W. Fetter, "Some Neglected Aspects of Gresham's Law", *Quarterly Journal of Economics,* May 1932, pp. 480–495.

[38]If, as he is sometimes quoted, Gresham maintained that better money quite generally could not drive out worse, he was simply wrong, until we add his probably tacit presumption that a *fixed* rate of exchange was enforced.

[39]Cf. C. Bresciani-Turroni, *The Economics of Inflation* [1931], London: Allen & Unwin, 1937, p. 174: "In monetary conditions characterised by a great distrust in the national currency, the principle of Gresham's law is reversed and *good money drives out bad,* and the value of the latter continually depreciates". But even he does not point out that the critical difference is not the "great distrust" but the presence or absence of effectively enforced fixed rates of exchange.

(which the expert but not the layman could ascertain). Most princes had tried to establish a fixed legal rate of exchange between gold and silver coins, thereby creating what came to be called a bimetallic system. But since, in spite of very early suggestions that this rate be fixed by an international treaty,[40] governments established different exchange rates, each country tended to lose all the coins of the metal it under-valued relatively to the rates prevailing in other countries. The system was for that reason more correctly described as an alternative standard, the value of a currency depending on the metal which for the time being was over-valued. Shortly before it was finally abandoned in the second half of the nineteenth century, a last effort was made to establish internationally a uniform rate of exchange of 15-1/2 between gold and silver. That attempt might have succeeded so long as there were no big changes in production. The comparatively large share of the total stocks of either metal that were in monetary use meant that, by an inflow or outflow into or from that use, their relative values could probably have been adjusted to the rate at which they were legally exchangeable as money.

Parallel Currencies

In some countries, however, gold and silver had also been current for long periods side by side, their relative value fluctuating with changing conditions. This situation prevailed, for example, in England from 1663 to 1695 when, at last, by decreeing a rate of exchange between gold and silver coins at which gold was over-valued, England inadvertently established a gold standard.[41] The simultaneous circulation of coins of the two metals without a fixed rate of exchange between them was later called, by a scholar from Hanover where such a system existed until 1857, parallel currencies (*Parallelwährung*), to distinguish it from bimetallism.[42]

This is the only form in which parallel currencies were ever widely used, but it proved singularly inconvenient for a special reason. Since for most of the time gold was by weight more than 15 times as valuable as silver, it was evidently necessary to use the former for large and silver for the smaller (and copper for the still smaller) units. But, with variable values for the different kinds of coins, the smaller units were not constant fractions of the larger ones. In other words, the gold and the silver coins were parts of different systems without smaller or larger coins respec-

[40] In 1582 by Gasparo Scaruffi, *L'Alitinonfo: per far ragione e concordandanza d'oro e d'argento* (Reggio: Hercoliano Bartoli, 1582).

[41] A. E. Feaveryear, *The Pound Sterling* (London: Oxford University Press, 1931), p. 142.

[42] Hermann Grote, *Die Geldlehre* (Leipzig: Hahn'sche Verlagshandlung, 1865).

tively of the same system being available.[43] This made any change from large to small units a problem, and nobody was able, even for his own purposes, to stick to one unit of account.

Except for a few instances in the Far East in recent times,[44] there seem to have been very few instances of concurrent circulation of currencies, and the memory of the parallel circulation of gold and silver coins has given the system rather a bad name. It is still interesting because it is the only important historical instance in which some of the problems arose that are generally raised by concurrent currencies. Not the least of them is that the concept of *the* quantity of money of a country or territory has strictly no meaning in such a system, since we can add the quantities of different monies in circulation only after we know the relative value of the different units.

Trade Coins

Nor are the somewhat different but more complex instances of the use of various trade coins[45] of much more help: the Maria Theresa Thaler in the regions around the Red Sea and the Mexican Dollar in the Far East, or the simultaneous circulation of two or more national currencies in some frontier districts or tourist centres. Indeed, our experience is so limited that we can do no better than fall back upon the usual procedure of classical economic theory and try to put together, from what we know from our common experience of the conduct of men in relevant situations, a sort of mental model (or thought experiment) of what is likely to happen if many men are exposed to new alternatives.

VIII. Putting Private Token Money into Circulation

I shall assume for the rest of this discussion that it will be possible to establish a number of institutions in various parts of the world which are free to issue notes in competition and similarly to carry cheque accounts

[43]For a time during the Middle Ages gold coins issued by the great commercial republics of Italy were used extensively in international trade and maintained over fairly long periods at a constant gold content, while at the same time the petty coins, mostly of silver, used in local retail trade suffered the regular fate of progressive debasement. Carlo M. Cipolla, *Money, Prices and Civilization in the Mediterranean World: Fifth to Seventeenth Century* [1956] (New York: Gordian Press, 1967), pp. 34 ff.

[44]Gordon Tullock, "Paper Money—A Cycle in Cathay", op. cit., and "Competing Monies", *Journal of Money, Credit and Banking,* November 1976, pp. 521–525; compare Benjamin Klein, "The Competitive Supply of Money", *Journal of Money, Credit and Banking,* November 1974, pp. 423–453.

[45]A convenient summary of information on trade coins is in Nussbaum, *Money in the Law, National and International,* op. cit., p. 315.

in their individual denominations. I shall call these institutions simply 'banks', or 'issue banks' when necessary to distinguish them from other banks that do not choose to issue notes. I shall further assume that the name or denomination a bank chooses for its issue will be protected like a brand name or trade mark against unauthorised use, and that there will be the same protection against forgery as against that of any other document. These banks will then be vying for the use of their issue by the public by making them as convenient to use as possible.

The Private Swiss 'Ducat'

Since readers will probably at once ask how such issues can come to be generally accepted as money, the best way to begin is probably to describe how I would proceed if I were in charge of, say, one of the major Swiss joint stock banks. Assuming it to be legally possible (which I have not examined), I would announce the issue of non-interest-bearing certificates or notes, and the readiness to open current cheque accounts, in terms of a unit with a distinct registered trade name such as 'ducat'. The only legal obligation I would assume would be to redeem these notes and deposits on demand with, at the option of the holder, either 5 Swiss francs of 5 D-marks or 2 dollars per ducat. This redemption value would however be intended only as a floor below which the value of the unit could not fall because I would announce at the same time my intention to regulate the quantity of the ducats so as to keep their (precisely defined) purchasing power as nearly as possible constant. I would also explain to the public that I was fully aware I could hope to keep these ducats in circulation only if I fulfilled the expectation that their real value would be kept approximately constant. And I would announce that I proposed from time to time to state the precise commodity equivalent in terms of which I intended to keep the value of the ducat constant, but that I reserved the right, after announcement, to alter the composition of the commodity standard as experience and the revealed preferences of the public suggested.

It would, however, clearly be necessary that, though it seems neither necessary nor desirable that the issuing bank legally commits itself to maintain the value of its unit, it should in its loan contracts specify that any loan could be repaid either at the nominal figure in its own currency, or by corresponding amounts of any other currency or currencies sufficient to buy in the market the commodity equivalent which at the time of making the loan it had used as its standard. Since the bank would have to issue its currency largely through lending, intending borrowers might well be deterred by the formal possibility of the bank arbitrarily raising the value of its currency, that they may well have to be explicitly reassured against such a possibility.

These certificates or notes, and the equivalent book credits, would be made available to the public by short-term loans or sale against other currencies. The units would presumably, because of the option they offered, sell from the outset at a premium above the value of any one of the currencies in which they were redeemable. And, as these governmental currencies continued to depreciate in real terms, this premium would increase. The real value at the price at which the ducats were first sold would serve as the standard the issuer would have to try to keep constant. If the existing currencies continued to depreciate (and the availability of a stable alternative might indeed accelerate the process) the demand for the stable currency would rapidly increase and competing enterprises offering similar but differently-named units would soon emerge.

The sale (over the counter or by auction) would initially be the chief form of issue of the new currency. After a regular market had established itself it would normally be issued only in the course of ordinary banking business, i.e., through short-term loans.

Constant but Not Fixed Value

It might be expedient that the issuing institution should from the outset announce precisely the collection of commodities in terms of which it would aim to keep the value of the 'ducat' constant. But it would be neither necessary nor desirable that it tie itself legally to a particular standard. Experience of the response of the public to competing offers would gradually show which combination of commodities constituted the most desired standard at any time and place. Changes in the importance of the commodities, the volume in which they were traded, and the relative stability or sensitivity of their prices (especially the degree to which they were determined competitively or not) might suggest alterations to make the currency more popular. On the whole I would expect that, for reasons to be explained later (Section XIII), a collection of raw material prices, such as has been suggested as the basis of a commodity reserve standard,[46] would seem most appropriate, both from the point of view of the issuing bank and from that of the effects of the stability of the economic process as a whole.

Control of Value by Competition

In most respects, indeed, the proposed system should prove a more practicable method of achieving all that was hoped from a commodity reserve

[46]Cf. F. A. Hayek, this volume, chapter 2.

standard or some other form of 'tabular standard'. At the same time it would remove the necessity of making it fully automatic by taking the control from a monopolistic authority and entrusting it to private concerns. The threat of the speedy loss of their whole business if they failed to meet expectations (and how any government organisation would be certain to abuse the opportunity to play with raw material prices!) would provide a much stronger safeguard than any that could be devised against a government monopoly. Competition would certainly prove a more effective constraint, forcing the issuing institutions to keep the value of their currency constant (in terms of a stated collection of commodities), than would any obligation to redeem the currency in those commodities (or in gold). And it would be an infinitely cheaper method than the accumulation and the storing of valuable materials.

The kind of trust on which private money would rest would not be very different from the trust on which today all private banking rests (or in the United States rested before the governmental deposit insurance scheme!). People today trust that a bank, to preserve its business, will arrange its affairs so that it will at all times be able to exchange demand deposits for cash, although they know that banks do not have enough cash to do so if everyone exercised his right to demand instant payment at the same time. Similarly, under the proposed scheme, the managers of the bank would learn that its business depended on the unshaken confidence that it would continue to regulate its issue of ducats, etc., so that their purchasing power remained approximately constant.

Is the risk in the venture therefore too big to justify entry by men with the kind of conservative temper its successful conduct probably requires?[47] It is not to be denied that, once announced and undertaken, the decision on how large the commitment was to grow would be taken out of the hands of the issuing institution. To achieve its announced aim

[47]On the question of its attractiveness the discussion by Stanley Fischer in "The Demand for Index Bonds", *Journal of Political Economy,* June 1975, pp. 509–534, of the notorious reluctance of enterprise to issue indexed bonds is somewhat relevant. It is true that a gradual increase of the value of the notes issued by a bank in terms of other concurrent currencies might produce a situation in which the aggregate value of its outstanding notes (*plus* its liabilities from other sources) would exceed its assets. The bank would of course not be legally liable to redeem its notes at this value, but it could preserve this business only if it did in fact promptly buy at the current rate any of its notes offered to it. So long as it succeeded in maintaining the real value of its notes, it would never be called upon to buy back more than a fraction of the outstanding circulation. Probably no one would doubt that an art dealer who owns the plates of the engravings of a famous artist could, so long as his works remained in fashion, maintain the market value of these engravings by judiciously selling and buying, even though he could never buy up all the existing prints. Similarly, a bank could certainly maintain the value of its notes even though it could never buy back all the outstanding ones.

of maintaining the purchasing power of its currency constant, the amount would have to be promptly adapted to any change of demand, whether increase or decrease. Indeed, so long as the bank succeeded in keeping the value of its currency constant, there would be little reason to fear a sudden large reduction of the demand for it (though successful competitors might well make considerable inroads on its circulation). The most embarrassing development might be a rapid growth of demand beyond the limits a private institution likes to handle. But we can be fairly sure that, in the event of such success, new competition would soon relieve a bank of this anxiety.

The issuing bank could, at first, at no prohibitive cost keep in cash a 100 per cent reserve of the currencies in terms of which it had undertaken to redeem its issue and still treat the premiums received as freely available for general business. But once these other currencies had, as the result of further inflation, substantially depreciated relative to the ducat, the bank would have to be prepared, in order to maintain the value of the ducat, to buy back substantial amounts of ducats at the prevailing higher rate of exchange. This means that it would have to be able rapidly to liquidate investments of very large amounts indeed. These investments would therefore have to be chosen very carefully if a temporary rush of demand for its currency were not to lead to later embarrassment when the institution that had initiated the development had to share the market with imitators. Incidentally, the difficulty of finding investments of an assured stable value to match similar obligations would not be anything like as difficult for such a bank as we are considering as present-day bankers seem to find it: All the loans made in its own currency would of course represent such stable assets. The curious fact that such an issuing bank could have claims and obligations in terms of a unit the value of which it determined itself, though it could not do so arbitrarily or capriciously without destroying the basis of its business, may at first appear disturbing but should not create real difficulties. What may at first appear somewhat puzzling accounting problems largely disappear when it is remembered that such a bank would of course keep its accounts in terms of its own currency. The outstanding notes and deposits of such a bank are not claims on it in terms of some other unit of value; it determines itself the value of the unit in terms of which it has debts and claims and keeps its books. This will cease to seem shocking when we remember that this is precisely what practically all central banks have been doing for nearly half a century—their notes were of course redeemable in precisely nothing. But notes which may appreciate relatively to most other capital assets may indeed present to accountants problems with which they never before had to deal. Initially the issuing bank would of course be under a legal obligation to redeem its currency in terms of the other currencies against which it was at first issued. But after it has existed for some time their value may have shrunk to very little or they may have altogether disappeared.[48]

IX. Competition between Banks Issuing Different Currencies

It has for so long been treated as a self-evident proposition that the supply of money cannot be left to competition that probably few people could explain why. As we have seen, the explanation appears to be that it has always been assumed that there must be only *one* uniform kind of currency in a country, and that competition meant that its amount was to be determined by several agencies issuing it independently. It is, however, clearly not practicable to allow tokens with the same name and readily exchangeable against each other to be issued competitively, since nobody would be in a position to control their quantity and therefore be responsible for their value. The question we have to consider is whether competition between the issuers of clearly distinguishable kinds of currency consisting of *different* units would not give us a better kind of money than we have ever had, far outweighing the inconvenience of encountering (but for most people not even having to handle) more than one kind.

In this condition the value of the currency issued by one bank would not necessarily be affected by the supplies of other currencies by different institutions (private or governmental). And it should be in the power of each issuer of a distinct currency to regulate its quantity so as to make it most acceptable to the public— and competition would force him to do so. Indeed, he would know that the penalty for failing to fulfil the expectations raised would be the prompt loss of the business. Successful entry into it would evidently be a very profitable venture, and success would depend on establishing the credibility and trust that the bank was able and determined to carry out its declared intentions. It would seem that

[48]A real difficulty could arise if a sudden large increase in the demand for such a stable currency, perhaps due to some acute economic crisis, had to be met by selling large amounts of it against other currencies. The bank would of course have to prevent such a rise in the value and could do so only by increasing the supply. But selling against other currencies would give it assets likely to depreciate in terms of its own currency. It probably could not increase its short-term lending very rapidly, even if it offered to lend at a very low rate of interest—even though in such a situation it would be safer to lend even at a small negative rate of interest than to sell against other currencies. And it would probably be possible to grant long-term loans at very low rates of interest against negotiable securities (in terms of its own currency) which it should be easy to sell if the sudden increase of demand for its currency should be as rapidly reversed.

in this situation sheer desire for gain would produce a better money than government has ever produced.[49]

Effects of Competition

It seems to me to be fairly certain that

(a) a money generally expected to preserve its purchasing power approximately constant would be in continuous demand so long as the people were free to use it;

(b) with such a continuing demand depending on success in keeping the value of the currency constant one could trust the issuing banks to make every effort to achieve this better than would any monopolist who runs no risk by depreciating his money;

(c) the issuing institution could achieve this result by regulating the quantity of its issue; and

(d) such a regulation of the quantity of each currency would constitute the best of all practicable methods of regulating the quantity of media of exchange for all possible purposes.

Clearly a number of competing issuers of different currencies would have to compete in the quality of the currencies they offered for loan or sale. Once the competing issuers had credibly demonstrated that they provided currencies more suitable to the needs of the public than govern-

[49]Apart from notes and cheque deposits in its distinctive currency, an issuing bank would clearly also have to provide fractional coins; and the availability of convenient fractional coins in that currency might well be an important factor in making it popular. It would also probably be the habitual use of one sort of fractional coins (especially in slot machines, fares, tips, etc.) which would secure the predominance of one currency in the retail trade of one locality. The effective competition between different currencies would probably be largely confined to inter-business use, with retail trade following the decisions about the currency in which wages and salaries were to be paid.

Certain special problems would arise where present sales practices are based on the general use of uniform coins of a few relatively small standard units, as, e.g., in vending machines, transportation, or telephones. Probably even in localities in which several different currencies were in general use, one set of small coins would come to dominate. If, as seems probable, most of these competing currencies were kept at practically the same value, the technical problem of the use of coins might be solved in any one of various ways. One might be that one institution, e.g., an association of retailers, specialized in the issue of uniform coins at slightly fluctuating market prices. Tradesmen and transport and communication undertakings of a locality might join to sell, at market prices and probably through the banks, a common set of tokens for all automats in the locality. We can certainly expect commercial inventiveness rapidly to solve such minor difficulties. Another possible development would be the replacement of the present coins by plastic or similar tokens with electronic markings which every cash register and slot machine would be able to sort out, and the 'signature' of which would be legally protected against forgery as any other document of value.

ment has ever provided, there would be no obstacle to their becoming generally accepted in preference to the governmental currencies—at least in countries in which government had removed all obstacles to their use. The appearance and increasing use of the new currencies would, of course, decrease the demand for the existing national ones and, unless their volume was rapidly reduced, would lead to their depreciation. This is the process by which the unreliable currencies would gradually all be eliminated. The condition required in order that this displacement of the government money should terminate before it had entirely disappeared would be that government reformed and saw to it that the issue of its currency was regulated on the same principles as those of the competing private institutions. It is not very likely that it would succeed, because to prevent an accelerating depreciation of its currency it would have to respond to the new currencies by a rapid contraction of its own issue.

"A Thousand Hounds": the Vigilant Press

The competition between the issuing banks would be made very acute by the close scrutiny of their conduct by the press and at the currency exchange. For a decision so important for business as which currency to use in contracts and accounts, all possible information would be supplied daily in the financial press, and have to be provided by the issuing banks themselves for the information of the public. Indeed, a thousand hounds would be after the unfortunate banker who failed in the prompt responses required to ensure the safeguarding of the value of the currency he issues. The papers would probably print a table daily, not only of the current rates of exchange between the currencies but also of the current value, and the deviation of each of the currencies likely to be used by their readers from the announced standard of value in terms of commodities. These tables might look something like Table I (with the initials of the issuing institution given after the name of the currency it issues).

Nothing would be more feared by the bankers than to see the quotation of their currency in heavy type to indicate that the real value had fallen below the standard of tolerance set by the paper publishing the table.

Three Questions

This sketch of the competition between several private issuing institutions presupposes answers to a number of questions we shall have to examine in more detail in succeeding sections.

—The first is whether a competing institution issuing its distinctive currency will always be able to regulate its value by controlling its quantity so as to make it more attractive to people than other currencies, and how

Table I
Illustration of Possible Currency Price Deviations

Currency	*Deviation from* *Announced Standard (%)*	*Our Test Standard (%)*
Ducats (SGB)	−0.04	−0.04
Florins (FNB)	+0.02	+0.03
Mengers (WK)	+0.10	+0.10
Piasters (DBS)	−0.06	−0.12
Reals (CNB)	−1.02	−1.01
Shekels (ORT)	−0.45	−0.45
Talents (ATBC)	+0.26	+0.02

far other issuers of currencies can by their policy interfere with these efforts.

—The second is which value (or other attribute of a currency) the public will prefer if different banks announce that it is their intention (and demonstrate their ability) to keep announced values of their currency constant.

—A third and no less important question is whether the kind of money most people will individually prefer to use will also best serve the aims of all. Though one might at first think that this must necessarily be so, it is not inevitably true. It is conceivable that the success of people's efforts will depend not only on the money they themselves use but also on the effects of the money others use, and the benefits they derive for themselves from using a particular kind of money may conceivably be more than offset by the disturbances caused by its general use. I do not believe this to be the case in the present instance, but the question certainly requires explicit consideration.

Before we can discuss further the interaction between currencies it will be expedient to devote a section to precisely what we mean by money or currency and its different kinds, and the various ways in which they may differ from one another.

X. A Digression on the Definition of Money

Money is usually defined as *the* generally acceptable medium of exchange,[50] but there is no reason why within a given community there

[50]This definition was established by Carl Menger (*Principles of Economics* [1871] (Glencoe, Ill.: The Free Press, 1950)), whose work also ought to have finally disposed of the medieval conception that money, or the value of money, was a creation of the state. Vissering, op. cit., p. 9, reports that in early times the Chinese expressed their notions of money by a term meaning literally "current merchandise". The now more widely used expression that money is the most liquid asset comes, of course (as W. W. Carlile pointed out as early as 1901, *The Evolution of Modern Money* (London: Macmillan, 1901)), to the same thing. To serve as a

should be only one kind of money that is generally (or at least widely) accepted. In the Austrian border town in which I have been living for the past few years, shopkeepers and most other business people will usually accept D-Marks as readily as Austrian schillings, and only the law prevents German banks in Salzburg from doing their business in D-Marks in the same manner as they do ten miles away on the German side of the border. The same is true of hundreds of other tourist centres in Austria frequented mainly by Germans. In most of them dollars will also be accepted nearly as readily as D-Marks. I believe the situation is not very different on both sides of long stretches of the border between the United States and Canada or Mexico, and probably along many other frontiers.

But though in such regions everybody may be ready to accept several currencies at the current rate of exchange, individuals may use different kinds of money to hold (as liquidity reserves), to make contracts for deferred payments, or to keep their accounts in, and the community may respond in the same manner to changes in the amounts of the different currencies.

By referring to different kinds of money we have in mind units of different denomination whose relative values may fluctuate against one another. These fluctuating values must be emphasised because they are not the only way in which media of exchange may differ from one another. They may also, even when expressed in terms of the same unit, differ widely in their degree of acceptability (or liquidity, i.e., in the very quality which makes them money), or the groups of people that readily accept them. This means that different kinds of money can differ from one another in more than one dimension.

No Clear Distinction between Money and Non-money

It also means that, although we usually assume there is a sharp line of distinction between what is money and what is not—and the law generally tries to make such a distinction—so far as the causal effects of monetary events are concerned, there is no such clear difference. What we find

---

widely accepted medium of exchange is the only function which an object must perform to qualify as money, though a generally accepted medium of exchange will generally acquire also the further functions of unit of account, store of value, standard of deferred payment, etc. The definition of money as "means of payment" is, however, purely circular, since this concept presupposed debts incurred in terms of money. Cf. Ludwig von Mises, *The Theory of Money and Credit* [1912] (London: Jonathan Cape, 1952), pp. 34ff.

The definition of money as the generally acceptable medium of exchange does not, of course, necessarily mean that even within one national territory there must be a single kind of money which is more acceptable than all others; there may be several equally acceptable kinds of money (which we may more conveniently call currencies), particularly if one kind can be quickly exchanged into the others at a known, though not fixed, rate.

is rather a continuum in which objects of various degrees of liquidity, or with values which can fluctuate independently of each other, shade into each other in the degree to which they function as money.[51]

I have always found it useful to explain to students that it has been rather a misfortune that we describe money by a noun, and that it would be more helpful for the explanation of monetary phenomena if 'money' were an adjective describing a property which different things could possess to varying *degrees*.[52] 'Currency' is, for this reason, more appropriate, since objects can 'have currency' to varying degrees and through different regions or sectors of the population.

Pseudo-exactness, Statistical Measurement, and Scientific Truth

Here we encounter a difficulty we frequently meet in our efforts to explain the ill-defined phenomena of economic life. In order to simplify our exposition of what are very complex interconnections that otherwise would become difficult to follow, we introduce sharp distinctions where in real life different attributes of the objects shade into each other. A similar situation arises where we try to draw sharp distinctions between such objects as commodities and services, consumers' goods and capital goods, durable and perishable, reproducible and non-reproducible, specific and versatile, or substitutable and non-substitutable goods. All are very important distinctions but they can become very misleading if, in the popular striving for pseudo-exactness, we treat these classes as measurable quantities. This involves a simplification which is perhaps sometimes necessary but always dangerous and has led to many errors in economics. Though the differences are significant, this does not mean we can neatly and unambiguously divide these things into two, or any other number of, distinct classes. We often do, and perhaps often must, talk as if this division were true, but the usage can be very deceptive and produce wholly erroneous conclusions.[53]

[51] Cf. John R. Hicks, "A Suggestion for Simplifying the Theory of Money", *Economica*, February 1935, pp. 1–19.

[52] Machlup for this reason speaks occasionally, of "moneyness" and "near-moneyness". Fritz Machlup, "Euro-Dollar Creation: A Mystery Story", *Banca Nazionale del Lavoro Quarterly Review,* September 1970, p. 225.

[53] It is a practice particularly congenial to statisticians, the applicability of whose techniques frequently depends on using it. Though the popular tendency in economics to accept only *statistically* testable theories has given us some useful gross approximations to the truth, such as the quantity theory of the value of money, they have acquired a quite undeserved reputation. The idea discussed in the text makes most quantitative formulations of economic theory inadequate in practice. To introduce sharp distinctions which do not exist in the real world in order to make a subject susceptible to mathematical treatment is not to make it more scientific but rather less so.

Legal Fictions and Defective Economic Theory

Similarly, the legal fiction that there is one clearly defined thing called 'money' that can be sharply distinguished from other things, a fiction introduced to satisfy the work of the lawyer or judge, was never true so far as things are to be referred to which have the characteristic effects of events on the side of money. Yet it has done much harm through leading to the demand that, for certain purposes, only 'money' issued by government may be used, or that there must always be some single kind of object which can be referred to as *the* 'money' of the country. It has also, as we shall see, led to the development in economic theory of an explanation of the value of units of money which, though under its simplified assumptions it gives some useful approximations, is of no help for the kind of problems we have to examine here.

For what follows it will be important to keep in mind that different kinds of money can differ from one another in two distinct although not wholly unrelated dimensions: acceptability (or liquidity) and the expected behaviour (stability or variability) of its value. The expectation of stability will evidently affect the liquidity of a particular kind of money, but it may be that in the short run liquidity may sometimes be more important than stability, or that the acceptability of a more stable money may for some reason be confined to rather limited circles.

Meanings and Definitions

This is perhaps the most convenient place to add explicit statements concerning the meanings in which we shall use other frequently recurring terms. It will have become clear that in the present connection it is rather more expedient to speak of 'currencies' than 'monies', not only because it is easier to use the former term in the plural but also because, as we have seen, 'currency' emphasises a certain attribute. We shall also use 'currency', perhaps somewhat in conflict with the original meaning of the term, to include not only pieces of paper and other sorts of 'hand-to-hand money', but also bank balances subject to cheque and other media of exchange that can be used for most of the purposes for which cheques are used. There is, however, as we have just pointed out, no need for a very sharp distinction between what is and what is not money. The reader will do best if he remains aware that we have to deal with a range of objects of varying degrees of acceptability which imperceptibly shade at the lower end into objects that are clearly not money.

Although we shall frequently refer to the agencies issuing currency simply as 'banks', this is not meant to imply that all banks will be issuing money. The term 'rate of exchange' will be used throughout for rates of exchange between currencies, and the term 'currency exchange' (analogous to stock exchange) for the organised currency market. Occasionally we shall also speak of 'money substitutes' when we have to consider borderline cases in the scale of liquidity—such as travellers' cheques, credit cards, and overdrafts—where it would be quite arbitrary to assert that they either are or are not part of the circulation of currency.

XI. The Possibility of Controlling the Value of a Competitive Currency

The chief attraction the issuer of a competitive currency has to offer to his customers is the assurance that its value will be kept stable (or otherwise be made to behave in a predictable manner). We shall leave for Section XII the question of precisely what kind of stability the public will probably prefer. For the moment we shall concentrate on whether an issuing bank in competition with other issuers of similar currencies will have the power to control the quantity of its distinctive issue so as to determine the value it will command in the market.

The expected value of a currency will, of course, not be the only consideration that will lead the public to borrow or buy it. But the expected value will be the decisive factor determining how much of it the public will wish to hold, and the issuing bank will soon discover that the desire of the public to *hold* its currency will be the essential circumstance on which its value depends. At first it might perhaps seem obvious that the exclusive issuer of a currency, who as such has complete control over its supply, will be able to determine its price so long as there is anyone who wants it at that price. If, as we shall provisionally assume, the aim of the issuing bank is to keep constant the aggregate price in terms of its currency of a particular collection of commodities it would, by regulating the amount of the currency in circulation, have to counteract any tendency of that aggregate price to rise or fall.

Control by Selling/Buying Currency and (Short-Term) Lending

The issuing bank will have two methods of altering the volume of its currency in circulation: It can sell or buy its currency against other currencies (or securities and possibly some commodities); and it can contract or expand its lending activities. In order to retain control over its outstanding circulation, it will on the whole have to confine its lending to relatively short-time contracts so that, by reducing or temporarily stopping new lending, current repayments of outstanding loans would bring about a rapid reduction of its total issue.

To assure the constancy of the value of its currency the main consideration would have to be never to increase it beyond the total the public is prepared to hold without increasing expenditure in it so as to drive up prices of commodities in terms of it; it must also never reduce its supply below the total the public is prepared to hold without reducing expenditure in it and driving prices down. In practice, many or even most of the commodities in terms of which the currency is to be kept stable would be currently traded and quoted chiefly in terms of some other competing currencies (especially if, as we suggest in Section XIII, it will be mainly prices of raw materials or wholesale prices of foodstuffs). The bank would therefore have to look to the effect of changes in its circulation, not so much directly on the prices of other *commodities*, but on the rates of exchange with the *currencies* against which they are chiefly traded. Though the task of ascertaining the appropriate rates of exchange (considering the given rates of exchange between the different currencies) would be complex, computers would help with almost instantaneous calculation, so the bank would know hour by hour whether to increase or decrease the amounts of its currency to be offered as loans or for sale. Quick and immediate action would have to be taken by buying or selling on the currency exchange, but a lasting effect would be achieved only by altering the lending policy.

Current Issuing Policy

Perhaps I ought to spell out here in more detail how an issuing bank would have to proceed in order to keep the chosen value of its currency constant. The basis of the daily decisions on its lending policy (and its sales and purchases of currencies on the currency exchange) would have to be the result of a constant calculation provided by a computer into which the latest information about commodity prices and rates of exchange would be constantly fed as it arrived. The character of this calculation can be illustrated by the following abridged table (Table II). (I am neglecting here the question how far the costs of transport from the chief market to some common centre, or perhaps separate items representing the costs of different forms of transport, should be considered or not.)

The essential information would be the guide number at the lower right-hand corner, resulting either from the quantities of the different commodities being so chosen that at the base date their aggregate price in ducats was 1,000 or 1,000 was used as the base of an index number. This figure and its current changes would serve as a signal telling all executive officers of the bank what to do. A 1,002 appearing on the screen would tell them to contract or tighten controls, i.e., restrict loans by making them dearer or being more selective, and selling other currencies more freely; 997 would tell them that they could slightly relax and ex-

Table II
Illustration of a Currency Stabilization Scheme

Commodity	*Quantity*	*Currency in which quoted*	*Price in that currency*	*Rate of exchange*	*Price in own currency*
Aluminium	x tons	$	·	·	·
Beef	·	£	·	·	·
Camphor	·	Ducats	—	—	·
Cocoa	·	·	·	·	·
Coffee	·	·	·	·	·
Coal	·	·	·	·	·
Coke	·	·	·	·	·
Copper	·	·	·	·	·
Copra	·	·	·	·	·
Corn	·	Ducats	—	—	·
Etc.	·	·	·	·	·
				Total	1,000

pand. (A special write-out of the computer in the chairman's office would currently inform him which of his officers did promptly respond to these instructions.) The effect of this contraction or expansion on commodity prices would be chiefly indirect through the rates of exchange with the currencies in which these commodities were chiefly traded, and direct only with regard to commodities traded chiefly in ducats.

The same signal would appear on the currency exchange and, if the bank was known for taking prompt and effective measures to correct any deviation, would lead to its efforts being assisted by more of its currency being demanded when it was expected to appreciate because its value was below normal (the guide number showing 1,002), and less being demanded when it was expected slightly to depreciate (because the guide number had fallen to 997). It is difficult to see how such a policy consistently pursued would not result in the fluctuations of the value of the currency around the chosen commodity standard being reduced to a very small range indeed.

The Crucial Factor: Demand for Currency to Hold

But, whether directly or indirectly *via* the price of other currencies, it would seem clear that, if an institution acts in the knowledge that the public preparedness to hold its currency, and therefore its business, depends on maintaining the currency value, it will be both able and compelled to assure this result by appropriate continuous adjustments of the quantity in circulation. The crucial point it must keep in mind will be that, to keep a large and growing amount of its currency in circulation, it will be not the demand for *borrowing* it but the willingness of the public to *hold* it that will be decisive. An incautious increase of the current issue may therefore make the flow back to the bank grow faster than the public demand to hold it.

The press, as pointed out, would closely watch the results of the efforts of each issuing bank and daily quote how much the various currencies deviate from the self-set standards. From the point of view of the issuing banks it would probably be desirable to allow a small, previously-announced, tolerance or standard of deviation in either direction. For in that event, and so long as a bank demonstrated its power and resolution to bring rates of exchange (or commodity prices in terms of its currency) promptly back to its standard, speculation would come to its aid and relieve it of the necessity to take precipitate steps to assure absolute stability.

So long as the bank had succeeded in keeping the value of its currency at the desired level, it is difficult to see that it should for this purpose have to contract its circulation so rapidly as to be embarrassed. The usual cause of such developments in the past was circumstances which increased the demand for liquid 'cash', but the bank would have to reduce the aggregate amount outstanding only to adjust it to a shrunken total demand for both forms of its currency. If it had lent mainly on short term, the normal repayment of loans would have brought this result fairly rapidly. The whole matter appears to be very simple and straightforward so long as we assume that all the competing banks try to control their currencies with the aim of keeping their values in some sense constant.

Would Competition Disrupt the System?

What, however, would be the consequences if one competitor attempted to gain in this competition by offering other advantages such as a low rate of interest, or if it granted book credits or perhaps even issued notes (in other words, incurred debts payable on demand) in terms of the currency issued by another bank? Would either practice seriously interfere with the control the issuing banks can exercise over the value of their currencies?

There will of course always be a strong temptation for any bank to try and expand the circulation of its currency by lending cheaper than competing banks; but it would soon discover that, insofar as the additional lending is not based on a corresponding increase of saving, such attempts would inevitably rebound and hurt the bank that over-issued. While people will no doubt be very eager to *borrow* a currency offered at a lower rate of interest, they will not want to *hold* a larger proportion of their liquid assets in a currency of the increased issue of which they would soon learn from various reports and symptoms.

It is true that, so long as the currencies are almost instantaneously exchangeable against one another at a known rate of exchange, the relative prices of commodities in terms of them will also remain the same. Even on the commodity markets the prices of those commodities (or, in regions where a high proportion of the demand is expressed in terms of the increased currency, prices in terms of all currencies) will tend to rise compared with other prices. But the decisive events will take place on the currency exchange. At the prevailing rate of exchange the currency that has increased in supply will constitute a larger proportion of the total of all currencies than people have habitually held. Above all, everybody indebted in the currencies for which a higher rate of interest has to be paid will try to borrow cheap in order to acquire currencies in which he can repay the more burdensome loans. And all the banks that have not reduced their lending rate will promptly return to the bank that lends more cheaply all of its currency they receive. The result must be the appearance on the currency exchange of an excess supply of the over-issued currency, which will quickly bring about a fall in the rate at which it can be exchanged into the others. And it will be at this new rate that commodity prices normally quoted in other currencies will be translated into the offending currency; while, as a result of its over-issue, prices normally quoted in it will be immediately driven up. The fall in the market quotation and the rise of commodity prices in terms of the offending currency would soon induce habitual holders to shift to another currency. The consequent reduction in the demand for it would probably soon more than offset the temporary gain obtained by lending it more cheaply. If the issuing bank nevertheless pursued cheap lending, a general flight from the currency would set in; and continued cheap lending would mean that larger and larger amounts would be dumped on the currency exchange. We can confidently conclude that it would not be possible for a bank to pull down the real value of other currencies by over-issue of its currency—certainly not if their issuers are prepared, so far as necessary, to counter such an attempt by temporarily curtailing their issues.

Would Parasitic Currencies Prevent Control of Currency Value?

A more difficult question, the answer to which is perhaps not so clear, is how far the unavoidable appearance of what one may call parasitic currencies, i.e., the pyramiding of a superstructure of circulating credit through other banks carrying cheque accounts and perhaps even issuing notes in the denomination of the currency of the original issuer, would interfere with the issuer's control over the value of his own currency. So long as such parasitic issues were clearly labelled as debts to be paid in the currency of the issuer it is difficult to see how this could be or should be prevented by law.

Clearly not all banks would wish to issue, or probably could issue, a currency of their own. Those that did not would have no choice but to accept deposits and grant credits in terms of some other currency, and would prefer to do so in the best currency available. Nor would the original issuer wish altogether to prevent this, although he might dislike the issue of notes more than the mere running of accounts subject to cheque in terms of his currency. Notes issued by a secondary issuer would, of course, have to show clearly that they were not the original ducats issued by the bank that owned that trade mark, but merely claims for ducats, since otherwise they would simply be a forgery. Yet I do not see how the ordinary legal protection of brand names or trade marks could prevent the issue of such claims in the form of notes, and very much doubt whether it would be desirable to prevent it by law, especially in view of the essential similarity between such notes and deposits subject to cheque which even the issuing banks would hardly wish to prevent.

What the original issuer of such a currency could do and would have to do is not to repeat the mistakes governments have made, as a result of which control of these secondary or parasitic issues has slipped from their hands. It must make clear that it would not be prepared to bail out secondary issuers by supplying the 'cash' (i.e., the original notes) they will need to redeem their obligations. We shall see later (Section XVI) how governments were led into this trap and allowed their monopoly of the issue of money to be watered down in the most undesirable manner. (They shared the responsibility for control of the total amount of the standard denomination, yielding to the constant pressure for cheap money that was supposed to be met by the rapid spread of banks which they assisted by securing their liquidity; and in the end nobody had full power over the total quantity of money.)

The answer to the most serious problem arising from the scheme seems to me that, though private issuers will have to tolerate the appearance of parasitic circulations of deposits and notes of the same denomination, they ought not to assist but rather restrain it by making it clear in advance that they would not be prepared to provide the notes needed to redeem parasitic issues except against 'hard cash', i.e., by sale against some other reliable currency. By adhering strictly to this principle they would force the secondary issuer to practise something very close to '100 per cent banking'. So far as there would still be limited fiduciary parasitic issues they would have to be kept in circulation by a policy which assured that their value was never questioned. Though this policy might limit the circulation and thus the profit of the original issuer, it should not seriously impair his ability to keep the value of his currency constant.

To achieve this the original issuer of a currency with a certain label would have to anticipate the effects of the over-issue of such a parasitic currency (or any other currency claiming to maintain a value equal to its own) and ruthlessly to refuse to buy it at par even before the expected depreciation manifests itself in the rise of some commodity prices in terms of that other currency. The dealings of an issue bank in other currencies would therefore never be a purely mechanical affair (buying and selling at constant prices) guided only by the observed changes in the purchasing power of the other currencies; nor could such a bank undertake to buy any other currency at a rate corresponding to its current buying power over the standard batch of commodities; but it would require a good deal of judgement effectively to defend the short-run stability of one's own currency, and the business will have to be guided in some measure by prediction of the future development of the value of other currencies.

XII. Which Sort of Currency Would the Public Select?

Since it is my thesis that the public would select from a number of competing private currencies a better money than governments provide, I must now examine the process and the criteria by which such a selection would take place.

This is a question on which we have little empirical knowledge. It would be of little use to try asking the people (perhaps by an opinion poll). Never having been in such a position, most people have never thought or formed an opinion about what they would do. We can merely attempt to derive the probable character of individual decisions from our general knowledge of the purpose for which people want money, and the manner in which they act in similar situations. This is, after all, the procedure by which most of economic theory has been built up and has arrived at conclusions usually confirmed by later experience. We must not, of course, assume that people will at once act rationally in a new situation. But, if not by insight, they would soon learn by experience and imitation of the most successful what conduct best serves their interests.[54] A major change like the one considered here might at first cause much uncertainty and confusion. Yet I do not think there is much reason to

[54]Cf. C. Menger, *Principles of Economics*, op. cit., p. 261: "There is no better way in which men can become more enlightened about their economic interests than by observation of the economic success of those who employ the correct means of achieving their ends".

doubt that people would soon discover what rational consideration could have told them at once. Whether in practice the process would be fast or slow may differ from country to country.[55]

Four Uses of Money

There are four kinds of uses of money that would chiefly affect the choice among available kinds of currency: Its use, first, for cash purchases of commodities and services; second, for holding reserves for future needs; third, in contracts for deferred payments; and, finally, as a unit of account, especially in keeping books. To treat these uses as different 'functions' of money is common but not really expedient. They are in effect simply consequences of the basic function of money as a medium of exchange, and will only in exceptional conditions, such as a rapid depreciation of the medium of exchange, come to be separated from it. They are also interdependent in such a way that, although at first different attributes of money may seem desirable for its different uses, money renders one service, namely as a unit of account, which makes stability of value the most desirable of all. Although at first convenience in daily purchases might be thought decisive in the selection, I believe it would prove that suitability as a unit of account would rule the roost.

(i) Cash purchases

To the great mass of wage- and salary-earners the chief interest will probably be that they can make their daily purchases in the currency in which they are paid, and that they find prices everywhere indicated in the currency they use. Shopkeepers, on the other hand, so long as they know they can instantaneously exchange any currency at a known rate of exchange against any other, would be only too willing to accept any currency at an appropriate price. Electronic cash registers would probably be developed rapidly, not only to show instantaneously the equivalent of any price in any currency desired, but also to be connected through the computer with banks so that firms would immediately be credited with the equivalent in the currency in which they kept their accounts. (Cash balances in the currencies would be collected every evening.) On the

[55]We must not entirely overlook the possibility that the practices and expectations of business men based on past experience, and particularly the experience of the last fifty years or so, are so much adjusted to the probability of a continuous upward trend of prices, that the realization that average prices in future are likely to remain constant may at first have a discouraging effect. This may even make some business men prefer to deal and keep accounts in a slowly depreciating currency. I believe, however, that in the end those who have chosen a stable currency will prove more successful.

other hand, shopkeepers would find it expedient, if two or three currencies were in common local use, to mark their wares in an easily distinguishable manner, for example in different colours for each currency, so as to ease price comparisons between shops and currencies.

(ii) Holding reserves for future payments

Beyond the desire to use his regular receipts for his ordinary expenditure, the wage- and salary-earner would probably be interested chiefly in stability. And although in his mortgage and instalment payments he might for a while profit from a depreciating currency, his wage or salary contract would incline his wishes towards an appreciating currency.

All holders of cash, that is, everybody, would prefer an appreciating currency and for this reason there might be a substantial demand for such money; but it would clearly not be to the advantage of borrowers to borrow in it, or for banks to have to maintain a value higher than that at which they issued a currency. It is conceivable that a limited amount of notes of such an appreciating currency might be issued and used for special purposes, but it would seem most unlikely that they would become generally used. The chief demand for holding would probably be for the currency in which people expected to have to pay debts.

(iii) Standard of deferred payments

When we come to the third use, as a standard of deferred payments, the primary interests of the parties to the contract would of course be precisely opposite: Lenders preferring an appreciating and borrowers a depreciating currency. But each group would be of a very mixed composition, the creditors including all wage- and salary-earners as well as the owners of capital, and the debtors including the banks as well as enterprises and farmers. It therefore seems unlikely that market forces would produce a predominant bias in one direction. And, though they would all in the short run either lose or gain from changes in the value of the currency on their borrowing or lending business, they would probably all soon discover that these losses or gains were merely temporary and tended to disappear as soon as interest rates adapted themselves to expected price movements.

(iv) A reliable unit of account

It seems to me that the decisive factor that would create a general preference for a currency stable in value would be that only in such a currency is a realistic calculation possible, and therefore in the long run a successful choice between alternative currencies for use in production and trade. In particular, the chief task of accounting, to ensure that the stock of capital of the business is not eaten into and only true net gains shown as profits available for disposal by the shareholders, can be realized only if the value of the unit of account is approximately stable.

An attempt to explain further why successful economic calculation is possible only with a stable value of money raises the question of what precisely we mean by 'the value of money' and the various respects in which it may be kept stable. This we must leave to Section XIII. For the present we content ourselves with the empirical fact that effective capital maintenance and cost control is possible only if accounts are kept in a unit that in some sense remains tolerably stable. So we will provisionally leave the present subject with the conclusion that, in the long run at least, the effective choice between competitive offers of currencies will be the usual one of competition. The currency that will prevail will be the one preferred by the people who are helped to succeed and who in consequence will be imitated by others.

XIII. Which Value of Money?

Strictly speaking, in a scientific sense, there is no such thing as a perfectly stable value of money—or of anything else. Value is a relationship, a rate of equivalence, or, as W. S. Jevons said, "an indirect mode of expressing a ratio",[56] which can be stated only by naming the quantity of one object that is valued equally with the 'equivalent' quantity of another object. Two objects may keep a constant relative value in terms of each other, but unless we specify the other, the statement that the value of something is unchanged has no definite meaning.

What we mean when we habitually but carelessly use such expressions as "Beer is more stable in value than beetroot" (and this is the most we can ever assert with any meaning) is that the relative value of beer, or its rate of exchange, tends to remain more stable with a larger number of other goods or over longer periods, than is true of beetroot and many other goods. For ordinary goods or services we have in mind in the first instance usually their relation to money. When we apply the term 'value' to money itself what is meant is that the price of most commodities will not tend to change predominantly in one direction, or will change only little, over short periods.

[56]W. S. Jevons, *Money and the Mechanism of Exchange,* op. cit., p. 11. See also p. 68: "Value merely expresses the essentially variable ratio in which two commodities exchange, so that there is no reason to suppose that any substance does for two days together retain the same value".

"A Stable Value of Money"

But some prices always change on a free market. We will sometimes feel that the value of money has remained approximately constant although many prices have changed, and at other times that the value of money has definitely decreased or increased, although the prices of only a few important commodities have changed but all in the same direction. What then do we call, in a world of constantly changing individual prices, a stable value of money?

In a rough sense it is of course fairly obvious that the command over commodities in general conferred by a sum of money has decreased if it brings a smaller amount of most of them and more of only a few of them. It is then sensible to say that the command over commodities has remained about the same if these two changes in command over commodities just balance. But for our purposes we need, of course, a more precise definition of "a stable value of money" and a more exact definition of the benefits we expect from it.

Balancing Errors

As we have seen, the chief disturbances which changes in the value of money will cause operate through the effects on contracts for deferred payments and on the use of money units as the basis of calculation and accounting. Decisions in both have to cope with the unalterable truth that for the individual the future movement of most prices is unpredictable (because they serve as signals of events of most of which he cannot know). The resulting risk can best be reduced by basing calculations on expectations of future prices from which current prices are quite as likely to deviate in the one direction as in the other by any given percentage. The median value of probable future changes will be correctly estimated only if it is zero and thus coincides with the probable behaviour of the large number of prices that are fairly rigid or sluggish (chiefly public utility rates but also the prices of most branded articles, goods sold by mail-order houses, and the like).

The position is best illustrated by two diagrams. If the value of money is so regulated that an appropriate average of prices is kept constant, the probabilities of future price movements with which all planning of future activities will have to cope can be represented as in Figure 1. Though in this case the unpredictability of particular future prices, inevitable in a functioning market economy, remains, the fairly high long-run chances are that for people in general the effects of the unforeseen price changes will just about cancel out. They will at least not cause a general error

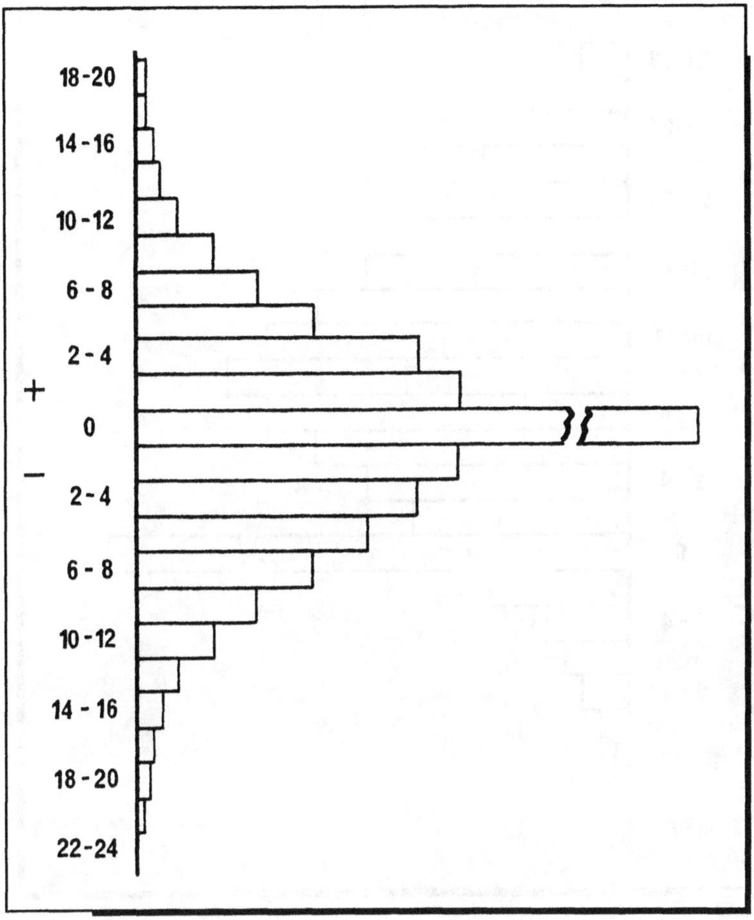

Figure 1 Aggregate Price of Commodities Sold at Prices Changed (Against Previous Period) by Percentage Indicated: Stable Prices

of expectations in one direction but on the whole make fairly successful calculations based on the assumption of the continuance of prices (where no better information is available).

Where the divergent movement of individual prices results in a *rise* in the average of all prices, it will look somewhat as in Figure 2.

Since the individual enterprise will have as little foundation for correctly foreseeing the median of all the movements as for predicting the movements of individual prices, it could also not base its calculations and decisions on a known median from which individual movements of prices

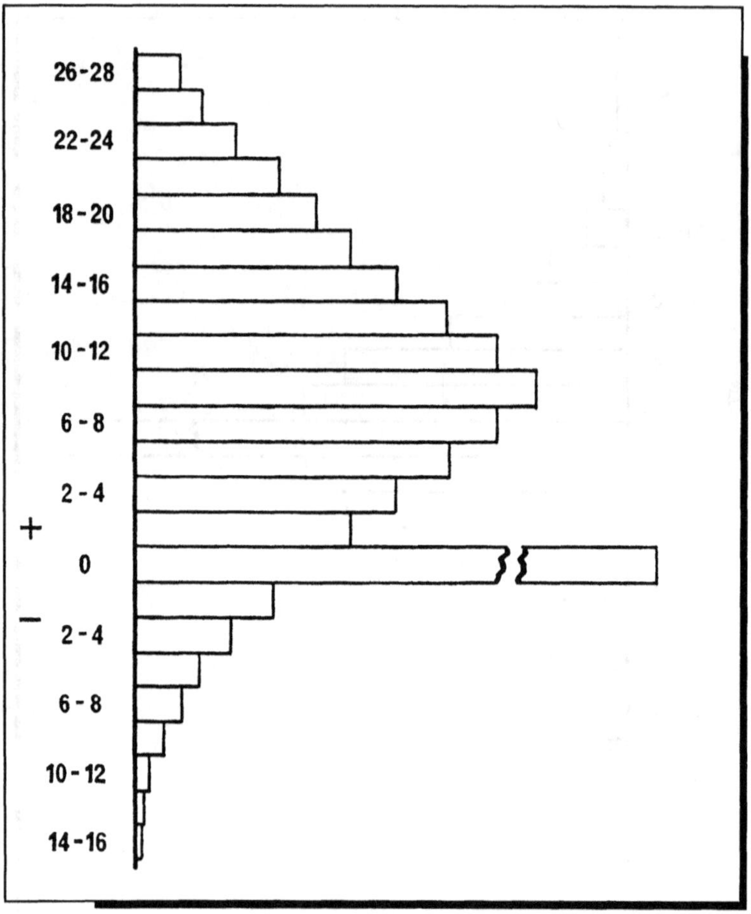

Figure 2 Aggregate Price of Commodities Sold at Prices Changed (Against Previous Period) by Percentage Indicated: Increase in Prices

were as likely to diverge in the one direction as in the other. Successful calculations, or effective capital and cost accounting, would then become impossible. People would more and more wish for a unit of account whose value moved more closely together with the general trend, and might even be driven to use as the unit of account something that could not be used as a medium of exchange.[57]

[57]The curve representing the dispersion of price changes by showing the percentage of all sales effected at one period at prices increased or decreased compared with an earlier period would, of course, if drawn on a logarithmic scale, have the same shape whether we

Criteria of Choice

These skewed shifts of the distribution of price changes to one side of constancy which changes in the quantity of money may cause, and the resulting difficulty of foresight, calculation, and accounting, must not be confused with the merely temporary changes in the structure of relative prices the same process also brings about which will cause misdirections of production. We shall have to consider (Section XVII) how a stabilization of the value of money will also substantially prevent those misdirections of production which later inevitably lead to reversals of the process of growth, the loss of much investment, and periods of unemployment. We shall argue that this would be one of the chief benefits of a stable currency. But it is hardly possible to argue that the users of money will for this reason select a currency with a stable value. This is an effect they are not likely to perceive and take into account in their individual decision of what money to use—although the observation of the smooth course of business in regions using a stable currency may induce the people of other regions to prefer a similar currency. The individual also could not protect himself against this effect by himself using a stable currency, because the structure of relative prices will be the same in terms of the different concurrent currencies and those distortions cannot therefore be avoided so long as side by side with stable currencies fluctuating currencies are used to a significant extent.

The reason why people will tend to prefer a currency with a value stable in terms of commodities will thus be that it will help them to minimise the effects of the unavoidable uncertainty about price movements because the effect of errors in opposite directions will tend to cancel each other out. This cancelling will not take place if the median around which

---

used money or any commodity as the measure of price. If we used as standard the commodity whose price had fallen more than that of any other, all price changes would merely appear as increases, but an increase of the relative price compared with that of another would still be shown as, say, a 50 per cent increase, whatever measure we used. We would probably obtain a curve of the general shape of a normal (Gaussian) curve of error—the, so far as we could have predicted, accidental deviations from the mode on either side just offsetting each other and becoming less numerous as the deviations increase. (Most price chances will be due to a shifting of demand with corresponding falls of some prices and rises of others; and relatively small transfers of this kind seem likely to be more frequent than large ones.) In terms of a money with stable value in this sense, the price of the commodities represented by the mode would then be unchanged, while the amount of transactions taking place at prices increased or decreased by a certain percentage would just balance each other. This will minimize errors, not necessarily of particular individuals, but in the aggregate. And though no practicable index number can fully achieve what we have assumed, a close approximation to the effect ought to be possible.

the deviation of individual prices clusters is not zero but some unknown magnitude. Even if we agree that the stable money people will prefer to use will be such that they expect the individual prices in which they are chiefly interested to be as likely to increase in terms of it as to decrease, this does not yet tell us which price level most people will want to see constant. Different people or enterprises will evidently be interested in the prices of different commodities. And the aggregate prices of different collections of commodities would of course move differently.

Effectiveness for Accounting Again Decisive

While one probably is at first again inclined to think in terms of retail prices or cost of living, and even most individual consumers might prefer a money stable in these terms, it is not likely that an extensive circulation could be built up for a currency so regulated. The cost of living differs from place to place and is apt to change at varying rates. Business would certainly prefer a money acceptable over wide regions. What would be most important for calculation and accounting in each enterprise (and therefore for the efficient use of resources), relying on the general stability of prices rather than its specialized knowledge of a particular market, would be the prices of widely traded products such as raw materials, agricultural foodstuffs and certain standardized semi-finished industrial products. They have the further advantage that they are traded on regular markets, their prices are promptly reported and, at least with raw materials, are particularly sensitive and would therefore make it possible by early action to forestall tendencies towards general price movements (which often show themselves in such commodities first).

Indeed it may well be that a regulation of the issue which directly aimed at stabilizing raw material prices might result in a greater stability even of the prices of consumers' goods than a management which aimed directly at the latter object. The considerable lag which experience has shown to prevail between changes in the quantity of money and changes in the price level of consumers' goods may indeed mean that, if adjustment of circulation were postponed until the effects of an excess or shortage of the issue showed itself in changes in the prices of consumers' goods, quite noticeable changes in their prices could not be avoided; while, in the case of raw materials, where this lag seems to be shorter, an earlier warning would make prompter precautionary measures possible.

Wage- and salary-earners would probably also discover that it was advantageous to conclude collective bargains in average raw material prices or a similar magnitude, which would secure for earners of fixed incomes an automatic share in an increase of industrial productivity. (The underdeveloped countries would also prefer an international currency that gave raw materials in general an increasing purchasing power over industrial products—though they are likely to spoil the possibility by insisting on the stabilization of individual raw material prices.) I hope, at any rate, that this will be the predominant choice because a currency stable in terms of raw material prices is probably also the nearest approach we can hope to achieve to one conducive to stability of general economic activity.

Wholesale Commodity Prices as Standard of Value for Currencies over International Regions

My expectation would be that, at least for large regions much exceeding present national territories, people would agree on a standard set of wholesale prices of commodities to treat as the standard of value in which they would prefer to have their currencies kept constant. A few banks that had established wide circulation by accommodating this preference, and issued currencies of different denominations but with roughly constant rates of exchange with one another, might continue to try and refine the precise composition of the standard 'basket' of commodities whose price they tried to keep constant in their currency.[58] But this practice would not cause substantial fluctuations in the relative values of the chief currencies circulating in the region. Regions with different compositions of the currencies in circulation would, of course, overlap, and currencies whose value was based chiefly on commodities important for one way of life, or for one group of predominant industries, might fluctuate relatively more against others but yet retain their distinct clientele among people with particular occupations and habits.

XIV. The Uselessness of the Quantity Theory for Our Purposes

The usual assumptions of monetary theory, that there is only one kind of currency, *the* money, and that there is no sharp distinction between full money and mere money substitutes, thus disappear. So does the applicability of what is called the quantity theory of the value of money—even as a rough approximation to a theoretically more satisfactory explanation of the determination of the value of money, which is all that it can ever be.[59]

The quantity theory presupposes, of course, that there is only one kind

[58]Indeed emulation would probably lead them to refine the technique for maintaining maximum stability to a point far beyond any practical advantage.

[59]But, as I wrote 45 years ago in *Prices and Production* (London: Routledge, 1931), p. 3, and would still maintain, "... from a practical point of view, it would be one of the worst things which could befall us if the general public should ever again cease to believe in the elementary propositions of the quantity theory".

of money in circulation within a given territory, the quantity of which can be ascertained by counting its homogeneous (or near-homogeneous) units. But if the different currencies in circulation within a region have no constant relative value, the aggregate amount in circulation can only be derived from the relative value of the currencies and has no meaning apart from it. A theory which is of use only in a particular situation, even if it happened to prevail during a long period, evidently suffers from a serious defect. Though we are apt to take it for granted, it is by no means of the essence of money that within a given territory there should exist only one kind, and it is usually true only because governments have prevented the use of other kinds. Even so, it is never fully true because there are always significant differences in the demand for different forms of money and money substitutes of varying degrees of liquidity. But if we assume that issuers of currency continually compete with one another for additional users of their currency, we cannot also assume, as the quantity theory can assume with some justification with respect to a currency of a single denomination, that there exists a fairly constant demand for money in the sense that the aggregate value of the total stock will tend to be approximately constant (or change in a predictable manner with the size of the population, the gross national product, or similar magnitudes).

The Cash Balance Approach . . .

For the problems discussed in this *Paper* we certainly require a more generally applicable tool. It is fortunately available in the form of a theory which is more satisfactory even for dealing with the simpler situations: the cash balance approach deriving from Carl Menger, Leon Walras, and Alfred Marshall. It enables us not merely to explain the ultimate effect of changes in 'the quantity of money' on 'the' general price level, but also to account for the process by which changes in the supplies of various kinds of money will successively affect different prices. It makes possible an analysis which admittedly cannot pretend to the pseudo-exactness of the quantity theory, but which has a much wider reach and can take account of the preferences of individuals for different kinds of money.

The decisive consideration to keep in mind for our present purpose is that in a multi-currency system there is no such thing as *the* magnitude of the demand for money. There will be different demands for the different kinds of currency; but since these different currencies will not be perfect substitutes, these distinct demands cannot be added up into a single sum. There may be little demand for (but large supply of) depreciating currencies, there will, we hope, be an equality of demand and supply for stable currencies (which is what will keep their values stable), and a large demand for (but little supply of) appreciating currencies. Though, so long as there exists a free market for currencies, people will be prepared to *sell* (at some price) for any currency, they will not be prepared to *hold* any currency; and the character of the available substitutes would affect the demand for any particular currency. There would therefore be no single quantity the magnitude of which could be said to be decisive for the value of money.

. . . and the Velocity of Circulation

It can be maintained that the analyses in terms of the demand for cash balances and the use of the concept of velocity of circulation by the quantity theory are formally equivalent. The difference is important. The cash balance approach directs attention to the crucial causal factor, the individual's desire for holding stocks of money. The velocity of circulation refers to a resultant statistical magnitude which experience may show to be fairly constant over the fairly long periods for which we have useful data—thus providing some justification for claiming a simple connection between 'the' quantity of money and 'the' price level—but which is often misleading because it becomes so easily associated with the erroneous belief that monetary changes affect only the *general* level of prices. [Monetary changes] are then often regarded as harmful chiefly for this reason, as if they raised or lowered all prices *simultaneously* and by the *same* percentage. Yet the real harm they do is due to the *differential* effect on different prices, which change successively in a very irregular order and to a very different degree, so that as a result the whole structure of relative prices becomes distorted and misguides production into wrong directions.

Unfortunately, Lord Keynes made practically no use of this most important contribution to monetary theory of the Cambridge tradition deriving from Marshall. Though criticizing the alleged tendency of all contemporary monetary theory to argue as if prices all changed simultaneously, he moved almost entirely within the framework of (or argued against) the Irving Fisher type of quantity theory. It is one of the chief damages the Keynesian flood has done to the understanding of the economic process that the comprehension of the factors determining both the value of money and the effects of monetary events on the value of particular commodities has been largely lost. I cannot attempt here even a concentrated restatement of this central chapter of monetary theory but must content myself with recommending economists who have had the misfortune to study monetary theory at institutions wholly dominated by Keynesian views but who still wish to understand the theory of the value of money to fill this gap by first working through the two volumes of A. W. Marget's *Theory of Prices*[60] and then skip most of the literature of the next 25 years until Professor Axel Leijonhufvud's recent book,[61] which will guide them to works of the interval they ought not to miss.

A Note on 'Monetarism'

It has become usual, since the reaction against the dominance of the 'Keynesian' dogma set in, to lump together as 'monetarists' all who regard as mistaken Keynes's denial "that an inflationary or deflationary movement was normally caused or necessarily accompanied" by "changes in the quantity of money and velocity of its circulation".[62] This 'monetarism' is of course a view held before Keynes by almost all economists except a very few dissenters and cranks, including in particular those Continental economists who by their advice on policy became responsible for the great inflations of the 1920s. I agree with these 'monetarists' in particular on what is now probably regarded as their defining characteristic, namely that they believe that all inflation is what is now called 'demand-pull' inflation, and that there is, so far as the economic mechanism is concerned, no such thing as a 'cost-push' inflation—unless one treats as part of the economic causation the political decision to increase the quantity of money in response to a rise of wages which otherwise would cause unemployment.[63]

[60]Arthur W. Marget, *The Theory of Prices*, 2 vols (New York and London: Prentice Hall, 1938 and 1942).

[61]Axel Leijonhufvud, *On Keynesian Economics and the Economics of Keynes* (New York and London: Oxford University Press, 1968). [A short guide to Professor Leijonhufvud's book is his *Keynes and the Classics*, Occasional Paper 30, Institute of Economic Affairs, 1969 (6th Impression, 1977). —Ed.]

[62]Roy F. Harrod, *The Life of John Maynard Keynes* (London: Macmillan, 1951), p. 513. [Hayek's review of this work is published in F. A. Hayek, *Contra Keynes and Cambridge*, ed. Bruce Caldwell, being vol. 9 of the Collected Works of F. A. Hayek, op. cit. —Ed.]

[63]In another sense I stand, however, outside the Keynes-monetarist controversy: Both are macroeconomic approaches to the problem, while I believe that monetary theory neither needs nor ought to employ such an approach, even if it can hardly wholly dispense with such an essentially macroeconomic concept. Macroeconomics and microeconomics are alternative methods of dealing with the difficulty that, in the case of such a complex phenomenon as the market, we never command all the factual information which we would need to provide a full explanation. Macroeconomics attempts to overcome this difficulty by referring to such magnitudes as aggregates or averages which are statistically available. This gives us a useful approximation to the facts, but as a theoretical explanation of causal connections is unsatisfactory and sometimes misleading, because it asserts empirically observed correlations with no justification for the belief that they will always occur.

The alternative microeconomic approach which I prefer relies on the construction of models which cope with the problem raised by our inescapable ignorance of all the relevant

Where I differ from the majority of other 'monetarists' and in particular from the leading representative of the school, Professor Milton Friedman, is that I regard the simple quantity theory of money, even for situations where in a given territory only one kind of money is employed, as no more than a useful rough approximation to a really adequate explanation, which, however, becomes wholly useless where several concurrent distinct kinds of money are simultaneously in use in the same territory. Though this defect becomes serious only with the multiplicity of concurrent currencies which we are considering here, the phenomenon of substitution of things not counted as money by the theory for what is counted as money by it always impairs the strict validity of its conclusions.

Its chief defect in any situation seems to me to be that by its stress on the effects of changes in the quantity of money on the general level of prices it directs all-too exclusive attention to the harmful effects of inflation and deflation on the creditor-debtor relationship, but disregards the even more important and harmful effects of the injections and withdrawals of amounts of money from circulation on the structure of relative prices and the consequent misallocation of resources and particularly the misdirection investments which it causes.

This is not an appropriate place for a full discussion of the fine points of theory on which there exist considerable differences within the 'monetarist' school, though they are of great importance for the evaluation of the effects of the present proposals. My fundamental objection to the adequacy of the pure quantity theory of money is that, even with a single currency in circulation within a territory, there is, strictly speaking, no such thing as *the* quantity of money, and that any attempt to delimit certain groups of the media of exchange expressed in terms of a single unit as if they were homogeneous or perfect substitutes is misleading even for the usual situation. This objection becomes of decisive importance, of course, when we contemplate different concurrent currencies.

A stable price level and a high and stable level of employment do not require or permit the total quantity of money to be kept constant or to change at a constant rate. It demands something similar yet still significantly different, namely that the quantity of money (or rather the aggregate value of all the most liquid assets) be kept such that people will not

facts by "reducing the scale" by diminishing the number of independent variables to the minimum required to form a structure which is capable of producing all the *kinds* of movements or changes of which a market system is capable. It is, as I have tried to explain more fully elsewhere, a technique which produces merely what I have called 'pattern' predictions but is incapable of producing those predictions of specific events which macroeconomics claims, as I believe mistakenly, be able to produce. See *Studies in Philosophy, Politics and Economics,* Part 1, op. cit.

reduce or increase their outlay for the purpose of adapting their balances to their altered liquidity preferences. Keeping the quantity of money constant does not assure that the money-stream will remain constant, and in order to make the volume of the money-stream behave in a desired manner the supply of money must possess considerable elasticity.

Monetary management cannot aim at a particular predetermined volume of circulation, not even in the case of a territorial monopolist of issue, and still less in the case of competing issues, but only at finding out what quantity will keep prices constant. No authority can beforehand ascertain, and only the market can discover, the 'optimal quantity of money'. It can be provided only by selling and buying at a fixed price the collection of commodities the aggregate price of which we wish to keep stable.

As regards Professor Friedman's proposal of a legal limit on the rate at which a monopolistic issuer of money was to be allowed to increase the quantity in circulation, I can only say that I would not like to see what would happen if under such a provision it ever became known that the amount of cash in circulation was approaching the upper limit and that therefore a need for increased liquidity could not be met.[64]

Why Indexation Is Not a Substitute for a Stable Currency

The usual emphasis on the most generally perceived and most painfully felt harm done by inflation, its effect on debtor-creditor relations and in particular on the receivers of fixed incomes, has led to the suggestion that these effects be mitigated by stipulating long-term obligations in terms of a "tabular standard", the nominal sum of the debt being continuously corrected according to the changes in anindex number of prices. It is, of course, correct that such a practice would eliminate the most glaring injustices caused by inflation and would remove the most severe suffering visibly due to it. But these are far from being the most severe damage which inflation causes, and the adoption of such a partial remedy for some of the symptoms would probably weaken the resistance against inflation, thus prolonging and increasing it, and in the long run considerably magnify the damage it causes and particularly the suffering it produces by bringing about unemployment.

Everybody knows of course that inflation does not affect all prices at

[64]To such a situation the classic account of Walter Bagehot would apply: "In a sensitive state of the English money market the near approach to the legal limit of reserve would be a sure incentive to panic; if one-third were fixed by law, the moment the banks were close to one-third, alarm would begin and would run like magic". (*Lombard Street* [1873], London: Kegan Paul, Trench, Trübner & Co., 1906, penultimate paragraph.)

the same time but makes different prices rise in succession, and that it therefore changes the relation between prices—although the familiar statistics of *average* price movements tend to conceal this movement in *relative* prices. The effect on relative incomes is only one, though to the superficial observer the most conspicuous, effect of the distortion of the whole structure of relative prices. What is in the long run even more damaging to the functioning of the economy and eventually tends to make a free market system unworkable is the effect of this distorted price structure in misdirecting the use of resources and drawing labour and other factors of production (especially the investment of capital) into uses which remain profitable only so long as inflation accelerates. It is this effect which produces the major waves of unemployment,[65] but which the economists using a macroeconomic approach to the problem usually neglect or underrate.

This crucial damage done by inflation would in no way be eliminated by indexation. Indeed, government measures of this sort, which make it easier to live with inflation, must in the long run make things worse. They would certainly not make it easier to fight inflation, because people would be less aware that their suffering was due to inflation. There is no justification for Professor Friedman's suggestion that

> by removing distortions in relative prices produced by inflation, widespread escalator clauses would make it easierfor the public to recognize changes in the rate of inflation, would thereby reduce the time-lag in adapting to such changes, and thus make the nominal price level more sensitive and variable.[66]

Such inflation, with some of its visible effect mitigated, would clearly be less resisted and last correspondingly longer.

It is true that Professor Friedman explicitly disclaims any suggestion

[65]A remarkable recognition of this fundamental truth occurs in the opening paragraphs of the final communique of the Downing Street 'summit' meeting of May 8, 1977, chaired by the Prime Minister of the United Kingdom and attended by the President of the United States of America, the Chancellor of West Germany, the President of France, the Prime Minister of Japan and the Prime Minister of Italy. The first few lines said: "Inflation is not a remedy for unemployment, but is one of its major causes". This is an insight for which I have been fighting, almost single-handed, for more than 40 years. Unfortunately, however, that statement over-simplified the issue. In many circumstances inflation indeed leads to a *temporary* reduction of unemployment, but only at the price of causing much more unemployment later. This is exactly what makes inflation so seductive and politically almost irresistible, but for that reason particularly insidious.

[66]Milton Friedman, *Monetary Correction: A proposal for escalator clauses to reduce the costs of ending inflation,* Occasional Paper 41 (London: Institute of Economic Affairs, 1974), p. 31.

that indexation is a substitute for stable money,[67] but he attempts to make it more tolerable in the short run, and I regard any such endeavour as exceedingly dangerous. In spite of his denial, it seems to me that to some degree it would even speed up inflation. It would certainly strengthen the claims of groups of workers whose real wages ought to fall (because their kind of work has become less valuable) to have their real wages kept constant. But that means that all relative increases of any wages relatively to any others would have to find expression in an increase of the nominal wages of all except those workers whose wages were the lowest, and this itself would make continuous inflation necessary.

It seems to me, in other words, like any other attempts to accept wage and price rigidities as inevitable and to adjust monetary policy to them, the attitude from which 'Keynesian' economics took its origin, to be one of those steps apparently dictated by practical necessity but bound in the long run to make the whole wage structure more and more rigid and thereby lead to the destruction of the market economy. But the present political necessity ought to be no concern of the economic scientist. His task ought to be, as I will not cease repeating, to make politically possible what today may be politically impossible. To decide what can be done at the moment is the task of the politician, not of the economist, who must continue to point out that to persist in their direction will lead to disaster.

I am in complete agreement with Professor Friedman on the inevitability of inflation under the existing political and financial institutions. But I believe that it will lead to the destruction of our civilization unless we change the political framework. In this sense I will admit that my radical proposal concerning money will probably be practicable only as part of a much more far-reaching change in our political institutions, but an essential part of such a reform which will be recognized as necessary before long. The two distinct reforms which I am proposing in the economic and the political order[68] are indeed complementary: The sort of monetary system I propose may be possible only under a limited government such as we do not have, and a limitation of government may require that it be deprived of the monopoly of issuing money. Indeed the latter should necessarily follow from the former.

The Historical Evidence

Professor Friedman has since more fully explained his doubts about the efficacy of my proposal and claimed that

[67] *Ibid.*, p. 28.

[68] F. A. Hayek, *Law, Legislation and Liberty*, op. cit., vol. 3.

> we have ample empirical and historical evidence that suggests that [my] hopes would not in fact be realised—that private currencies which offer purchasing power security would not drive out governmental currencies.[69]

I can find no such evidence that anything like a currency of which the public has learnt to understand that the issuer can continue his business only if he maintains its currency constant, for which all the usual banking facilities are provided and which is legally recognized as an instrument for contracts, accounting and calculation has not been preferred to a deteriorating official currency, simply because such a situation seems never to have existed. It may well be that in many countries the issue of such a currency is not actually prohibited, but the other conditions are rarely if ever satisfied. And everybody knows that if such a private experiment promised to succeed, governments would at once step in to prevent it.

If we want historical evidence of what people will do where they have free choice of the currency they prefer to use, the displacement of sterling as the general unit of international trade since it began continuously to depreciate seems to me strongly to confirm my expectations. What we know about the behaviour of individuals having to cope with a bad national money, and in the face of government using every means at its disposal to force them to use it, all points to the probable success of any money which has the properties the public wants if people are not artificially deterred from using it. Americans may be fortunate in never having experienced a time when everybody in their country regarded some national currency other than their own as safer. But on the European Continent there were many occasions in which, if people had only been permitted, they would have used dollars rather than their national currencies. They did in fact do so to a much larger extent than was legally permitted, and the most severe penalties had to be threatened to prevent this habit from spreading rapidly—witness the billions of unaccounted-for dollar notes undoubtedly held in private hands all over the world.

I have never doubted that the public at large would be slow in recognizing the advantages of such a new currency and have even suggested that at first, if given the opportunity, the masses would turn to gold rather than any form of other paper money. But as always the success of the few who soon recognize the advantages of a really stable currency would in the end induce the others to imitate them.

I must confess, however, that I am somewhat surprised that Professor Friedman of all people should have so little faith that competition will

[69] In an interview given to *Reason* magazine, August 1977, p. 28.

make the better instrument prevail when he seems to have no ground to believe that monopoly will ever provide a better one and merely fears the indolence produced by old habits.

The Desirable Behaviour of the Supply of Currency

We have so far provisionally assumed that the kind of money individuals will prefer to use will also be most conducive to the smooth functioning of the market process as a whole. Although this is plausible and, as we shall see, approximately true in practice, it is not self-evident. We have still to examine the validity of this belief. It is at least conceivable that the use of one particular kind of currency might be most convenient for each separate individual but that each might be better off if all the others used a different kind.

We have seen (Section XIII) that successful economic action (or the fulfillment of the expectations which prompted it) depends largely on the approximately correct prediction of future prices. These predictions will be based on current prices and the estimation of their trend, but future prices must always be to some degree uncertain because the circumstances which determine them will be unknown to most individuals. Indeed, the function of prices is precisely to communicate, as rapidly as possible, signals of changes of which the individual cannot know but to which his plans must be adjusted. This system works because on the whole current prices are fairly reliable indications of what future prices will probably be, subject only to those 'accidental' deviations which, as we have seen, if average prices remain constant, are likely to offset each other. We have also seen how such an offsetting of opposite disappointments becomes impossible if a substantial general movement of prices in one direction takes place.

But the current prices of particular commodities or groups of commodities can also be positively misleading if they are caused by non-recurring events, such as temporary inflows or outflows of money to the system. For such apparent changes in demand from a particular direction are in a peculiar manner self-reversing: They systematically channel productive efforts into directions where they cannot be maintained. The most important recurrent misdirections of the use of resources of this sort occur when, by the creation (or withdrawal) of amounts of money, the funds available for investment are increased substantially above (or decreased substantially below) the amounts currently transferred from consumption to investment, or saved.

Although this is the mechanism by which recurrent crises and depressions are caused, it is not a specific effect of a particular kind of currency which the users are likely to be aware of and which might therefore lead them to switch to another. We can expect the selection of the currency they use to be influenced only by such attributes as recognizably affect their actions, but not by indirect effects of changes of its amount which will operate largely through their effects on the decisions of others.

The Supply of Currency, Stable Prices, and the Equivalence of Investment and Saving

While the modern author who first drew attention to the crucial importance of these divergences between investment and saving, Knut Wicksell, believed that they would disappear if the value of money were kept constant, this has unfortunately proved to be not strictly correct. It is now generally recognized that even those additions to the quantity of money that in a growing economy are necessary to secure a *stable* price level may cause an excess of investment over saving. But though I was among those who early pointed out this difficulty,[70] I am inclined to believe that it is a problem of minor practical significance. If increases or decreases of the quantity of money never exceeded the amount necessary to keep average prices approximately constant, we would come as close to a condition in which investment approximately corresponded to saving as we are likely to do by any conceivable method. Compared, anyhow, with the divergences between investment and saving which necessarily accompany the major swings in the price level, those which would still occur under a stable price level would probably be of an order of magnitude about which we need not worry.

'Neutral Money' Fictitious

My impression is that economists have become somewhat over-ambitious concerning the degree of stability that is either achievable or even desirable under any conceivable economic order, and that they have unfortunately encouraged political demands concerning the certainty of employment at a hoped-for wage which in the long run no government can satisfy. That perfect matching or correspondence of the individual plans which the theoretical model of a perfect market equilibrium derives on the assumption that the money required to make indirect exchange possible has no influence on relative prices is a wholly fictitious picture to which nothing in the real world can ever correspond. Although I have myself given currency to the expression 'neutral money' (which, as I dis-

[70]F. A. Hayek, *Monetary Theory and the Trade Cycle* [1929] (London: Jonathan Cape, 1933), pp. 114ff. [Reprinted, New York: Augustus M. Kelley, 1966. —Ed.]

covered later, I had unconsciously borrowed from Wicksell), it was intended to describe this almost universally made assumption of theoretical analysis and to raise the question whether any real money could ever possess this property, and not as a model to be aimed at by monetary policy.[71] I have long since come to the conclusion that no real money can ever be neutral in this sense, and that we must be content with a system that rapidly corrects the inevitable errors. The nearest approach to such a condition which we can hope to achieve would appear to me to be one in which the average prices of the 'original factors of production' were kept constant. But as the average price of land and labour is hardly something for which we can find a statistical measure, the nearest practicable approximation would seem to be precisely that stability of raw material and perhaps other wholesale prices which we could hope competitively issued currencies would secure.

I will readily admit that such a provisional solution (on which the experimentation of competition might gradually improve), though giving us an infinitely better money and much more general economic stability than we have ever had, leaves open various questions to which I have no ready answer. But it seems to meet the most urgent needs much better than any prospects that seemed to exist while one did not contemplate the abolition of the monopoly of the issue of money and the free admission of competition into the business of providing currency.

Increased Demand for Liquidity

To dispel one kind of doubt which I myself at one stage entertained about the possibility of maintaining a stable price level, we may briefly consider here what would happen if at one time most members of a community wished to keep a much larger proportion of their assets in a highly liquid form than they did before. Would this not justify, and even require, that the value of the most liquid assets, that is, of all money, should rise compared with that of commodities?

The answer is that such needs of all individuals could be met not only by increasing the *value* of the existing liquid assets, money, but also by increasing the *amounts* they can hold. The wish of each individual to have a larger share of his resources in a very liquid form can be taken care of by additions to the total stock of money. This, paradoxically, increases the sum of the value to the individuals of all existing assets and thereby also the share of them that is highly liquid. Nothing, of course, can increase the liquidity of a closed community as a whole, if that concept has any

[71] F. A. Hayek, "Über Neutrales Geld", *Zeitschrift für Nationalökonomie,* vol. 4, no. 5, 1933. [Translated as "On Neutral Money", chapter 6 of *Good Money, Part I,* being vol. 5 of the Collected Works of F. A. Hayek, op. cit. —Ed.]

meaning whatsoever, except, perhaps, if one wishes to extend its meaning to a shift from the production of highly specific to very versatile goods which would increase the ease of adaptation to unforeseen events.

There is no need to be afraid of spurious demands for more money on the ground that more money is needed to secure adequate liquidity. The amount required of any currency will always be that which can be issued or kept in circulation without causing an increase or decrease of the aggregate (direct or indirect) price of the 'basket' of commodities supposed to remain constant. This rule will satisfy all legitimate demands that the variable 'needs of trade' be satisfied. And this will be true in so far as the stated collection of goods can be bought or sold at the stated aggregate price, and the absorption or release of currency from cash balances does not interfere with this condition.

It remains true, however, that so long as good and bad currencies circulate side by side, the individual cannot wholly protect himself from the harmful effects of the bad currencies by using only the good ones in his own transactions. Since the relative prices of the different commodities must be the same in terms of the different concurrent currencies, the user of a stable currency cannot escape the effects of the distortion of the price structure by the inflation (or deflation) of a widely used competing currency. The benefit of a stable course of the economic activities which, we shall argue, the use of a stable money would produce, would therefore be achieved only if the great majority of transactions were effected in stable currencies. Such a displacement of most bad money by good would, I believe, come about fairly soon, but occasional disturbances of the whole price structure and in consequence of general economic activity cannot be wholly excluded until the public has learnt rapidly to reject tempting offers of cheap money.

XVI. Free Banking

Some of the problems we are encountering were discussed extensively in the course of a great debate on 'free banking' during the middle of the last century, mainly in France and Germany.[72] This debate turned on the question whether commercial banks should have the right to issue bank notes redeemable in the established national gold or silver currency. Bank notes were then very much more important than the scarcely yet developed use of checking accounts which became important only after (and

[72]A good survey of this discussion will be found in Vera C. Smith, *Rationale of Central Banking*, op. cit. [On the subject of free banking, an extensive literature has developed. See George A. Selgin, *The Theory of Free Banking* (Totowa, N.J.: Roman and Littlefield with the Cato Institute, 1988) and Lawrence H. White, *Competition and Currency* (New York and London: New York University Press with the Cato Institute, 1989). —Ed.]

in part perhaps because) the commercial banks were in the end definitely denied the right to issue bank notes. This outcome of the debate resulted in the establishment in all European countries of a single bank privileged by government to issue notes. (The United States followed only in 1914.)

A Single National Currency, Not Several Competing Currencies

It should be specially observed that the demand for free banking at that time was wholly a demand that the commercial banks should be allowed to issue notes in terms of the single established national currency. So far as I am aware, the possibility of competing banks issuing *different* currencies was never contemplated. That was of course a consequence of the view that only bank notes redeemable in gold or silver were practicable, and therefore that notes for other than the standard quantity of precious metal would seem to be merely inconvenient and not serve any useful purpose.

The older legitimate argument for freedom of the note issue by banks became, however, invalid once the notes they issued were no longer to be redeemed in gold or silver, for the supply of which each individual bank of issue was fully responsible, but in terms of a legal tender money provided by a privileged central bank of issue, which then was in effect under the necessity of supplying the cash needed for the redemption of the notes of the private banks of issue. That would have been a wholly indefensible system which was prevented (at least so far as the issue of notes, though not the issue of cheque deposits, was concerned) by the prohibition of private note issue.

The demands for free banking (i.e., for the free issue of bank notes) were mostly based on the ground that banks would thereby be enabled to provide more and cheaper credit. They were for the same reason resisted by those who recognized that the effect would be inflationary—although at least one advocate of the freedom of note issue had supported it on the ground that

> what is called freedom of banking would result in the total suppression of bank notes in France. I want to give everybody the right to issue bank notes so that nobody would take any bank notes any longer.[73]

The idea was, of course, that the inevitable abuse of this right, i.e., the issue of an amount of notes which the banks could not redeem from their own reserves, would lead to their failure.

The ultimate victory of the advocates of the centralization of the na-

[73] Henri Cernuschi, *Contre le billet de banque* (Paris: F. Lacroix, Verboeckhoven et cie, 1866), as quoted by Ludwig von Mises, *Human Action* (Edinburgh: William Hodge, 1949; Chicago: Henry Regnery, 1966), p. 446; also Vera C. Smith, op. cit., p. 91.

tional note issue was, however, in effect softened by a concession to those who were mainly interested in the banks being able to provide cheap credit. It consisted in the acknowledgement of a duty of the privileged bank of issue to supply the commercial banks with any notes they needed in order to redeem their demand deposits—rapidly growing in importance. This decision, or rather recognition of a practice into which central banks had drifted, produced a most unfortunate hybrid system in which responsibility for the total quantity of money was divided in a fatal manner so that nobody was in a position to control it effectively.

Demand Deposits Are Like Bank Notes or Cheques

This unfortunate development came about because for a long time it was not generally understood that deposits subject to cheque played very much the same role, and could be created by the commercial banks in exactly the same manner, as bank notes. The consequent dilution of what was still believed to be a government monopoly of the issue of all money resulted in the control of the total circulation of money being divided between a central bank and a large number of commercial banks whose creation of credit it could influence only indirectly. Not till much later did it come to be understood that the "inherent instability of credit"[74] under that system was a necessary outcome of this feature; that liquid means was mostly supplied by institutions which themselves had to keep liquid in terms of another form of money, so that they had to *reduce* their outstanding obligations precisely when everybody else also desired to be *more* liquid. By that time this kind of structure had become so firmly established that, in spite of the "perverse elasticity of the supply of credit"[75] it produced, it came to be regarded as unalterable. Walter Bagehot had clearly seen this dilemma a hundred years ago but despaired of the possibility of remedying this defect of the firmly established banking structure.[76] And Wicksell and later von Mises made it clear that this arrange-

[74]The expression was originally coined by Ralph G. Hawtrey [in *Currency and Credit* (London: Longmans), 3rd edition, 1928. —Ed.]

[75]Lauchlin Currie, *The Supply and Control of Money in the United States,* Harvard Economic Studies, vol. 47 (Cambridge, Mass.: Harvard University Press, 1934).

[76]Walter Bagehot, op. cit., p. 160: "I have tediously insisted that the natural system of banking is that of many banks keeping their own reserves, with the penalty of failure before them if they neglect it. I have shown that our system is that of a single bank keeping the whole reserve under no effectual penalty of failure. And yet I propose to retain that system and only attempt to mend and palliate it . . . because I am quite sure that it is of no manner of use proposing to alter it . . . there is no force to be found adequate to so vast a reconstruction, and so vast a destruction, and therefore it is useless proposing them". That was almost certainly true so long as the prevailing system worked tolerably, but not after it had broken down.

ment must lead to violent recurring fluctuations of business activity—the so-called 'trade-cycle'.

New Controls over Currencies; New Banking Practices

Not the least advantage of the proposed abolition of the government monopoly of the issue of money is that it would provide an opportunity to extricate ourselves from the impasse into which this development had led. It would create the conditions in which responsibility for the control of the quantity of the currency is placed on agencies whose self-interest would make them control it in such a manner as to make it most acceptable to the users.

This also shows that the proposed reform requires a complete change in the practices not only of the banks which take up the business of issuing currency but also of those which do not. For the latter could no longer rely on being bailed out by a central bank if they could not meet from their own reserves their customers' demands for cash—not even if they chose to keep their accounts in terms of the currency issued by a still existing governmental central bank which, to maintain its circulation, would have to adopt the practices of the other issuing banks with which it competed.

Opposition to New System from Established Bankers . . .

This necessity of all banks to develop wholly new practices will undoubtedly be the cause of strong opposition to the abolition of the government monopoly. It is unlikely that most of the older bankers, brought up in the prevailing routine of banking, will be capable of coping with those problems. I am certain that many of the present leaders of the profession will not be able to conceive how it could possibly work and therefore will describe the whole system as impracticable and impossible.

Especially in countries where competition among banks has for generations been restricted by cartel arrangements, usually tolerated and even encouraged by governments, the older generation of bankers would probably be completely unable even to imagine how the new system would operate and therefore be practically unanimous in rejecting it. But this foreseeable opposition of the established practitioners ought not to deter us. I am also convinced that if a new generation of young bankers were given the opportunity they would rapidly develop techniques to make the new forms of banking not only safe and profitable but also much more beneficial to the whole community than the existing one.

. . . and from Banking Cranks

Another curious source of opposition, at least once they had discovered that the effects of 'free banking' would be exactly the opposite of those they expected, would be all the numerous cranks who had advocated 'free banking' from inflationist motives.[77] Once the public had an alternative, it would become impossible to induce it to hold cheap money, and the desire to get rid of currency that threatened to depreciate would indeed rapidly turn it into a dwindling money. The inflationists would protest because in the end only very 'hard' money would remain. *Money is the one thing competition would not make cheap, because its attractiveness rests on its preserving its 'dearness'.*

The Problem of a 'Dear' (Stable) Money

A competition the chief merit of which is that it keeps the products of the competitors dear raises various interesting questions. In what will the suppliers compete once they have established somewhat similar reputations and trust for keeping their currencies stable? The profits from the issuing business (which amounts to borrowing at zero interest) will be very large and it does not seem probable that very many firms can succeed in it. For this reason services to the enterprises basing their accounting on a bank's currency would be likely to become the chief weapon of competition, and I should not be surprised if the banks were practically to take over the accounting for their customers.

Though even very large profits of the successfully established issuers of currency would not be too high a price for a good money, they would inevitably create great political difficulties. Quite apart from the inevitable outcry against the profits of the money monopoly, the real threat to the system would be the cupidity of Ministers of Finance who would soon claim a share in them for the permission to allow a currency to circulate in their country, which would of course spoil everything. It might indeed prove to be nearly as impossible for a democratic government not to interfere with money as to regulate it sensibly.

[77]The list is very long and, in addition to works by well-known writers Clifford H. Douglas, Silvio Gesell, Henry Meulen, and H. Rittershausen, the series of studies by Edwin Clarence Riegel (1879–1953) published between 1929 and 1944 deserves special mention as an instance of how the results of acute insights and long reflection which seem to have gained the attention of an economist of the rank of Irving Fisher may be completely invalidated by an ignorance of elementary economics. A posthumous volume by Riegel, entitled *Flight from Inflation. The Monetary Alternative,* has been announced by the Heather Foundation, San Pedro, California.

The real danger is thus that, while today the people submissively put up with almost any abuse of the money prerogative by government, as soon as it will be possible to say that money is issued by 'rich financial institutions', the complaint about their abuse of the alleged monopoly will become incessant. To wring from the money power their alleged privilege will become the constant demand of demagogues. I trust the banks would be wise enough not to desire even a distant approach to the monopoly position, but to limit the volume of their business may become one of their most delicate problems.

XVII. No More General Inflation or Deflation?

Neither a *general* increase nor a *general* decrease of prices appears to be possible in normal circumstances so long as several issuers of different currencies are allowed freely to compete without the interference of government. There will always be one or more issuers who find it to their advantage to regulate the supply of their currency so as to keep its value constant in step with the aggregate price of a bundle of widely used commodities. This would soon force any less provident issuers of competing currencies to put a stop to a slide in the value of their currency in either direction if they did not wish to lose the issue business altogether or to find the value of their currency falling to zero.

No Such Thing as Oil-Price (or Any Other) Cost-Push Inflation

It is, of course, taken for granted here that the average prices in terms of a currency can always be controlled by appropriate adjustments of its quantity. Theoretical analysis and experience seem to me alike to confirm this proposition. We need therefore pay no attention to the views always advanced in periods of prolonged inflation in attempts to exculpate governments by contending that the continued rise in prices is not the fault of policy but the result of an initial rise in costs. To this claim it must be replied emphatically that, in the strict sense, there is simply no such a thing as 'cost-push' inflation. Neither higher wages nor higher prices of oil, or perhaps of imports generally, can drive up the aggregate price of all goods *unless the purchasers are given more money to buy them.* What is called a cost-push inflation is merely the effect of increases in the quantity of money which governments feel forced to provide in order to prevent the unemployment resulting from a rise in wages (or other costs), which preceded it and which was conceded in the expectation that government would increase the quantity of money. They mean thereby to make it possible for all the workers to find employment through a rise in the demand for their products. If government did not increase the quantity of money such a rise in the wages of a group of workers would not lead to a rise in the general price level but simply to a reduction in sales and therefore to unemployment.

It is, however, worth considering a little more fully what would happen if a cartel or other monopolistic organisation, such as a trade union, did succeed in substantially raising the price of an important raw material or the wages of a large group of workers, fixing them in terms of a currency which the issuer endeavours to keep stable. In such circumstances the stability of the price level in terms of this currency could be achieved only by the reduction of a number of other prices. If people have to pay a larger amount of money for the oil or the books and printed papers they consume, they will have to consume less of some other things.

The Problem of Rigid Prices and Wages

No currency, of course, can remove the rigidity of some prices which has developed. But it can make impossible the policies which have assisted this development by making it necessary for those who hold prices rigid in the face of a reduced demand to accept the consequent loss of sales.

The whole difference of approach between the dominant Keynesian school and the view underlying the present exposition rests in the last resort on the position taken with regard to the phenomenon of rigid prices and wages. Keynes was largely led to his views by his belief that the increasing rigidity of wages was an unalterable fact which had to be accepted and the effect of which could be mitigated only by accommodating the rate of money expenditure to the given rate of wages. (This opinion was in some measure justified in the British position in the 1920s, when, as a result of an injudicious attempt to raise the external value of the pound, most British wages had become out of line with international commodity prices.) I have maintained ever since that such an adaptation of the quantity of money to the rigidity of some prices and particularly wages would greatly extend the range of such rigidities and must therefore, in the long run, entirely destroy the functioning of the market.

The Error of the 'Beneficial Mild Inflation'

All inflation is so very dangerous precisely because many people, including many economists, regard a mild inflation as harmless and even beneficial. But there are few mistakes of policy with regard to which it is more important to heed the old maxim *principiis obsta*.[78] Apparently, and sur-

[78]["Resist beginnings" (or, colloquially, "nip it in the bud"): Ovid, *Remedia Amoris,* 91, trans. Showerman, *Oxford Dictionary of Quotations.* —Ed.]

prisingly, the self-accelerating mechanism of all engineered inflation is not yet understood even by some economists. The initial general stimulus which an increase of the quantity of money provides is chiefly due to the fact that prices and therefore profits turn out to be higher than expected. Every venture succeeds, including even some which ought to fail. But this can last only so long as the continuous rise of prices is not generally expected. Once people learn to count on it, even a continued rise of prices at the same rate will no longer exert the stimulus that it gave at first.

Monetary policy is then faced with an unpleasant dilemma. In order to maintain the degree of activity it created by mild inflation, it will have to accelerate the rate of inflation, and will have to do so again and again at an ever-increasing rate every time the prevailing rate of inflation comes to be expected. If it fails to do so and either stops accelerating or ceases to inflate altogether, the economy will be in a much worse position than when the process started. Not only has inflation allowed the ordinary errors of judgement to accumulate which are normally promptly eliminated and will now all have to be liquidated at the same time; it will in addition have caused misdirection of production and drawn labour and other resources into activities which could be maintained only if the additional investment financed by the increase in the quantity of money could be maintained.

Since it has become generally understood that whoever controls the total supply of money of a country has thereby power to give in most situations almost instantaneous relief to unemployment, even if only at the price of much unemployment later, the political pressure on such an agency must become irresistible. The threat of that possibility has always been understood by some economists, who for this reason have ever been anxious to restrain the monetary authorities by barriers they could not break. But since the betrayal, or ignorance, of this insight by a school of theorists which thereby bought themselves temporary popularity, political control of the supply of money has become too dangerous to the preservation of the market order to be any longer tolerated. However much political pressure might be brought on the most important private banks of issue to make them relax their credit conditions and extend their circulation, if a *non-monopolistic* institution gave in to such pressure it would soon cease to be one of the most important issuers.

The 'money illusion', i.e., the belief that money represents a constant value, could arise only because it was useless to worry about changes in the value of money so long as one could not do anything about it. Once people have a choice they will become very much aware of the different changes of the value of the different currencies accessible to them. It would, as it should, become common knowledge that money needs to be watched, and would be regarded as a praiseworthy action rather than as an unpatriotic deed to warn people that a particular currency was suspect.

Responsibility for Unemployment Would Be Traced Back to Trade Unions

Depriving government of the power of thus counteracting the effects of monopolistically enforced increases in wages or prices by increasing the quantity of money would place the responsibility for the full use of resources back to where it belongs: where the causally effective decisions are taken—the monopolists who negotiate the wages or prices. We ought to understand by now that the attempt to combat by inflation the unemployment caused by the monopolistic actions of trade unions will merely postpone the effects on employment to the time when the rate of inflation required to maintain employment by continually increasing the quantity of money becomes unbearable. The sooner we can make impossible such harmful measures, probably unavoidable so long as government has the monetary power to take them, the better for all concerned.

The scheme proposed here would, indeed, do somewhat more than prevent only inflations and deflations in the strict sense of these terms. Not all changes in the general level of prices are caused by changes in the quantity of money, or its failure to adapt itself to changes in the demand for holding money; and only those brought about in this manner can properly be called inflation or deflation. It is true that there are nowadays unlikely to be large simultaneous changes in the supply of many of the most important goods, as happened when variations in harvests could cause dearths or gluts of most of the main foodstuffs and clothing materials. And, even today, perhaps in wartime in a country surrounded by enemies or on an island, an acute scarcity (or glut) of the products in which the country has specialized is perhaps conceivable. At least if the index number of the commodity prices that guided the issue of the currency in the country were based chiefly on national prices, such a rule might lead to changes in the supply of currency designed to counteract price movements not caused by monetary factors.

Preventing General Deflation

The reader may not yet feel fully reassured that, in the kind of competitive money system we are here contemplating, a general deflation will be as impossible as a general inflation. Experience seems indeed to have shown that, in conditions of severe uncertainty or alarm about the future, even very low rates of interest cannot prevent a shrinking of a bank's outstanding loans. What could a bank issuing its own distinct currency do when it finds itself in such a situation, and commodity prices in terms of its currency threaten to fall? And how strong would be its interest in stopping such a fall of prices if the same circumstances affected the competing institutions in the same way?

There would of course be no difficulty in placing additional money at a time when people in general want to keep very liquid. The issuing bank, on the other hand, would not wish to incur an obligation to maintain by redemption a value of its currency higher than that at which it had issued it. To maintain profitable investments, the bank would presumably be driven to buy interest-bearing securities and thereby put cash into the hands of people looking for other investments as well as bring down the long-term rates of interest, with a similar effect. An institution with a very large circulation of currency might even find it expedient to buy for storage quantities of commodities represented in the index that tended to fall particularly strongly in price.

This would probably be sufficient to counteract any downward tendency of general prices produced by the economic process itself, and if it achieved this effect it is probably as much as can be accomplished by any management of money. But it is of course not to be wholly excluded that some events may cause such a general state of discouragement and lethargy that nothing could induce people to resume investment and thereby stop an impending fall of prices. So far as this were due to extraneous events, such as the fear of an impending world catastrophe or of the imminent advent of communism, or in some region the desire to convert all private possessions into cash to be prepared for flight, probably nothing could prevent a general fall in the prices of possessions that are not easily portable. But so long as the general conditions for the effective conduct of capitalist enterprise persisted, competition would provide a money that caused as little disturbance to its working as possible. And this is probably all we can hope.[79]

XVIII. Monetary Policy Neither Desirable Nor Possible

It is true that under the proposed arrangements monetary policy as we now know it could not exist. It is not to be denied that, with the existing sort of division of responsibility between the issues of the basic money and those of a parasitic circulation based on it, central banks must, to

[79]The remaining doubt concerns the question whether in such circumstances the holders of cash might wish to switch towards an appreciating currency, but such a currency would then probably not be available.

prevent matters from getting completely out of hand, try deliberately to forestall developments they can only influence but not directly control. But the central banking system, which only 50 years ago was regarded as the crowning achievement of financial wisdom, has largely discredited itself. This is even more true since, with the abandonment of the gold standard and fixed exchange rates, the central banks have acquired fuller discretionary powers than when they were still trying to act on firm rules. And this is true no less where the aim of policy is still a reasonable degree of stability, as in countries overwhelmed by inflation.

Government the Major Source of Instability

We have it on the testimony of a competent authority who was by no means unsympathetic to those modern aspirations that, during the recent decade 1962 to 1972 when the believers in a 'fine tuning' of monetary policy had an influence which we must hope they will never have again, the larger part of the fluctuations were a consequence of budgetary and monetary policy.[80] And it is certainly impossible to claim that the period since the abandonment of the semi-automatic regulation of the quantity of money has *generally* been more stable or free from monetary disturbances than the periods of the gold standard or fixed rates of exchange.

We indeed begin to see how completely different an economic landscape the free issue of competitive currencies would produce when we realize that under such a system what is known today as monetary policy would neither be needed nor even possible. The issuing banks, guided solely by their striving for gain, would thereby serve the public interest better than any institution has ever done or could do that supposedly aimed at it. There neither would exist a definable quantity of money of a nation or region, nor would it be desirable that the individual issuers of the several currencies should aim at anything but to make as large as possible the aggregate value of their currency that the public was prepared to hold at the given value of the unit. If we are right that, being able to choose, the public would prefer a currency whose purchasing

[80]Otto Eckstein, "Instability in the Private and Public Sector", *Swedish Journal of Economics*, vol. 75, no. 1, 1973, especially p. 19: "Traditionally, stabilization theory has viewed private, capitalist economy as a mechanism which produces fluctuations. . . . There is no question that government is a major source of instability". And p. 25: "The rate of inflation [in the United States between 1962 and 1972] would have been substantially less, real growth would have been smoother, the total amount of unemployment experienced would have been little changed but the variations would have been milder, and the terminal conditions at the end of the period would have made it possible to avoid the wage and price controls".

power it could expect to be stable, this would provide a better currency and secure more stable business conditions than have ever existed before.

The supposed chief weakness of the market order, the recurrence of periods of mass unemployment, is always pointed out by socialists and other critics as an inseparable and unpardonable defect of capitalism.[81] It proves in fact wholly to be the result of government preventing private enterprise from working freely and providing itself with a money that would secure stability. We have seen that there can be no doubt that free enterprise would have been both able to provide a money securing stability and that striving for individual gain would have driven private financial institutions to do so if they had been permitted. I am not sure that private enterprise would adopt the manner of performing the task I have suggested, but I am inclined to think that, by its habitual procedure of selecting the most successful, it would in time throw up better solutions to these problems than anyone can foresee today.

Monetary Policy a Cause of Depressions

What we should have learned is that monetary policy is much more likely to be a cause than a cure of depressions, because it is much easier, by giving in to the clamour for cheap money, to cause those misdirections of production that make a later reaction inevitable, than to assist the economy in extricating itself from the consequences of overdeveloping in particular directions. *The past instability of the market economy is the consequence of the exclusion of the most important regulator of the market mechanism, money, from itself being regulated by the market process.*

A single monopolistic governmental agency can neither possess the information which should govern the supply of money nor would it, if it knew what it ought to do in the general interest, usually be in a position to act in that manner. Indeed, if, as I am convinced, the main advantage of the market order is that prices will convey to the acting individuals the relevant information, only the constant observation of the course of current prices of particular commodities can provide information on the direction in which more or less money ought to be spent. Money is not a tool of policy that can achieve particular foreseeable results by control of its quantity. But it should be part of the self-steering mechanism by which individuals are constantly induced to adjust their activities to circumstances on which they have information only through the abstract signals of prices. It should be a serviceable link in the process that communicates

[81]The long depression of the 1930s, which led to the revival of Marxism (which would probably have been dead today without it), was wholly due to the mismanagement of money by government—before as well as after the crisis of 1929.

the effects of events never wholly known to anybody and that is required to maintain an order in which the plans of participating persons match.

Government Cannot Act in the General Interest

Yet even if we assumed that government could know what should be done about the supply of money in the general interest, it is highly unlikely that it would be able to act in that manner. As Professor Eckstein, in the article quoted above, concludes from his experience in advising governments:

> Governments are not able to live by the rules even if they were to adopt the philosophy [of providing a stable framework].[82]

Once governments are given the power to benefit particular groups or sections of the population, the mechanism of majority government forces them to use it to gain the support of a sufficient number of them to command a majority. The constant temptation to meet local or sectional dissatisfaction by manipulating the quantity of money so that more can be spent on services for those clamouring for assistance will often be irresistible. Such expenditure is not an appropriate remedy but necessarily upsets the proper functioning of the market.

In a true emergency such as war, governments would of course still be able to force upon people bonds or other pieces of paper for unavoidable payments which cannot be made from current revenues. Compulsory loans and the like would probably be more compatible with the required rapid readjustments of industry to radically changed circumstances than an inflation that suspends the effective working of the price mechanism.

No More Balance-of-Payment Problems

With the disappearance of distinct territorial currencies there would of course also disappear the so-called 'balance-of-payment problems' believed to cause intense difficulties to present-day monetary policy. There would, necessarily, be continuous redistributions of the relative and absolute quantities of currency in different regions as some grew relatively richer and others relatively poorer. But this would create no more difficulties than the same process causes today within any large country. People who grew richer would have more money and those who grew poorer would have less. That would be all. The special difficulties caused by the fact that under existing arrangements the reduction of the distinct

[82] Eckstein, "Instability in the Private and Public Sector", op. cit., p. 26.

cash basis of one country requires a contraction of the whole separate superstructure of credit erected on it would no longer exist.

Similarly, the closer connections of the structure of the prices prevailing within any one country as against prices in neighbouring countries, and with it the statistical illusion of the relative movement of distinct national price levels, would largely disappear. Indeed it would be discovered that 'balance-of-payment problems' are a quite unnecessary effect of the existence of distinct national currencies, which is the cause of the wholly undesirable closer coherence of national prices than of international prices. From the angle of a desirable international economic order, the 'balance-of-payment problem' is a pseudo-problem about which nobody need worry but a monopolist of the issue of money for a given territory. And not the least advantage of the disappearance of distinct national currencies would be that we could return to the happy days of statistical innocence in which nobody could know what the balance of payment of his country or region was and thus nobody could worry or would have to care about it.

The Addictive Drug of Cheap Money

The belief that cheap money is always desirable and beneficial makes inevitable and irresistible the pressure on any political authority or monopolist known to be capable of making money cheap by issuing more of it. Yet loanable funds made artificially cheap by creating more money for lending them, not only help those to whom they are lent, though at the expense of others, but for a while have a general stimulating effect on business activity. That at the same time such issues have the effect of destroying the steering mechanism of the market is not so easily seen. But supplies of such funds for additional purchases of goods produce a distortion of the structure of relative prices which draws resources into activities that cannot be lastingly maintained and thereby become the cause of an inevitable later reaction. These indirect and slow effects are, however, in their nature very much more difficult to recognize or understand than the immediate pleasant effects and particularly the benefits to those to whom the additional money goes in the first instance.

To provide a medium of exchange for people who want to hold it until they wish to buy an equivalent for what they have supplied to others is a useful service like producing any other good. If an increase in the demand for such cash balances is met by an increase of the quantity of money (or a reduction of the balances people want to hold by a corresponding decrease of the total amount of money), it does not disturb the correspondence between demand and supply of all other commodities or services. But it is really a crime like theft to enable some people to buy more than they have earned by more than the amount which other people have at the same time foregone to claim.

When committed by a monopolistic issuer of money, and especially by government, it is however a very lucrative crime which is generally tolerated and remains unpunished because its consequences are not understood. But for the issuer of a currency which has to compete with other currencies, it would be a suicidal act, because it would destroy the service for which people did want to hold his currency.

Because of a lack of general understanding, the crime of over-issue by a monopolist is still not only tolerated but even applauded. That is one of the chief reasons why the smooth working of the market is so frequently upset. But today almost any statesman who tries to do good in this field, and certainly anyone forced to do what the large organized interests think good, is therefore likely to do much more harm than good. On the other hand, anyone who merely knows that the success of his business of issuing money rests wholly on his ability to keep the buying power of his currency constant will do more for the public good by aiming solely at large profits for himself than by any conscious concern about the more remote effects of his actions.

The Abolition of Central Banks

Perhaps a word should be explicitly inserted here about the obvious corollary that the abolition of the government monopoly of the issue of money should involve also the disappearance of central banks as we know them, both because one might conceive of some private bank assuming the function of a central bank and because it might be thought that, even without a government monopoly of issue, some of the classic functions of central banks, such as that of acting as 'lender of last resort' or of 'holder of the ultimate reserve',[83] might still be required.

The need for such an institution is, however, entirely due to the commercial banks incurring liabilities payable on demand in a unit of currency which some other bank has the sole right to issue, thus in effect creating money redeemable in terms of another money. This, as we shall have still to consider, is indeed the chief cause of the instability of the existing credit system, and through it of the wide fluctuations in all economic activity. Without the central bank's (or the government's) monopoly of issuing money, and the legal tender provisions of the law, there

[83]The standard description of this function and of how it arose is still W. Bagehot, who could rightly speak (op. cit., p. 142) of "a natural state of banking, that in which all the principal banks kept their own reserve".

would be no justification whatever for the banks to rely for their solvency on the cash to be provided by another body. The "one reserve system", as Walter Bagehot called it, is an inseparable accompaniment of the monopoly of issue but unnecessary and undesirable without it.

It might still be argued that central banks are necessary to secure the required 'elasticity' of the circulation. And though this expression has probably in the past been more abused than any other to disguise inflationist demands, we must not overlook its valid kernel. The manner in which elasticity of supply and stability of value of the money can be reconciled is a genuine problem, and it will be solved only if the issuer of a given currency is aware that his business depends on so regulating the quantity of his currency that the value of its unit remains stable (in terms of commodities). If an addition to the quantity would lead to a rise of prices, it would clearly not be justified, however urgently some may feel that they need additional cash—which then will be cash to spend and not to add to their liquidity reserves. What makes a currency a universally acceptable, that is really liquid, asset will be precisely that it is preferred to other assets because its buying power is expected to remain constant.

What is necessarily scarce is not liquidity but buying power—the command over goods for consumption or use in further production, and this is limited because there is no more than a given amount of these things to buy. So far as people want more liquid assets solely to hold them but not to spend them, they can be manufactured without thereby depreciating their value. But if people want more liquid assets in order to spend them on goods, the value of such credits will melt between their fingers.

No Fixing of Rates of Interest

With the central banks and the monopoly of the issue of money would, of course, disappear also the possibility of deliberately determining the rate of interest. The disappearance of what is called "interest policy" is wholly desirable. The rate of interest, like any other price, ought to record the aggregate effects of thousands of circumstances affecting the demand for and supply of loans which cannot possibly be known to any one agency. The effects of most price changes are unpleasant to some, and, like other price changes, changes in the rate of interest convey to all concerned that an aggregate of circumstances which nobody knows has made them necessary. The whole idea that the rate of interest ought to be used as an instrument of policy is entirely mistaken, since only competition in a free market can take account of all the circumstances which ought to be taken account of in the determination of the rate of interest.

So long as each separate issue bank in its lending activity aimed at regulating the volume of its outstanding currency so as to keep its buying power constant, the rate of interest at which it could do so would be determined for it by the market. And, on the whole, the lending for investment purposes of all the banks together, if it was not to drive up the price level, could not exceed the current volume of savings (and conversely, if it was not to depress the price level, must not fall short of the current volume of savings) by more than was required to increase aggregate demand in step with a growing volume of output. The rate of interest would then be determined by balancing the demand for money for spending purposes with the supply required for keeping the price level constant. I believe this would assure as close an agreement between saving and investment as we can hope to achieve, leaving a balance of change in the quantity of money to take account of changes in the demand for money caused by changes in the balances people want to hold.

Of course, government would still affect this market rate of interest by the net volume of its borrowing. But it could no longer practice those most pernicious manipulations of the rate of interest which are intended to enable it to borrow cheaply—a practice which has done so much harm in the past that this effect alone would seem an adequate reason why government should be kept away from the tap.

A Better Discipline than Fixed Rates of Exchange

Readers who know of my consistent support over more than 40 years of fixed rates of exchange between national currencies, and of my critique of a system of flexible rates of foreign exchange,[84] even after most of my fellow defenders of a free market had become converts to this system, will probably feel at first that my present position is in conflict with, or even represents a complete reversal of, my former views. This is not so. In two respects my present proposal is a result of the further development of the considerations which determined my former position.

In the first instance, I have always regarded it as thoroughly undesirable that the structure of the prices of commodities and services in one country should be lifted and lowered as a whole relatively to the price structure of other countries in order to correct some alteration in the

[84]The first systematic exposition of my position will be found in my 1937 Geneva lectures on *Monetary Nationalism and International Stability* [now published as chapter 1, this volume]. It contains a series of lectures hastily and badly written on a topic to which I had earlier committed myself but which I had to write when I was preoccupied with other problems. I still believe that it contains important arguments against flexible exchange rates between national currencies which have never been adequately answered, but I am not surprised that few people appear ever to have read it.

supply of or demand for a particular commodity. This was erroneously thought to be necessary chiefly because the availability of statistical information in the form of index numbers of the *average* movement of prices in one country gave the misleading impression that 'the internal value' of one currency as such had to be changed relatively to the value of other currencies, while what was required were primarily changes of the relations between particular prices in all the countries concerned. So far as the assumed necessity of changes in relation between general prices in the countries was true, this was an artificial and undesirable effect of the imperfection of the international monetary system which the gold standard with a superstructure of deposit money produced. We will consider these questions further in the next section.

Remove Protection of Official Currency from Competition

Secondly, I had regarded fixed rates of exchange as necessary for the same reason for which I now plead for completely free markets for all kinds of currency, namely that it was required to impose a very necessary discipline or restraint on the agencies issuing money. Neither I, nor apparently anybody else, then thought of the much more effective discipline that would operate if the providers of money were deprived of the power of shielding the money they issued against the rivalry of *competing currencies*.

The compulsion to maintain a fixed rate of redemption in terms of gold or other currencies has in the past provided the only discipline that effectively prevented monetary authorities from giving in to the demand of the ever-present pressure for cheap money. The gold standard, fixed rates of exchange, or any other form of obligatory conversion at a fixed rate served no other purpose than to impose upon the issuers of money such a discipline and, by making its regulation automatic, to deprive them of the power arbitrarily to change the quantity of money. It is a discipline that has proved too weak to prevent governments from breaking it. Yet, though the regulations achieved by those automatic controls were far from ideal or even tolerably satisfactory, so long as currencies were thus regulated they were much more satisfactory than anything the discretionary powers of governmental monopolies have ever achieved for any length of time. Nothing short of the belief that it would be a national disgrace for a country not to live up to its obligations has ever sufficed adequately to strengthen the resistance of monetary authorities against pressures for cheap money. I should never have wanted to deny that a very wise and politically independent monetary authority might do better than it is compelled to do in order to preserve a fixed parity with gold or another currency. But I can see no hope of monetary authorities in the real world prevailing for any length of time in their good intentions.

Better Even Than Gold—the 'Wobbly Anchor'

It ought by now of course to be generally understood that the value of a currency redeemable in gold (or in another currency) is not *derived* from the value of that gold, but merely kept at the same value through the automatic regulation of its quantity. The superstition dies only slowly, but even under a gold standard it is no more true (or perhaps even less true) that the value of the currency is determined by the value in other uses of the gold it contains (or by its costs of production) than is the converse, that the value of gold is determined by the value of the currencies into which it can be converted. Historically it is true that all the money that preserved its value for any length of time was metallic (or money convertible into metal—gold or silver); and governments sooner or later used to debase even metallic money, so that all the kinds of paper money of which we have experience were so much worse. Most people therefore now believe that relief can come only from returning to a metallic (or other commodity) standard. But not only is a metallic money also exposed to the risks of fraud by government; even at its best it would never be as good a money as one issued by an agency whose whole business rested on its success in providing a money the public preferred to other kinds. Though gold is an anchor—and any anchor is better than a money left to the discretion of government—it is a very wobbly anchor. It certainly could not bear the strain if the majority of countries tried to run their own gold standard. There just is not enough gold about. An international gold standard could today mean only that a few countries maintained a real gold standard while the others hung on to them through a gold exchange standard.

Competition Would Provide Better Money Than Would Government

I believe we can do much better than gold ever made possible. Governments cannot do better. Free enterprise, i.e., the institutions that would emerge from a process of competition in providing good money, no doubt would. There would in that event also be no need to encumber the money supply with the complicated and expensive provision for convertibility which was necessary to secure the automatic operation of the gold standard and which made it appear as at least more practicable than what would ideally seem much more suitable—a commodity reserve standard. A very attractive scheme for storing a large variety of raw materials and other standard commodities had been worked out for such a standard to ensure the redeemability of the currency unit by a fixed combination of such commodities and thereby the stability of the currency. Storage would however be so expensive, and practicable only for such a small collection of commodities, as to reduce the value of the proposal.[85] But some such precaution to force the issuer to regulate the amount of his currency appears necessary or desirable only so long as his interest would be to increase or decrease its value above or below the standard. Convertibility is a safeguard necessary to impose upon a *monopolist*, but unnecessary with *competing* suppliers who cannot maintain themselves in the business unless they provide money at least as advantageous to the user as anybody else.

Government Monopoly of Money Unnecessary

Not so very long ago, in 1960, I myself argued that it is not only impracticable but probably undesirable even if possible to deprive governments of their control over monetary policy.[86] This view was still based on the common tacit assumption that there must be in each country a single uniform kind of money. I did not then even consider the possibility of true competition between currencies within any given country or region. If only one kind of money is permitted, it is probably true that the monopoly of its issue must be under the control of government. The concurrent circulation of several currencies might at times be slightly inconvenient, but careful analysis of its effects indicates that the advantages appear to be so very much greater than the inconveniences that they hardly count in comparison, though unfamiliarity with the new situation makes them appear much bigger than they probably would be.

Difference between Voluntarily Accepted and Enforced Paper Money

Much as all historical experience appears to justify the deep mistrust most people harbour against paper money, it is well founded only with regard to money issued by government. Frequently the term 'fiat money' is used as if it applied to all paper money, but the expression refers of course only to money which has been given currency by the arbitrary decree or other act of authority. Money which is current only because people have been forced to accept it is wholly different from money that has come to be accepted because people trust the issuer to keep it stable.

[85] See Milton Friedman, "Commodity Reserve Currency" [1951], in *Essays in Positive Economics* (Chicago: University of Chicago Press, 1953). [The original scheme was proposed independently by Benjamin Graham and Frank Graham. See this volume, chapter 2. —Ed.]

[86] F. A. Hayek, *The Constitution of Liberty*, op. cit., pp. 324 et seq.

Voluntarily accepted paper money therefore ought not to suffer from the evil reputation governments have given paper money.

Money is valued because, and in so far as, it is known to be scarce, and is for this reason likely to be accepted at the going value by others. And any money which is voluntarily used only because it is trusted to be kept scarce by the issuer, and which will be held by people only so long as the issuer justifies that trust, will increasingly confirm its acceptability at the established value. People will know that the risk they run in holding it will be smaller than the risk they run in holding any other good on which they do not possess special information. Their willingness to hold it will rest on the experience that other people will be ready to accept it at an approximately known range of prices because they also have learnt to hold the same expectation, and so on. This is a state of affairs that can continue indefinitely and will even tend to stabilize itself more and more as confirmed expectations increase the trust.

Some people apparently find it difficult to believe that a mere token money which did not give the holder a legal claim for redemption in terms of some object possessing an intrinsic value equal to its current value could ever be generally accepted for any length of time or preserve its value. They seem to forget that for the past 40 years in the whole Western World there has been no other money than such irredeemable tokens. The various paper currencies we have had to use have preserved a value which for some time was only slowly decreasing not because of any hope of ultimate redemption, but only because the monopolistic agencies authorised to issue the exclusive kind of currency of a particular country did in some inadequate degree restrict its amount. But the clause on a pound-note saying "I promise to pay to the bearer on demand the sum of one pound", or whatever the figure be, signed for the Governor and Company of the Bank of England by their Chief Cashier, means of course no more than that the promise to exchange that piece of paper for other pieces of paper.

It is entirely at the discretion of these institutions or governments to regulate the total amount of their issues in circulation by exchanging some of the notes for other kinds of money or for securities. This sort of redemption is just a method of regulating the quantity of money in the hands of the public, and, so long as public opinion was not misguided by specious theories, it has always been taken as a matter of course that, e.g., "the value of [greenbacks] changes as the government chooses to enlarge or to contract the issue".[87]

History certainly disproves the suggestion that in this respect govern-

[87] Walter Bagehot, op. cit., p. 12.

ment, which only profits from excessive issues, can be trusted more than a private issuer whose whole business depends on his not abusing that trust. Does anyone really believe that in the industrial countries of the West, after the experience of the last half-century, anybody trusts the value of government-sponsored money more than he would trust money issued by a private agency whose business was understood to depend wholly on its issuing good money?

XX. Should There Be Separate Currency Areas?

We are so used to the existence in each country of a distinct currency in which practically all internal transactions are conducted that we tend to regard it also as natural and necessary for the whole structure of internal prices to move together relatively to the price structure of other countries. This is by no means a necessary or in any sense natural or desirable state of affairs.

National Currencies Not Inevitable or Desirable

At least without tariffs or other obstructions to the free movement of goods and men across frontiers, the tendency of national prices to move in unison is an *effect* of, rather than a justification for, maintaining separate national currency systems. And it has led to the growth of national institutions, such as nationwide collective bargaining, which have intensified these differences. The reason for this development is that the control over the supply of money gives national governments more power over actions which are wholly undesirable from the point of view of international order and stability. It is the kind of arrangement of which only *ètatists* of various complexions can approve but which is wholly inimical to frictionless international relations.

There is indeed little reason why, apart from the effects of monopolies made possible by national protection, territories that happen to be under the same government should form distinct national economic areas which would benefit by having a common currency distinct from that of other areas. In an order largely dependent on international exchange, it was rather absurd to treat the often accidental agglomeration of different regions under the same government as a distinct economic area. The recognition of this truth has however only recently led a few economists to ask what would be desirable currency areas—a question they found rather difficult to answer.[88]

[88]Ronald I. McKinnon, "Optimum Currency Areas", *American Economic Review,* September 1963, pp. 717–725, and Robert A. Mundell, "A Theory of Optimum Currency Areas", *American Economic Review,* September 1961, pp. 657–665.

While historically distinct national currencies were simply an instrument to enhance the power of national governments, the modern argument for monetary nationalism favours an arrangement under which *all* prices in a region can simultaneously be raised or lowered *relatively* to *all* prices in other regions. This is regarded as an advantage because it avoids the necessity to lower a group of particular prices, especially wages, when foreign demand for the products concerned has fallen and shifted to some other national region. But it is a political makeshift; in practice it means that, instead of lowering the *few* prices immediately affected, a very much *larger* number of prices will have to be raised to restore international equilibrium after the international price of the local currency has been reduced. The original motive for the agitation for flexible rates of exchange between national currencies was therefore purely inflationist, although a foolish attempt was made to place the burden of adjustment on the surplus countries. But it was later also taken up in countries which wanted to protect themselves against the effects of the inflationist policies of others.

There is no better case for preventing the decrease of the quantity of money circulating in a region or sector of a larger community than there is for governmental measures to prevent a decrease of the money incomes of particular individuals or groups—even though such measures might temporarily relieve the hardships of the groups living there. It is even essential for honest government that nobody should have the power of relieving groups from the necessity of having to adapt themselves to unforeseen changes, because, if government can do so, it will be forced by political necessity to do so all the time.

Rigidity of Wage-Rates: Raising National Price Structure Is No Solution

Experience has shown that what was believed to be the easy way out from the difficulties created by the rigidity of wages, namely, raising the *whole* national price level, is merely making matters worse, since in effect it relieves trade unions of the responsibility for the unemployment their wage demands would otherwise cause and creates an irresistible pressure on governments to mitigate these effects by inflation. I remain therefore as opposed to monetary nationalism[89] or flexible rates of exchange between national currencies as ever. But I prefer now abolishing monetary frontiers altogether to merely making national currencies convertible into each other at a fixed rate. The whole conception of cutting out a particular sector from the international structure of prices and lifting or lowering

[89]The historical origin of the preoccupation with national price levels as well as the other aspects of *Monetary Nationalism* were discussed in my book with that title [this volume, chapter 1. —Ed.].

it, as it were, bodily against all the other prices of the same commodities still seems to me an idea that could be conceived only in the brains of men who have come to think exclusively in terms of national ('macro') price levels, not of individual ('micro') prices. They seem to have thought of national price levels as the acting determinants of human action and to have ceased to understand the function of relative prices.

Stable National Price Level Could Disrupt Economic Activity

There is really no reason why we should want the price level of a region interconnected by a large number of commodity streams with the rest of the world economy to have a stable price level. To keep this price level stable in spite of shifts of demand towards or away from the region only disturbs and does not assist the functioning of the market. The relation between regions or localities is in this respect not essentially different from the relations between countries. The transfer of demand for airplanes from Seattle to Los Angeles will indeed lead to a loss of jobs and a decline of incomes and probably of retail prices in Seattle; and if there is a fall in wages in Seattle, it will probably attract other industries. But nothing would be gained, except perhaps for the moment, by increasing the quantity of money in Seattle or the State of Washington. And it would not ease the problem if the whole Northwest of the United States had a currency of its own which it could keep constant or even increase to meet such a misfortune for some of its inhabitants.

But while we have no foundations for desiring particular areas to have their individual currencies, it is of course an altogether different question whether the free issue of competitive currencies in each area would lead to the formation of currency areas—or rather of areas where different currencies were predominant, although others could be used. As we have seen (Section XII), there might develop different preferences as regard the commodity equivalent of the currency that should be kept constant. In a primitive country where people used little but rice, fish, pork, cotton, and timber, they would be chiefly concerned about different prices—though local tendencies of this sort would probably be offset by those of the users to be guided in their preferences by the greater trust they had in an internationally reputed issuer of money than in one who adapted his currency specially to local circumstances. Nor would I be surprised to find that in large areas only one currency was generally used in ordinary dealings, so long as potential competition made its issuer keep it stable. As everywhere else, so long as it does not come to trying out innovations or improvements, competition *in posse*[90] is likely to be nearly as effective

[90][*In posse:* potential; *in esse:* in being. —Ed.]

as competition *in esse*. And the ready convertibility of the generally used currency would make all those who had any traffic beyond the region change their holdings quickly enough into another currency if their suspicions about the commonly accepted one were aroused.

Such areas in which one currency predominates would however not have sharp or fixed boundaries but would largely overlap, and their dividing lines would fluctuate. But once the principle were generally accepted in the economically leading countries, it would probably spread rapidly to wherever people could choose their institutions. No doubt there would remain enclaves under dictators who did not wish to let go their power over money—even after the absence of exchange control had become the mark of a civilized and honest country.

XXI. The Effects on Government Finance and Expenditure

The two goals of public finance and of the regulation of a satisfactory currency are entirely different from, and largely in conflict with, each other. To place both tasks in the hands of the same agency has in consequence always led to confusion and in recent years has had disastrous consequences. It has not only made money the chief cause of economic fluctuations but has also greatly facilitated an uncontrollable growth of public expenditure. If we are to preserve a functioning market economy (and with it individual freedom), *nothing can be more urgent than that we dissolve the unholy marriage between monetary and fiscal policy,* long clandestine but formally consecrated with the victory of 'Keynesian' economics.

We need not say much more about the unfortunate effects of the 'needs' of finance on the supply of money. Not only have all major inflations until recently been the result of governments covering their financial 'needs' by the printing press, but even during relatively stable periods the regular necessity for central banks to accommodate the financial 'needs' of government by keeping interest rates low has been a constant embarrassment: It has interfered with the banks' efforts to secure stability and has given their policies an inflationist bias that was usually checked only belatedly by the mechanism of the gold standard.

Good National Money Impossible under Democratic Government Dependent on Special Interests

I do not think it an exaggeration to say that it is wholly impossible for a central bank subject to political control, or even exposed to serious political pressure, to regulate the quantity of money in a way conducive to a smoothly functioning market order. A good money, like good law, must operate without regard to the effects that decisions of the issuer will have on known groups or individuals. A benevolent dictator might conceivably disregard these effects; no democratic government dependent on a number of special interests can possibly do so. But to use the control of the supply of money as an instrument for achieving particular ends destroys the equilibrating operation of the price mechanism, which is required to maintain the continuing process of ordering the market that gives individuals a good chance of having their expectations fulfilled.

Government Monopoly of Money and Government Expenditure

But we have probably said enough about the harm that monetary policy guided by financial considerations is likely to do. What we must still consider is the effect that power over the supply of money has had on financial policy. Just as the absence of competition has prevented the monopolist supplier of money from being subject to a salutary discipline, the power over money has also relieved governments of the necessity to keep their expenditure within their revenue. It is largely for this reason that Keynesian economics has become so rapidly popular among socialist economists. Indeed, since ministers of finance were told by economists that running a deficit was a meritorious act, and even that, so long as there were unemployed resources, extra government expenditure cost the people nothing, any effective bar to a rapid increase in government expenditure was destroyed.

There can be little doubt that the spectacular increase in government expenditure over the last 30 years, with governments in some Western countries claiming up to half or more of the national income for collective purposes, was made possible by government control of the issue of money. On the one hand, inflation has constantly pushed people with a given real income into much higher tax brackets than they anticipated when they approved the rates, and thus raised government revenue more rapidly than they had intended. On the other, the habitual large deficits, and the comparative ease with which budgeted figures could be exceeded, still further increased the share of the real output governments were able to claim for their purposes.

Government Money and Unbalanced Budgets

In a sense it is arbitrary to require governments to balance their budget for the calendar year. But the alternations of the seasons and the firmly established business practices of accounting provide a good reason; and the practice of business, where receipts and expenditure are regularly balanced over a period with known fluctuations, further supports the usage. If major economic fluctuations can be prevented by other arrangements, the conventional annual budget is still the best term for requiring such balancing. Assuming it to be true that the regulation of the supply of money by competition between private currencies would secure not only a stable value of money but also stable business conditions, the argument that government deficits are necessary to reduce unemployment amounts to the contention that a government control of money is needed to cure what it is itself causing. There is no reason why, with a stable money, it should ever be desirable to allow government to spend more than it has. And it is certainly more important that government expenditure does not become a cause of general instability than that the clumsy apparatus of government should (in the most unlikely event that it acts in time) be available to mitigate any slackening of economic activity.

The ease with which a minister of finance can today both budget for an excess of expenditure over revenue and exceed that expenditure has created a wholly new style of finance compared with the careful housekeeping of the past. And since the ease with which one demand after another is conceded evokes ever new expectations of further bounty, the process is a self-accelerating one which even men who genuinely wish to avoid it find it impossible to stop. Anyone who knows the difficulty of restraining a bureaucratic apparatus not controlled by profit-and-loss calculations from constantly expanding also knows that without the rigid barrier of strictly limited funds there is nothing to stop an indefinite growth of government expenditure.

Unless we restore a situation in which governments (and other public authorities) find that if they overspend they will, like everybody else, be unable to meet their obligations, there will be no halt to this growth which, by substituting collective for private activity, threatens to suffocate individual initiative. Under the prevailing form of unlimited democracy, in which government has power to confer special material benefits on groups, it is forced to buy the support of sufficient numbers to add up to a majority. Even with the best will in the world, no government can resist this pressure unless it can point to a firm barrier it cannot cross. While governments will of course occasionally be forced to borrow from the public to meet unforeseen requirements, or choose to finance some investments in that manner, it is highly undesirable in any circumstances that these funds should be provided by the creation of additional money. Nor is it desirable that those additions to the total quantity of money which are required in a growing economy to equip the suppliers of additional factors of production with the needed cash balances should be introduced into circulation in this manner.

Government Power over Money Facilitates Centralization

There can be little doubt also that the ability of central governments to resort to this kind of finance is one of the contributory causes of the advance in the most undesirable centralization of government. Nothing can be more welcome than depriving government of its power over money and so stopping the apparently irresistible trend towards an accelerating increase of the share of the national income it is able to claim. If allowed to continue, this trend would in a few years bring us to a state in which governments would claim 100 per cent (in Sweden and Britain it already exceeds 60 per cent) of all resources—and would in consequence become literally 'totalitarian'.[91] The more completely public finance can be separated from the regulation of the monetary circulation, the better it will be. It is a power which always has been harmful. Its use for financial purposes is always an abuse. And government has neither the *interest* nor the *capacity* to exercise it in the manner required to secure the smooth flow of economic effort.

The suggestion of depriving government of the monopoly of issuing money and of its power of making any money 'legal tender' for all existing debts has been made here in the first instance because governments have invariably and inevitably grossly abused that power throughout the whole of history and thereby gravely disturbed the self-steering mechanism of the market. But it may turn out that cutting off government from the tap which supplies it with additional money for its use may prove as important in order to stop the inherent tendency of unlimited government to grow indefinitely, which is becoming as menacing a danger to the future of civilization as the badness of the money it has supplied. Only if people are made to perceive that they must pay in undisguised taxes (or voluntarily lend) all the money government can spend can the process of buying majority support by granting special benefits to ever-increasing numbers with particular interests be brought to a stop.

XXII. Problems of Transition

For the vast majority of people the appearance of several concurrent currencies would merely offer them alternatives; it would not make necessary any change in their habitual use of money. Experience would gradually teach them how to improve their position by switching to other kinds of money. Retail merchants would soon be offered by the banks the appropriate calculating equipment which would relieve them of any initial difficulties in management or accounting. Since the issuer of the money they used would be interested in supplying assistance, they would prob-

[91]One alarming feature, the threat of which is not yet sufficiently appreciated, is the spreading tendency to regard a government pension as the *only* trustworthy provision for one's old age, because experience seems to demonstrate that political expedience will force governments to maintain or even to increase its real value.

ably discover they were better served than before. In manufacture, trade, and the service industries, learning to take full advantage of the new opportunities might take a little longer, but there would be no important necessary changes in the conduct of business or unavoidably difficult adaptations.

Preventing Rapid Depreciation of Formerly Exclusive Currency

The two activities that would be most profoundly affected, and in which an almost complete change of habitual practices and routines would be required, are public finance and the whole range of private finance, including banking, insurance, building societies, saving and mortgage banks as well. For government, apart from the changes in financial policy mentioned in Section XXI, the chief task would be to guard against a rapid displacement and consequent accelerating depreciation of the currency issued by the existing central bank. This could probably be achieved only by instantly giving it complete freedom and independence, putting it thus on the same footing with all other issue banks, foreign or newly created at home, coupled with a simultaneous return to a policy of balanced budgets, limited only by the possibility of borrowing on an open loan market which they could not manipulate. The urgency of these steps derives from the fact that, once the displacement of the hitherto exclusive currency by new currencies had commenced, it would be rapidly speeded up by an accelerating depreciation that would be practically impossible to stop by any of the ordinary methods of contracting the circulation. Neither the government nor the former central banks would possess the reserves of other currencies or of gold to redeem all the old money the public would want to get rid of as soon as it could change from a rapidly depreciating currency to one it had reason to believe would remain stable. It could be brought to trust such a currency only if the bank issuing it demonstrated a capacity to regulate it in precisely the same manner as the new issue banks competing with it.

Introduce New Currencies at Once, Not Gradually

The other important requirement of government action, if the transition to the new order is to be successful, is that all the required liberties be conceded at once, and no tentative and timid attempt be made to introduce the new order gradually, or to reserve powers of control 'in case anything goes wrong'. The possibility of free competition between a multiplicity of issuing institutions and the complete freedom of all movements of currency and capital across frontiers are equally essential to the success of the scheme. Any hesitant approach by a *gradual* relaxation of the existing monopoly of issue would be certain to make it fail. People would learn to trust the new money only if they were confident it was completely exempt from any government control. Only because they were under the sharp control of competition could the private banks be trusted to keep their money stable. Only because people could freely choose which currency to use for their different purposes would the process of selection lead to the good money prevailing. Only because there was active trading on the currency exchange would the issuing banks be warned to take the required action in time. Only because the frontiers were open to the movement of currency and capital would there be assurance of no collusion between local institutions to mismanage the local currency. And only because there were free commodity markets would stable average prices mean that the process of adapting supply to demand was functioning.

Commercial Bank Change in Policy

If the government succeeded in handing over the business of supplying money to private institutions without the existing currency collapsing, the chief problem for the individual commercial banks would be to decide whether to try and establish their own currency, or to select the other currency or currencies in which they would in future conduct their business. The great majority clearly would have to be content to do their business in other currencies. They would thus (Sections XI and XII) have to practise a kind of '100 per cent banking', and keep a full reserve against all their obligations payable on demand.

This necessity would probably prove the most far-reaching change in business practice required by competing currencies. Since these banks presumably would have to charge substantially for running chequing accounts, they would lose that business largely to the issuing banks and be reduced to the administration of less liquid kinds of capital assets.

So long as this change could be effected by a deliberate transition to the use of a currency of their choice, it might prove somewhat painful but not raise unmanageable problems. And to do away with banks which, in effect, create currency without bearing any responsibility for the results has been for more than a hundred years the desideratum of economists who perceived the inherent instability of the mechanism into which we had drifted but who usually saw no hope of ever getting out of it. An institution which has proved as harmful as fractional reserve banking without responsibility of the individual bank for the money (i.e., cheque deposits) it created cannot complain if the support by a government monopoly that has made its existence possible is withdrawn. There will certainly also have to develop generally a much sharper distinction between pure banking and the investment business, or between what used to be regarded as the English and the Continental types of banks (*Depositenbanken* and *Spekulationsbanken* as these types were once described in German). I expect that it will soon be discovered that the business of creating money does not go along well with the control of large investment portfolios or even control of large parts of industry.

A wholly different set of difficulties would of course arise if the government or its privileged bank did not succeed in preventing a collapse of its currency. This would be a possibility which the banks not able to issue their own currency would rightly fear, since a large part of their assets, namely all their loans, would dwindle away with most of their liabilities. But this would merely mean that the danger of a high inflation, of the kind that now always threatens and that others might avoid by shifting to other currencies, would for them become particularly threatening. But banks have usually claimed that they have more or less succeeded in bringing their assets through even a galloping inflation. Bankers who do not know how to do it might perhaps consult their colleagues in Chile and elsewhere where they have had plenty of experience with this problem. At any rate, to get rid of the present unstable structure is too important a task for it to be sacrificed to the interests of some special groups.

XXIII. Protection against the State

Though under the proposed arrangement the normal provision of money would be entirely a function of private enterprise, the chief danger to its smooth working would still be interference by the state.[92] If the international character of the issuing business should largely protect the issuing banks against direct political pressure (though it would certainly invite attacks by demagogues), the trust in any one institution would still largely depend on the trust in the government under which it was established. To obviate the suspicion of serving the political interests of the country in which they were established, it would clearly be important that banks with headquarters in different countries should compete with one another. The greatest confidence, at least so long as peace was regarded as assured, would probably be placed in institutions established in small

[92] I use here for once the term 'state' because it is the expression which in the context would be commonly used by most people who would wish to emphasize the probability of the beneficial nature of these public activities. Most people rapidly become aware of the idealistic and unrealistic nature of their argument if it is pointed out to them that the agent who acts is never an abstract state but always a very concrete government with all the defects necessarily inherent in this kind of political institution.

wealthy countries for which international business was an important source of income and that would therefore be expected to be particularly careful of their reputation for financial soundness.

Pressures for Return to National Monetary Monopolies

Many countries would probably try, by subsidies or similar measures, to preserve a locally established bank issuing a distinct national currency that would be available side by side with the international currencies, even if they were only moderately successful. There would then be some danger that the nationalist and socialist forces active in a silly agitation against multinational corporations would lead governments, by advantages conceded to the national institution, to bring about a gradual return to the present system of privileged national issuers of currency.

Recurring Governmental Control of Currency and Capital Movements

The chief danger, however, would threaten from renewed attempts by governments to control the international movements of currency and capital. It is a power which at present is the most serious threat not only to a working international economy but also to personal freedom; and it will remain a threat so long as governments have the physical power to enforce such controls. It is to be hoped that people will gradually recognize this threat to their personal freedom and that they will make the complete prohibition of such measures an entrenched constitutional provision. The ultimate protection against the tyranny of government is that at least a large number of able people can emigrate when they can no longer stand it. I fear that few Englishmen, most of whom thought the statement which I now repeat unduly alarmist and exaggerated when I published it more than 30 years ago, will still feel so:

> The extent of the control over all life that economic control confers is nowhere better illustrated than in the field of foreign exchanges. Nothing would at first seem to affect private life less than a state control of the dealings in foreign exchange, and most people will regard its introduction with complete indifference. Yet the experience of most continental countries has taught thoughtful people to regard this step as the decisive advance on the path to totalitarianism and the suppression of individual liberty. It is in fact the complete delivery of the individual to the tyranny of the state, the final suppression of all means of escape—not merely for the rich, but for everybody. Once the individual is no longer free to travel, no longer free to buy foreign books or journals, once all means of foreign contact can be restricted to those whom official opinion approves or for whom it is regarded as necessary, the effective

> control of opinion is much greater than that ever exercised by any of the absolutist governments of the seventeenth and eighteenth centuries.[93]

Next to the barrier to the excessive growth of government expenditure, the second fundamental contribution to the protection of individual freedom which the abolition of the government monopoly of issuing money would secure would probably be the intertwining of international affairs, which would make it more and more impossible for government to control international movements, and thus safeguard the ability of dissidents to escape the oppression of a government with which they profoundly disagreed.

XXIV. The Long-Run Prospects

A hope one may cherish is that, as competition usually does, it will lead to the discovery of yet unknown possibilities in currency. This makes any attempt at prediction of the long-run effects of the proposed reform exceedingly hazardous, but we will attempt to summarize briefly what would appear to be the probable long-run developments if it were adopted.

I believe that, once the system had fully established itself and competition had eliminated a number of unsuccessful ventures, there would remain in the free world several extensively used and very similar currencies. In various large regions one or two of them would be dominant, but these regions would have no sharp or constant boundaries, and the use of the currencies dominant in them would overlap in broad and fluctuating border districts. Most of these currencies, based on similar collections of commodities, would in the short run fluctuate very little in terms of one another, probably much less than the currencies of the most stable countries today, yet somewhat more than currencies based on a true gold standard. If the composition of the commodity basket on which they are based were adapted to the conditions of the region in which they are mainly used, they might slowly drift apart. But most of them would thus *concur,* not only in the sense of running side by side, but also in the sense of agreeing with one another in the movements of their values.

After the experimental process of finding the most favoured collection of commodities to the price of which the currency was to be tied, further changes would probably be rare and minor. Competition between the issuing banks would concentrate on the avoidance of even minor fluctuations of their value in terms of these commodities, the degree of informa-

[93] F. A. Hayek, *The Road to Serfdom* (Chicago: University of Chicago Press, and London: Routledge, 1944), p. 69n.

tion provided about their activities, and various additional services (such as assistance in accounting) offered to their customers. The currencies issued by any surviving government banks would often themselves be driven more and more to accept and even to seek payment in currencies other than those issued by a favoured national institution.

The Possibility of a Multiplicity of Similar Currencies

There exists, however, a possibility or even probability I did not consider in the First Edition. After certain currencies based on a particular batch of commodities have become widely accepted, many other banks might, under different names, issue currencies the value of which was based on the same collection of commodities as the one successful first, either in the same or smaller or larger units. In other words, competition might lead to the extensive use of the same commodity base by a large number of issue banks that would still compete for the favour of the public through the constancy of the value of their issues or other services they offer. The public might then learn to accept a considerable number of such moneys with different names (but all described as, say, of 'Zurich Standard') at constant rates of exchange; and shops might post lists of all the currencies which they were prepared to accept as representing that standard. So long as the press properly exercised its supervisory function and warned the public in time of any dereliction of duty on the part of some issuers, such a system might satisfactorily serve for a long time.

Considerations of convenience would probably also lead to the adoption of a standard unit, i.e., based not only on the same collection of commodities but also of the same magnitude. In this case most banks could issue, under distinct names, notes for these standard units which would be readily accepted locally as far as the reputation of the individual bank extended.

The Preservation of a Standard of Long-Term Debts Even While Currencies May Lose Their Value

With the availability of at least some stable currencies the absurd practice of making 'legal tender' a mere token which may become valueless but still remain effective for the discharge of debts contracted in what had been an object of a certain value is bound to disappear. It was solely the power of government to force upon people what they had not meant in their contracts which produced this absurdity. With the abolition of the government monopoly of issuing money, the courts will soon understand, and, I trust, statute law recognize, that justice requires debts to be paid in terms of the units of value which the parties to the contracts intended and not in what government says is a substitute for them. (The exception is where the contract explicitly provides for a stated number of tokens rather than for a value expressed in terms of an amount of tokens.)

After the development of a widely preferred common standard of value the courts would in most cases have no difficulty in determining the approximate magnitude of the abstract value intended by the parties to a contract for the value of such-and-such an amount of a widely accepted unit of currency. If one currency in terms of the value of which a contract had been concluded seriously depreciated beyond a reasonable range of fluctuation, a court would not allow the parties to gain or lose from the malpractice of the third party that issued the currency. They would without difficulty be able to determine the amount of some other currency or currencies with which the debtor was entitled and obliged to discharge his obligation.

As a result, even the complete collapse of one currency would not have the disastrous far-reaching consequences which a similar event has today. Though the holders of cash, either in the form of notes or demand deposits in a particular currency, might lose their whole value, this would be a relatively minor disturbance compared with the general shrinkage or wiping out of all claims to third persons expressed in that currency. The whole structure of long-term contracts would remain unaffected, and people would preserve their investments in bonds, mortgages, and similar forms of claims, even though they might lose all their cash if they were unfortunate to use the currency of a bank that failed. A portfolio of bonds and other long-term claims might still be a very safe investment even if it happened that some issuers of currency became insolvent and their notes and deposits valueless. Completely liquid assets would still involve a risk—but who wants, except perhaps temporarily, to keep all his assets in a very liquid form? There could never occur that complete disappearance of any common standard of debts or such a wiping out of all monetary obligations as has been the final effect of all major inflations. Long before this could happen, everybody would have deserted the depreciated unit and no old obligation could be discharged in terms of it.

New Legal Framework for Banking

While governments should not interfere in this development by any conscious attempts at control (i.e., any acts of intervention in the strict sense of the term), it may be found that new rules of law are needed to provide an appropriate legal framework within which the new banking practices could successfully develop. It would, however, seem rather doubtful whether it would assist developments if such rules were at once made generally applicable by international treaties and experimentation with alternative arrangements thereby provided.

How long it would take for some countries no longer to desire to have a currency of their own for purely nationalistic or prestige reasons, and for governments to stop misleading the public by complaining about an undue restriction of their sovereign power, is difficult to say.[94] The whole system is of course wholly irreconcilable with any striving for totalitarian powers of any sort.

XXV. Conclusions

The abolition of the government monopoly of money was conceived to prevent the bouts of acute inflation and deflation which have plagued the world for the past 60 years. It proves on examination to be also the much-needed cure for a more deep-seated disease: the recurrent waves of depression and unemployment that have been represented as an inherent and deadly defect of capitalism.

Gold Standard Not the Solution

One might hope to prevent the violent fluctuations in the value of money in recent years by returning to the gold standard or some regime of fixed exchanges. I still believe that, *so long as the management of money is in the hands of government,* the gold standard with all its imperfections is the only tolerably safe system. But we certainly can do better than that, though not through government. Quite apart from the undeniable truth that the gold standard also has serious defects, the opponents of such a move can properly point out that a central direction of the quantity of money is in the present circumstances necessary to counteract the inherent instability of the existing credit system. But once it is recognized that this inherent instability of credit is itself the effect of the structure of deposit banking determined by the monopolistic control of the supply of the hand-to-hand money in which the deposits must be redeemed, these objections fall to the ground. If we want free enterprise and a market economy to survive (as even the supporters of a so-called 'mixed economy' presumably also wish), we have no choice but to replace the governmental currency monopoly and national currency systems by free competition between private banks of issue. We have never had the control of money in the hands of agencies whose *sole* and *exclusive* concern was to give the public what currency it liked best among several kinds offered, and which at the same time staked their existence on fulfilling the expectations they had created.

It may be that, with free competition between different kinds of money,

[94]Indeed it would be the day of final triumph of the new system when governments began to prefer to receive taxes in currencies other than those they issue!

gold coins might at first prove to be the most popular. But this very fact, the increasing demand for gold, would probably lead to such a rise (and perhaps also violent fluctuations) of the price of gold that, though it might still be widely used for hoarding, it would soon cease to be convenient as the unit for business transactions and accounting. There should certainly be the same freedom for its use, but I should not expect this to lead to its victory over other forms of privately issued money, the demand for which rested on its quantity being successfully regulated so as to keep its purchasing power constant.

The very same fact which at present makes gold more trusted than government-controlled paper money, namely that its total quantity cannot be manipulated at will in the service of political aims, would in the long run make it appear inferior to token money used by competing institutions whose business rested on successfully so regulating the quantity of their issues as to keep the value of the units approximately constant.

Good Money Can Come Only from Self-Interest, Not from Benevolence

We have always had bad money because private enterprise was not permitted to give us a better one. In a world governed by the pressure of organized interests, the important truth to keep in mind is that we cannot count on intelligence or understanding but only on sheer self-interest to give us the institutions we need. Blessed indeed will be the day when it will no longer be from the benevolence of the government that we expect good money but from the regard of the banks for their own interest. "It is in this manner that we obtain from one another the far greater part of those good offices we stand in need of"[95]—but unfortunately not yet a money that we can rely upon.

It was not 'capitalism' but government intervention which has been responsible for the recurrent crises of the past, a theme repeatedly argued by the late Ludwig von Mises. Government has prevented enterprise from equipping itself with the instruments that it required to protect itself against its efforts being misdirected by an unreliable money and that it would be both profitable for the supplier and beneficial to all others to develop. The recognition of this truth makes it clear that the reform proposed is not a minor technicality of finance but a crucial issue which may decide the fate of free civilization. What is proposed here seems to me the only discernible way of completing the market order and freeing it from its main defect and the cause of the chief reproaches directed against it.

[95]Adam Smith, *The Wealth of Nations,* op. cit., p. 26.

Is Competitive Paper Currency Practicable?

We cannot, of course, hope for such a reform before the public understands what is at stake and what it has to gain. But those who think the whole proposal wholly impracticable and utopian should remember that 200 years ago in *The Wealth of Nations* Adam Smith wrote that, "to expect, indeed, that the freedom of trade should ever be entirely restored in Great Britain, is as absurd as to expect that an Oceana or Utopia should ever be established in it."[96] It took nearly 90 years from the publication of his work in 1776 until Great Britain became the first country to establish complete free trade in 1860. But the idea caught on rapidly; and if it had not been for the political reaction caused by the French Revolution and the Napoleonic Wars no doubt it would have taken effect much sooner. It was not until 1819 that an effective movement to educate the general public on these matters started and it was in the end due to the devoted efforts of a few men who dedicated themselves to spread the message by an organized Free Trade Movement that what Smith had called "the insolent outrage of furious and disappointed monopolists" was overcome.[97,98]

I fear that since 'Keynesian' propaganda has filtered through to the masses, has made inflation respectable and provided agitators with arguments which the professional politicians are unable to refute, the only way to avoid being driven by continuing inflation into a controlled and directed economy, and therefore ultimately in order to save civilization, will be to deprive governments of their power over the supply of money.[99]

[96]Adam Smith, op. cit., p. 471. The whole paragraph beginning with the sentence quoted and concluding with the phrase cited further on is well worth reading in the present connection.

[97]As John Porteous, a reviewer of the first edition of this essay, sensibly observed: "It would have seemed unthinkable 400 years ago that governments would ever relinquish control over religious belief" (*New Statesman*, January 14, 1977).

[98]It has been said that my suggestion to "construct" wholly new monetary institutions is in conflict with my general philosophical attitude. But nothing is further from my thoughts than any wish to design new institutions. What I propose is simply to remove the existing obstacles which for ages have prevented the evolution of desirable institutions in money.

[99]Recent experience also suggests that in future governments may find themselves exposed to international pressure to pursue monetary policies which, while harmful to their own citizens, are supposed to help some other country, and will be able to escape such pressure only by divesting themselves both of the power and the responsibility of controlling the supply of money. We have already reached a stage in which countries which have succeeded in reducing the annual rate of *inflation* to 5 per cent are exhorted by others who lustily continue to inflate at 15 per cent per annum to assist them by 'reflation'.

'Free Money Movement'

What we now need is a Free Money Movement comparable to the Free Trade Movement of the nineteenth century, demonstrating not merely the harm caused by acute inflation, which could justifiably be argued to be avoidable even with present institutions, but the deeper effects of producing periods of stagnation that are indeed inherent in the present monetary arrangements.

The alarm about current inflation is, as I can observe as I write, only too quickly dispelled whenever the rate of inflation slows down only a little. I have not much doubt that, by the time these lines appear in print, there will be ample cause for a renewal of this alarm (unless, which would be even worse, the resumed inflation is concealed by price controls). Probably even the new inflationary boom already initiated will again have collapsed. But it will need deeper insight into the superficially invisible effects of inflation to produce the result required to achieve the abolition of the harmful powers of government on the control of money. There is thus an immense educational task ahead before we can hope to free ourselves from the gravest threat to social peace and continued prosperity inherent in existing monetary institutions.

It will be necessary that the problem and the urgent need of reform come to be widely understood. The issue is not one which, as may at first appear to the layman, concerns a minor technicality of the financial system which he has never quite understood. It refers to the one way in which we may still hope to stop the continuous progress of all government towards totalitarianism which already appears to many acute observers as inevitable. I wish I could advise that we proceed slowly. But the time may be short. What is now urgently required is not the construction of a new system but the prompt removal of all the legal obstacles which have for two thousand years blocked the way for an evolution which is bound to throw up beneficial results which we cannot now foresee.

FIVE

TOWARD A FREE MARKET MONETARY SYSTEM[1]

When a little over two years ago, at the second Lausanne Conference of this group, I threw out, almost as a sort of bitter joke, that there was no hope of ever again having decent money, unless we took from government the monopoly of issuing money and handed it over to private industry, I took it only half seriously. But the suggestion proved extraordinarily fertile. Following it up I discovered that I had opened a possibility which in two thousand years no single economist had ever studied. There were quite a number of people who have since taken it up and we have devoted a great deal of study and analysis to this possibility. As a result I am more convinced than ever that if we ever again are going to have a decent money, it will not come from government: It will be issued by private enterprise, because providing the public with good money which it can trust and use can not only be an extremely profitable business; it imposes on the issuer a discipline to which the government has never been and cannot be subject. It is a business which competing enterprise can maintain only if it gives the public as good a money as anybody else. Now, fully to understand this, we must free ourselves from what is a widespread but basically wrong belief. Under the Gold Standard, or any other metallic standard, the value of money is not really derived from gold. The fact is that the necessity of redeeming the money they issue in gold places upon the issuers a discipline which forces them to control the quantity of money in an appropriate manner; I think it is quite as legitimate to say that under a gold standard it is the demand of gold for monetary purposes which determines that value of gold, as the common belief that the value which gold has in other uses determines the value of money. The gold standard is the only method we have yet found to place a discipline on the government, and government will behave reasonably only if it is forced to do so.

[1][A lecture delivered at the Gold and Monetary Conference, New Orleans, La., November 10, 1977. First printed in the *Journal of Libertarian Studies* (Burlingame, Ca.: Center for Libertarian Studies), vol. 3, no. 1 (spring 1979), pp. 1–8. —Ed.]

I am afraid I am convinced that the hope of ever again placing on government this discipline is gone. The public at large have learned to understand, and I am afraid a whole generation of economists have been teaching, that government has the power in the short run by increasing the quantity of money rapidly to relieve all kinds of economic evils, especially to reduce unemployment. Unfortunately this is true so far as the short run is concerned. The fact is that such expansions of the quantity of money which seems to have a short-run beneficial effect become in the long run the cause of a much greater unemployment. But what politician can possibly care about long run effects if in the short run he buys support?

My conviction is that the hope of returning to the kind of gold standard systems which has worked fairly well over a long period is absolutely vain. Even if, by some international treaty, the gold standard were reintroduced, there is not the slightest hope that governments will play the game according to the rules. And the gold standard is not a thing which you can restore by an act of legislation. The gold standard requires a constant observation by government of certain rules which include an occasional restriction of the total circulation which will cause local or national recession, and no government can nowadays do it when both the public and, I am afraid, all those Keynesian economists who have been trained in the last thirty years, will argue that it is more important to increase the quantity of money than to maintain the gold standard.

I have said that it is an erroneous belief that the value of gold or any metallic basis determines directly the value of the money. The gold standard is a mechanism which was intended and for a long time did successfully force governments to control the quantity of the money in an appropriate manner so as to keep its value equal with that of gold. But there are many historical instances which prove that it is certainly possible, if it is in the self-interest of the issuer, to control the quantity even of a token money in such a manner as to keep its value constant.

There are three such interesting historical instances which illustrate this and which in fact were very largely responsible for teaching the economists that the essential point was ultimately the appropriate control of the quantity of money and not its redeemability into something else, which was necessary only to force governments to control the quantity of money appropriately. This I think will be done more effectively not if some legal rule forces government, but if it is the self-interest of the issuer which makes him do it, because he can keep his business only if he gives the people a stable money.

Let me tell you in a very few words of these important historical instances. The first two I shall mention do not refer directly to the gold standard as we know it. They occurred when large parts of the world were still on a silver standard and when in the second half of the last century silver suddenly began to lose its value. The fall in the value of silver brought about a fall in various national currencies and on two occasions an interesting step was taken. The first, which produced the experience which I believe inspired the Austrian monetary theory, happened in my native country in 1879. The government happened to have a really good adviser on monetary policy, Carl Menger, and he told them, "Well, if you want to escape the effect of the depreciation of silver on your currency, stop the free coinage of silver, stop increasing the quantity of silver coin, and you will find that the silver coin will begin to rise above the value of their content in silver". And this the Austrian government did and the result was exactly what Menger had predicted. One began to speak about the Austrian *Gulden,* which was then the unit in circulation, as banknotes printed on silver, because the actual coins in circulation had become a token money containing much less value than corresponded to its value. As silver declined, the value of the silver *Gulden* was controlled entirely by the limitation of the quantity of the coin.

Exactly the same was done fourteen years later by British India. It also had had a silver standard, and the depreciation of silver brought the rupee down lower and lower till the Indian government decided to stop the free coinage; and again the silver coins began to float higher and higher above their silver value. Now, there was at that time neither in Austria nor in India any expectation that ultimately these coins would be redeemed at a particular rate in either silver or gold. The decision about this was made much later, but the development was the perfect demonstration that even a circulating metallic money may derive its value from an effective control of its quantity and not directly from its metallic content.

My third illustration is even more interesting, although the event was more short-lived, because it refers directly to gold. During World War I, the great paper money inflation in all the belligerent countries brought down not only the value of paper money but also the value of gold, because paper money was in large measure substituted for gold, and the demand for gold fell. In consequence, the value of gold fell and prices in gold rose all over the world. That affected even the neutral countries. Particularly Sweden was greatly worried: Because it had stuck to the gold standard, it was flooded by gold from all the rest of the world that moved to Sweden which had retained its gold standard; and Swedish prices rose quite as much as prices in the rest of the world. Now, Sweden also happened to have one or two very good economists at the time, and they repeated the advice which the Austrian economists had given concerning the silver in the 1870s, "Stop the free coinage of gold and the value of your existing gold coins will rise above the value of the gold which it contains". The Swedish government did so in 1916 and what happened was again exactly what the economists had predicted: the value of the gold coins began to float above the value of its gold content and Sweden, for the rest of the war, escaped the effects of the gold inflation.

I quote this only as illustration of what among the economists who understand their subject is now an undoubted fact, namely that the gold standard is a partly effective mechanism to make governments do what they ought to do in their control of money, and the only mechanism which has been tolerably effective in the case of a monopolist who can do with the money whatever he likes. Otherwise gold is not really necessary to secure a good currency. I think it is entirely possible for private enterprise to issue a token money which the public will learn to expect to preserve its value, provided both the issuer and the public understand that the demand for this money will depend on the issuer being forced to keep its value constant; because if he did not do so, the people would at once cease to use his money and shift to some other kind.

I have as a result of throwing out this suggestion at the Lausanne Conference worked out the idea in fairly great detail in a little book which came out a year ago, called *Denationalization of Money*. My thought has developed a great deal since then. I rather hoped to be able to have at this conference a much enlarged second edition available which may already have been brought out in London by the Institute of Economic Affairs, but which unfortunately has not yet reached this country. All I have is the proofs of the additions.

In this second edition I have arrived at one or two rather interesting new conclusions which I did not see at first.[2] In the first exposition in the speech two years ago, I was merely thinking of the effect of the selection of the issuer: that only those financial institutions which so controlled the distinctly named money which they issued, and which provided the public with a money, which was a stable standard of value, an effective unit for calculation in keeping books, would be preserved. I have now come to see that there is a much more complex situation, that there will in fact be two kinds of competition, one leading to the choice of standard which may come to be generally accepted, and one to the selection of the particular institutions which can be trusted in issuing money of that standard.

I do believe that if today all the legal obstacles were removed which prevent such an issue of private money under distinct names, in the first instance indeed, as all of you would expect, people would from their own

[2][Reprinted this volume, chapter 4. —Ed.]

experience be led to rush for the only thing they know and understand, and start using gold. But this very fact would after a while make it very doubtful whether gold was for the purpose of money really a good standard. It would turn out to be a very good investment, for the reason that because of the increased demand for gold the value of gold would go up; but that very fact would make it very unsuitable as money. You do not want to incur debts in terms of a unit which constantly goes up in value as it would in this case, so people would begin to look for another kind of money: if they were free to choose the money, in terms of which they kept their books, made their calculations, incurred debts or lent money, they would prefer a standard which remains stable in purchasing power. I have not got time here to describe in detail what I mean by being stable in purchasing power, but briefly, I mean a kind of money in terms which it is equally likely that the price of any commodity picked out at random will rise as that it will fall. Such a stable standard reduced the risk of unforeseen changes in the prices of particular commodities to a minimum, because with such a standard it is just as likely that any one commodity will rise in price or will fall in price and the mistakes which people at large will make in their anticipations of future prices will just cancel each other because there will be as many mistakes in overestimating as in underestimating. If such a money were issued by some reputable institution, the public would probably first choose different definitions of the standard to be adopted, different kinds of index numbers of price in terms of which it is measured; but the process of competition would gradually teach both the issuing banks and the public which kind of money would be the most advantageous.

The interesting fact is that what I have called the monopoly of government of issuing money has not only deprived us of good money but has also deprived us of the only process by which we can find out what would be good money. We do not even quite know what exact qualities we want because in the two thousand years in which we have used coins and other money, we have never been allowed to experiment with it, we have never been given a chance to find out what the best kind of money would be.

Let me here just insert briefly one observation: In my publications and in my lectures including today's I am speaking constantly about the government monopoly of issuing money. Now, this is legally true in most countries only to a very limited extent. We have indeed given the government, and for fairly good reasons, the exclusive right to issue gold coins. And after we had given the government that right I think it was equally understandable that we also gave the government the control over any money or any claims, paper claims, for coins or money of that definition. That people other than the government are not allowed to issue dollars if the government issues dollars is a perfectly reasonable arrangement, even if it has not turned out to be completely beneficial. And I am not suggesting that the other people should be entitled to issue dollars. All the discussion in the past about free banking was really about this idea that not only the government or government institutions but others should also be able to issue dollar notes. That, of course, would not work. But if private institutions began to issue notes under some other names without any fixed rate of exchange with the official money or each other, so far as I know this is in no major country actually prohibited by law. I think the reason why it has not actually been tried is that of course we know that if anybody attempted it, the government would find so many ways to put obstacles in the way of the use of such money that it could make it impracticable. So long, for instance, as debts in terms of anything but the official dollar cannot be enforced in legal process, it is clearly impracticable. Of course it would have been ridiculous to try to issue any other money if people could not make contracts in terms of it. But this particular obstacle has fortunately been removed now in most countries, so the way ought to be free for the issuing of private money.

If I were responsible for the policy of any one of the great banks in this country, I would begin to offer to the public both loans and current accounts in a unit which I undertook to keep stable in value in terms of a defined index number. I have no doubt, and I believe that most economists agree with me on that particular point, that it is technically possible so to control the value of any token money which is used in competition with other token monies as to fulfill the promise to keep its value stable. The essential point which I can not emphasize strongly enough is that we would get for the first time a money where the whole business of issuing money could be effected only by the issuer issuing good money. He would know that he would at once lose his extremely profitable business if it became known that his money was threatening to depreciate. He would lose it to a competitor who offered better money. As I said before, I believe this is our only hope at the present time. I do not see the slightest prospect that with the present type of, I emphasize, the present type of democratic government under which every little group can force the government to serve its particular needs, government, even if it were restricted by strict law, can ever again give us good money. At present the prospects are really only a choice between two alternatives: either continuing an accelerating open inflation, which is, as you all know, absolutely destructive of an economic system or a market order; but I think much more likely is an even worse alternative: government will not cease inflating, but will, as it has been doing, try to suppress the open effects of this inflation; it will be driven by continual inflation into price controls, into increasing direction of the whole economic system. It is therefore now not merely a question of giving us better money, under which the market system will function infinitely better than it has ever done before, but of warding off the gradual decline into a totalitarian, planned system, which will, at least in this country, not come because anybody wants to introduce it, but will come step by step in an effort to suppress the effect of the inflation which is going on.

I wish I could say that what I propose is a plan for the distant future, that we can wait. There was one very intelligent reviewer of my first booklet who said, "Well, three hundred years ago, nobody would have believed that government would ever give up its control over religion, so perhaps in three hundred years we can see that government will be prepared to give up its control over money". We have not got that much time. We are now facing the likelihood of the most unpleasant political development, largely as a result of an economic policy with which we have already gone very far. My proposal is not, as I would wish, merely a sort of standby arrangement of which I could say we must work it out intellectually to have it ready when the present system completely collapses. It is not merely an emergency plan. I think it is very urgent that it become rapidly understood that there is no justification in history of the existing position of a government monopoly of issuing money. It has never been proposed on the ground that government will give us better money than anybody else could. It has always, since the privilege of issuing money was first explicitly represented as a Royal prerogative, been advocated because the power to issue money was essential for the finance of the government—not in order to give us good money, but in order to give to government access to the tap where it can draw the money it needs by manufacturing it. That, ladies and gentlemen, is not a method by which we can hope ever to get good money. To put it into the hands of an institution which is protected against competition, which can force us to accept the money, which is subject to incessant political pressure, such an authority will not ever again give us good money.

I think we ought to start fairly soon, and I think we must hope that some of the more enterprising and intelligent financiers will soon begin to experiment with such a thing. The great obstacle is that it involves such great changes in the whole financial structure that, and I am saying this from the experience of many discussions, no senior banker, who understands only the present banking system, can really conceive how such a new system would work, and he would not dare to risk an experiment with it. I think we will have to count on a few younger and more flexible brains to begin and show that such a thing can be done.

In fact, it is already being tried in a limited form. As a result of my publication I have received from all kinds of surprising quarters letters from small banking houses, telling me that they are trying to issue gold accounts or silver accounts, and that there is a considerable interest for these. I am afraid they will have to go further, for the reasons I have sketched in the beginning. In the course of such a revolution of our monetary system, the values of the precious metals, including the value of gold, are going to fluctuate a great deal, mostly upwards, and therefore those of you who are interested in it from an investor's point of view need not fear. But those of you who are mainly interested in a good monetary system must hope that in the not too distant future we shall find generally applied another system of control over the monetary circulation, other than the redeemability in gold. The public will have to learn to select among a variety of monies, and to choose those which are good.

If we start on this soon we may indeed achieve a position in which at last capitalism is in a position to provide itself with the money it needs in order to function properly, a thing which it has always been denied. Ever since the development of capitalism it has never been allowed to produce for itself the money it needs; and if I had more time I could show you how the whole crazy structure we have as a result, this monopoly originally only of issuing gold money, is very largely the cause of the great fluctuations in credit, of the great fluctuations in economic activity, and ultimately of the recurring depressions. I think if the capitalists had been allowed to provide themselves with the money which they need, the competitive system would have long overcome the major fluctuations in economic activity and the prolonged periods of depression. At the present moment we have of course been led by official monetary policy into a situation where it has produced so much misdirection of resources that you must not hope for a quick escape from our present difficulties, even if we adopted a new monetary system.

SIX

THE FUTURE UNIT OF VALUE[1]

Twenty-one years ago, few people will have noticed that in a footnote to my *The Constitution of Liberty*[2], I wrote the following:

> Though I am convinced that modern credit banking as it has developed requires some public institutions such as central banks, I am doubtful whether it is necessary or desirable that they (or the government) should have a monopoly of the issue of any kind of money. The state has, of course, the right to protect the name of the unit of money which it (or anybody else) issues, and, if it issues 'dollars', to prevent anybody else from issuing tokens with the same name. As it is its task to enforce contracts, it must also be able to determine what is 'legal tender' for the discharge of any obligation contracted. But there seems to be no reason at all why the state should ever prohibit the use of other kinds of media of exchange, be it some commodity or money issued by another agency, domestic or foreign. One of the most effective measures for protecting the freedom of the individual, might indeed be to have constitutions prohibiting all peacetime restrictions on transactions in any kind of money or precious metals.

The idea seems to have been developing quietly in my mind, and sixteen years later, in growing despair about the continuing deterioration of the monetary situation, I threw out, almost as a bitter joke, the suggestion that, as things were developing, our only hope of ever again having good money probably required that we take from government the monopoly of issuing money and hand this task over to private enterprise. Once seriously examined, this proved to be a more and more attractive idea and finally appeared to me to be the only definite solution of the increasingly hopeless position we were encountering with monetary conditions every-

[1][This section was written from notes and a transcript of the lecture given by F. A. Hayek at the Institutum Europeaum on December 2, 1980, and from a paper delivered by Hayek at the Visa International Annual Conference, Athens, Greece, September 14, 1981. —Ed.]

[2]F. A. Hayek, *The Constitution of Liberty* (London: Routledge & Kegan Paul, 1960), p. 520, note 2.

where. I then systematically expounded the concept in a tract on *The Denationalization of Money,* a second expanded version of which was published in 1978.[3]

1. The Need for a Competitive Monetary System

In advocating the freedom of offering money to the public, I am of the opinion that everybody should be free to offer money of differing denominations to the public. It would be the public which would ultimately decide which of these monies would become generally accepted. The new feature of this proposal becomes clear when one realises that, in the discussions on free banking and the free issue of money, people are really only talking about private institutions issuing, for instance, dollars, pounds, etc. If that were true, they could be rightly accused of creating a situation leading to depreciation of these currencies and inflation. But if private institutions were to create their own currencies, under a distinctive name, the public would immediately recognise with whose currency it is dealing. In a truly competitive situation the issuer of money has to behave in such a way that his money is most attractive to the public and that it suits the public best to hold his money, instead of that of the other issuers.

Another important point is that a private institution which must issue money in competition with others can only remain in business if it provides the people with a stable money which it can trust. The slightest suspicion that the issuer was abusing his position when issuing money would lead to a depreciation of its value and would at once drive him out of business. It would make him lose what might be an extremely profitable kind of business.

The constant danger of losing the customers of one's business is a better disciplining force and will be more effective to maintain the value of money, than anything else. It would operate in such a way that, at the slightest rumor that one money was decreasing in value as compared to other currencies, everybody would try to get rid of the money threatened with depreciation and exchange it for a money which inspires more confidence.

There is no doubt that it will take people some time to adjust themselves to such a new situation, but it is certain that it would not really take very long. When you watch what is happening in a major inflationary period, you see how ingenious people are in finding alternatives to an

[3]F. A. Hayek, *Denationalization of Money,* 2nd edition, revised and extended (London: Institute of Economic Affairs, 1978). [This volume, chapter 3. —Ed.]

inflating currency which they are forced to use. I do not think it would take them long to learn to follow the quotations on the currency markets which would come into being, in order to inform themselves as to which currency they could trust to be a stable money and which not.

It is really extraordinary that, as long as the discussion on money has been going on, everyone has accepted the right of government to provide us with money on an exclusive basis. The creation of a monopoly in the issuance of money is, however, not an obvious solution to the problem of keeping our currencies stable.

If we go back to the first known currencies which were created by government, which occurred in the 6th century BC, we discover that coins of copper and bronze had already served as a means of exchange for at least 2000 years before then. Government issued its money by stamping coins with marks or crowns, or the portrait of their sovereign. I do not know a great deal about the first three or four hundred years of money-issuing by the government, but the governments may have assumed the monopoly of doing this fairly soon. Already in the 4th century BC money was described as the dice of the politicians. Governments prevented the people from searching for the right solutions and experimenting with a process of selection which would have led to continuous improvements. The monopoly prevented a spontaneous formation of money in ways similar to what we have seen in the area of law, language and morals, where, through a process of evolution, the more effective forms displaced the less effective forms. If we had been allowed to benefit from a similar form of selective evolution where money was concerned, we would have had a money which would have been entirely different from the money we have today.

In fact, in endeavouring to design a better monetary order we at once encounter the difficulty of not really knowing what we want. What would be a really good money? To the present day, money is that part of the market order that government has not allowed to find its most effective form, and on which silly rulers and economists have doctored most. Yet it was not economists or statesmen who invented the market, though some have come to understand it a little; nor is it our present knowledge which can show us the best solutions, but the discoveries made by free experimentation. Those who chiefly needed money as an indispensable tool of trade, and who had first discovered it as a means for making most trade possible, were soon forced to use what money government gave them. And government jealously guarded its monopoly for quite different purposes than those for which money had been introduced. Today, money is not mainly an effective medium of exchange, but chiefly a tool of government for fleecing us and for 'managing' the economy. The result is that we are obliged to admit that we have little empirical evidence of how the various conceivable methods of supplying money would operate, and almost none about which kind of money the public would select if it had an opportunity to choose freely between several different and clearly distinguishable kinds of money. For this we must rely largely on our theoretical imagination, and try to apply to a special problem that understanding of the functioning of competition which we have gained elsewhere.

The gold standard, for instance, is the ideal means to prevent governments from abusing their powers. However, even when governments were committed to the gold standard, we were unable to learn what kind of money would be the best. All discussions on the reform of our monetary order suffer from the very serious defect that we do not quite know what sort of money would really be the best. Should we look for a money which, as its prime characteristic, keeps its value? Or do we need a money which increases in value in proportion to the increase in the productivity of human labour? Should we desire a uniform international money or different monies of local significance? These are open questions. One of the first requirements of a monetary policy must therefore be that it offers a chance for experimenting and learning what money would be best.

Of course, government could, in justification of its policy, use the pretext that a single uniform kind of money used in all transactions constitutes such an advantage that it is worth sacrificing potential improvements. Yet it is very questionable whether this can still be accepted once we recognize how much avoidable harm is done by the kind of money we now have. And perhaps the most important reason for not having better money is that there has not been enough experimentation to lead to agreement about what kind would be desirable. Selective evolution was cut off by authority before we were able to explore adequately the different possible solutions of the problem. That, surely, was too high a price to pay for what may have been a temporary inconvenience.

I shall now turn to more practical aspects of the problem and develop a proposal for bringing about such a system of currency competition.

2. A Stable Purchasing Power

An important question—for which I must admit I have no clear-cut answer—is, if people had a free choice among several kinds of money, whether they would secure for themselves the money which would give a maximum stability of their purchasing-power. It is certainly appropriate to start with the question: What should we expect from a good money, and what is likely to induce individuals to select the good money? We know, of course, that the general reason why people use money as a medium of exchange is that such a commodity possesses a greater degree of acceptability or that it is likely to be more accepted than other commodities. In modern times the word acceptability is often replaced by liquidity, which is very useful because it brings out another aspect which has been neglected for a long time. It is the question about the distinction between a money and a commodity. There exists a whole range of types of liquidity which particular commodities possess. When you have perfect liquidity you really are at the start of the basic money. Then there are all sorts of more or less close substitutes. The range goes from gold, which is liquid, to commodities of a kind which are very illiquid. This distinction is important because it shows that another concept, that of the stability of money, is not an ambiguous concept. Commodities may, for instance, be stable in value provided we are not being forced to sell them rapidly. As regards money, if several currencies have the same degree of acceptability, they may have different degrees of stability.

Therefore the basic contention, on which the validity of my further argument rests, is that, if people were wholly free to choose which money they wished to use in their daily transactions, it would soon appear that those did best who preferred a money with a stable purchasing power. This aspect of liquidity which is usually indicated with the term stability of value is normally expressed in terms of index number of prices. It is often taken for granted that a good money should be approximately constant in purchasing power. That means that it should be approximately constant in terms of its average prices.

It so happens that sixty years ago I began my work on monetary theory by questioning this belief, then universally accepted, but I have since become convinced that a money of stable value is really the best we can hope for. This notion is sometimes being questioned, but on the whole people accept it, albeit without any explicit justification. This justification, in my opinion, is the following. People want, as a medium of exchange, something which reduces as much as possible the uncertainty of future prices. It is inevitable, however, that prices change. They even change unpredictably. The reason for this is that prices are instruments which inform us on events about which we have no information and which, by their nature, must be unexpected events. But the uncertainty about future prices can be reduced to a minimum, if the risk of making mistakes in anticipating future prices in one direction is balanced by the risk of making mistakes in other directions.

Therefore a stable money means a money through which the price of any commodity about which we have no special information would be as likely to rise as to fall, so that on balance the unforeseen price changes would simply be offset by each other. Such a stable level of average prices would, in other words, mean a situation in which a rise (or fall) of the money price of any commodity would indicate that it has also risen (or fallen) in price relative to most other commodities, and not, as is often the case today, become relatively cheaper (or dearer) than most other goods whose prices have changed more (or less). The disturbing influence which money can have—for instance, on relative prices in a situation of inflation—can be attenuated by providing a money which is stable in value in the way which has just been defined.

However, I am not quite certain that the often neglected way in which money can produce misleading effects can ultimately be completely corrected by the existence of a money of constant purchasing power. Money which keeps a constant purchasing power or remains constant in terms of its average price may distort the structure of relative prices, which means that it distorts the allocation of the factors of production. As I have written in my work on the relation between money and the trade cycle, changes in the quantity of money are bound to bring about temporary distortions in the relative price structures. An additional amount of money spent must temporarily raise the price of those goods on which the money is being spent. The resulting change in the structure of prices will be maintained as long as the increase in the quantity of money continues. That means that factors of production will be directed towards the production of those goods and that they will only be used in that production as long as inflation continues.

In a growing economy, with a growing population and a growing production, prices have a tendency to fall and they can only be kept constant by increasing the quantity of money. By such an increase one can indeed keep the value of money constant in terms of the average purchasing power, but only at the expense of distorting the structure of relative prices. This distortion will displace factors of production for as long as the increase in the quantity of money is being maintained. This is a very serious dilemma. The price of money must either fall or rise with the decrease or increase in productivity, or it can be kept stable at the cost of displacing factors of production. This means that my early hope for a fully neutral money, as regards the formation of prices, is a hope which can never be fully realized. All we can hope for is that the increase in the quantity of money will be minimized so as to disturb as little as possible the guide function of money in determining prices.

To the question whether a money with a stable purchasing power is really the ideal, I should now answer that it may not be an ideal, but that it is merely a means to do the trick in order to find a practical solution to the monetary problem. In short, the best we can hope for is a money of which the average purchasing power would remain constant.

Anyhow, the advantage of a stable money over all unstable ones would be particularly significant for the calculations of enterprise, but hardly less so for the holders of employment contracts and savers. And the most important consequence of a range of different currencies being available would not only be that people would prefer to make contracts in a currency they could trust, but even more that, though they might be ready to accept any currency for payment for their goods, they would not wish to hold any currency which they did not trust, but could rapidly exchange it for one which they did. This would very quickly either wholly drive out any currency whose issuer did not keep its purchasing power constant, or at least force him to alter his policy as soon as even a slight discount of its value became visible on the market.

If this should at first appear to be in conflict with the so-called law of Gresham, which says that 'bad money drives out the good' (already known to the ancient Greeks more than two thousand years ago) let me just point out that this law applies only to different moneys between which a fixed rate of exchange is enforced by government. Between different competing moneys whose relative value is determined by the market, precisely the opposite is true, and, as has been shown many times, the good money tends to drive out the bad.

I have no time here to consider the reasons why, almost since coins were first introduced more than two and a half thousand years ago, governments have invariably, with the exception only of the short periods during which they divested themselves of the discretion by making a fixed quantity of one of the precious metals the legal unit, shamelessly abused their monopoly, to the grave damage of people at large. Nor have I time to explain why, though the international gold standard which for a short period in the past provided us with a better money than we have ever had before or since, can in fact not be restored in an effective form. The gold standard requires a return to beliefs which have been destroyed, and it would also be likely to cause such fluctuations in the value of gold that it would break down before long. It has probably become easier by now to deprive governments altogether of their power over money than to attempt to prevent them from abusing their power.

3. An International Standard

The idea according to which the best money would be a money with a constant average purchasing power, of course opens the incidental question of choosing the commodity or the commodities which would play the role of a standard for assessing the average purchasing power. If one were to express the purchasing power in terms of a set of consumer goods, one would limit the conception of constant purchasing power to very small geographical regions. A money whose purchasing power would be kept constant in terms of consumer goods in Brussels, for instance, would not necessarily have the same stability in Paris or New York.

That, incidentally, raises the question whether we want regional or international monies. My option would be to aim for an international money. That means that we should look for prices which might remain fairly stable internationally. It must be clear that I am only giving a sketch here of my own provisional conclusions of what people would aim at, if they were free to select competing monies offered to them. I believe that such a competition would lead to the selection of a money which would be stable in purchasing power and preferably in a purchasing power expressed in terms of an international standard.

Since, in order to keep the world economy functioning efficiently, we clearly need some international standard, and the only part of the international price system on which we can obtain current information is the wholesale prices of the more widely traded standardized raw materials, the closest approach to a general stability of the purchasing power on a monetary unit would probably be a situation in which the index number of the prices of these raw materials would remain constant. Of course, such an index number would have to be what is called weighted, and neither its composition nor the weight attached to each of the different commodities could be kept constant indefinitely. The issuer of a money unit redeemable in such amounts of other currencies as would be required at any time to buy the whole collection of different raw materials defining the standard unit, would have to have the option of changing the list of different commodities and the weights attached to each as their importance in trade changed. The assurance he would have to give to the holders of the units, in order to protect them against concealed changes in value, would have to be that at the moment of any change the aggregate value of the new 'basket', at current market prices, would be the same as that of the old 'basket' (and, probably, that, for a limited short period, holders of the units would have the choice whether to demand redemption in terms of the new or old 'basket').

Any such new international unit provided by a particular issuer would of course have to have a distinct name, and for the purposes of this discussion I shall call it a *Solid*. The success of such an experiment might well depend greatly on the persuasiveness and suitability of the name chosen. I can think of one which in this respect is very much more attractive than any other I can invent; indeed, it would probably be worth millions. But as I have had legal advice that a protective trade mark (or copyright protection) can be obtained under current law only by persons or firms actively dealing in the article in question, I have no choice but to keep it secret for the time being and to use here as a second best name Solid in describing my scheme for a privately issued monetary unit which might well, in spite of the inevitable resistance of governments, be introduced—though at first not as circulating tokens but in the form of transferable deposits redeemable in the current kind of hand-to-hand money or tokens which, for the time being, governments will probably not allow private agencies to issue.

Though the different credit units of this kind issued would of course all have to bear different names, and might at first represent different collections of commodities, after a period of experimentation most of all that survived would probably keep constant value relations to each other, though the units might be of different magnitude. Once the advantages of such units with stable buying power were generally recognized, and some suppliers had demonstrated their capacity for maintaining the value of their units, and thereby established a flourishing business depending wholly on maintaining this trust, such a system would be preserved by the fact that any supplier of such stable credits who failed to maintain this trust would be rapidly driven out by a mass flight from his money.

Another question in this respect is, by whom it would be decided what money would become the generally accepted money. Would it be the consumers at large or the business community or a particular sector of business? I personally believe that the great mass of people would almost accept any kind of money which would be tolerably stable and generally accepted. The average consumer will be happy with any kind of money in which he will be paid and which he will spend on the market if it is tolerably stable. He will not substantially alter his demand for money according to whether it is slightly more or slightly less stable. The decisions on the money to become generally current would rather be formed by people for whom the nature of money is frightfully important for purposes of being able to calculate in it successfully and to hold liquid balances of it without losing or gaining output. That means that business or the preferences of those who use money for business purposes would determine the outcome of the selection process for money, if people were *free to choose* between different sorts of money.

4. Currency and Credit

My original proposal visualized that from the beginning the suppliers of private moneys would provide them not only in the form of book credits, but also by issuing corresponding notes or tokens for fractional values. But though years of further reflection of the problem have only confirmed my belief that this ought to be the final solution of our money problems, I cannot close my eyes to the fact that any hope for a voluntary abdication by governments of their present monopolies of the issues of circulating currency is utopian. Yet this is the only way in which we will ever get back to honest money again while at the same time ridding ourselves of the evils of depression, unemployment and general disorganisation on the market. Governments have become dependent on their power to create money for the finance of their own activities. They regard this ability as so essential a weapon of their economic policy, that they will probably defend to the last, not merely all the explicit power the law has conferred upon them, but also any other power which they can obtain. Though it may be doubtful whether most governments at present really possess a constitutional right to prohibit the private issue of an alternative circulating money, there can be little doubt that they could, through the manipulation of such rules as those of legal tender, prevent any such attempt from being successful.

But this applies, under present conditions, only to currency or hand-to-hand money. This is a misleading impression, however. The exclusive right to issue the tokens, which serve as legal tender for the discharge of obligations contracted in terms of them, does not preclude the use of credit accounts in other units as a general means of exchange. At least where no foreign exchange restrictions are in force—and even these presumably restrict only transactions in specified amounts of named national currencies, general laws do not seem to prohibit the keeping of accounts which entitle the creditor to receive on demand other monies; in particular such amounts as at the time would enable him to buy at current market rates a corresponding part (or multiple) of the 'basket' of raw materials by which the unit is defined and in which the account is kept.

5. Private Banks Guaranteeing a Stable Purchasing Power

I am now coming to the crucial problem: would it be possible and profitable for a banking institution to offer such accounts as *Solids, Ducats, Stables,* or whatever the name might be? I am referring here to a unit which it undertakes to redeem on demand with such amounts of the various other currencies as are required to buy on the established commodity exchanges the stated collection of the various raw materials by the aggregate price of which the unit in question is defined. The difficulties of this task derive from the circumstance that, in order to maintain any particular value of the unit, the offerer must stand ready to buy or sell at the states rates *any* amount of such units that is offered to (or demanded from) him.

The only control he can exercise would be through lending and borrowing (i.e., creating and extinguishing such deposits) at different terms, or at various rates of interest, and possibly charging an administration fee for running the account. The provider of such accounts would, of course, have to be constantly aware that he has no control over the total amount of such liquid assets available to the members of the community, or to the inhabitants of any clearly limitable region. His aim would be to offer in competition with other institutions a clearly distinguishable asset desired by the public as a liquid reserve because it was trusted to preserve its value. This assurance could be offered only by standing ready, at all times, to redeem these deposits by the 'cash' actually needed to buy the designated collection of raw materials. Yet, if a number of separate institutions succeeded in supplying their clientele with differently named, but in fact equivalent amounts of fully liquid units or media of exchange at market prices, the result would be that, in terms of anyone of these units, the general price level of commodities would remain stable.

Could any individual bank so control the volume of its on-demand commitments that it would at all times be able to deliver instantly the amounts of other currencies sufficient to buy at market prices the stated collection of commodities? The chief difficulty would arise from the fact that if it were to prevent the value of its unit from rising *above* the announced level, it could secure this only by being prepared to accept any amount on deposit that was offered to it at the announced terms. This might at times create the difficult problem of finding sufficient opportunities for investing these amounts in assets which themselves are likely to preserve their value. For controlling such fluctuations in the demand for its deposits, the bank would have in effect only the two instruments of varying the difference between the buying and selling prices of its own unit in terms of other kinds of money, and variations from a positive rate of interest paid on its deposits to a negative administration charge for keeping them, both stated as time rates.

It is clear that banks will have much to learn before they can be certain that they know how to deal successfully with these tasks. To be able to provide millions with their liquidity reserves and to earn the interest they may have to pay for the funds thus deposited with them, could well prove the greatest banking success ever for those who first solved these problems. I would gladly wish the highest gains to those who succeeded in conferring on the world the inestimable benefit of at last having a medium of exchange by the use of which the markets could be made to function as well as they should be able to. If such a stable money ever established itself, though it would exist under many different names, and each kind issued under the name and on the responsibility of a different institution, their successful suppliers could probably not for a long time be denied the right to issue corresponding tokens, representing fractional units which, because of their constant relation to the basic credit unit, would soon displace, at least locally, the traditional 'official' cash. And before long governments would probably learn to insist that their taxes be paid in the new stable units, which would constitute the final victory of the system.

I believe that complete freedom to offer to the public alternative monies would rapidly lead to a number of types of money, all of them essentially stable in value, all widely known for their quality and—this is perhaps a surprising feature—all of them stable in terms of each other. They would represent more or less the same store of value under different names and they would be kept stable in terms of this same basket of widely traded raw materials which experience will have proved to be the most acceptable to the public. These monies, I believe, would be partly expressed in denominations of the same magnitude, though bearing different names according to the issuer of a particular type of token or money. It is a strange picture, I admit, but the more one thinks about it, the more realisable it appears.

The main difficulty is that our present banking and credit structure are fully adapted to a monopolistic money where the government appears as the so-called lender of last resort, who has the double function of controlling the quantity of money and adjusting it to changing demands for liquidity.

Quite naturally then, the bankers are the group of people who find it most impossible to place themselves in the position of having to compete with each other in this respect under a new monetary system. Personally, I have only succeeded in convincing economists and young people who are at the point of entering economic life of the attractions of the competitive issue of money, about which there is indeed no basic difficulty. I must admit that I have not yet persuaded a single banker that this situation is practical. They all complain that it is so completely different to what is now regarded as banking and they fear that banking of the traditional sort would disappear. I wish to point out, however, that what we now call banking has only been in practice in the last century and a half since central banking has become universally established and banking has become a business which hinges on the fact that there is a so-called lender of last resort. Bankers have in particular forgotten a famous phrase, used by an English banker when Peel's Act of 1844 was passed: 'I don't need a reserve bank; I keep my reserves here', thereby pointing his finger down to the direction of the vaults of his bank. I believe that if we introduced a system of competing currencies and did away with the monopolistic provider of the ultimate liquid funds, we would indeed have a banking system where each issuer or banker of a particular money would invent the amount of reserves; in terms of commodities and/or collections of other monies as would be required by the necessity to guarantee the stability of his own money.

The development of our monetary system over the last hundred or hundred and fifty years has indeed made my proposal seem more peculiar and more impractical than it would have been a hundred and fifty years ago. At that time, people still clearly perceived the dangers of a national monopoly to issue money. An interesting illustration of this can be found in the writings of an American political economist who was one of the founding fathers of the American Republic. He expressed the opinion that 'to attach full confidence to an institution of this nature (meaning a central bank) appears to be an essential ingredient of this (monetary) structure. But we need private, not public direction of our monetary system and that under the guidance of the market and not of public policy'.

6. *The Collapse of a Private Currency*

Of the many other consequences, some of which I deal with more fully in my book,[4] I will consider here more in depth only one which initially I had not even perceived but which now appears to me to be the most important. It appears to me that the emergence of a new stable international unit of value which is not dependent on the arbitrary will of anybody, would have even more far-reaching effects than is at first obvious. If there were current in the world a large number of nominally different monetary units, all maintaining themselves in circulation only so long as they preserved the same value as most others, even the collapse of any one of them as a result of mistakes of policy or malfeasance would not do anywhere near as much harm as the collapse of any currency today. The holders of balances of a currency that lost part or all of its value would, of course, lose all that, just as they do today. But the greatest losses caused today by the devaluation of a currency are not those of the individuals

[4] *Denationalization of Money*, op. cit.

actually holding amounts of that money, but those who have contractual claims expressed in terms of it. As I explained in the second edition of *The Denationalization of Money* (pp. 124–125),

> With the availability of at least some stable currencies, the present absurd practice of making 'legal tender' a mere token which may become valueless but still effective for the discharge of debts contracted in what has been an object of a certain value, is bound to disappear. It was solely the power of governments to force upon people what they had not meant in the contracts that had produced this absurdity. With the abolition of the government monopoly of issuing money, the courts would soon learn to understand that justice requires all debts to be paid in terms of units of value which the contracting parties intended, and not in what government decrees make a substitute for them. After the development of a widely accepted common standard of values the courts would have in most cases no difficulty in determining the approximate magnitude of the abstract value intended by the parties to a contract by the value of such and such an amount of a widely accepted currency.
>
> If a currency in terms of which a contract had been made, depreciated seriously beyond a reasonable range, a court would not allow the parties to gain or lose from the malpractice of a third party that issued the currency. They would be able without difficulty to determine the amount of some other currency in which the debtor was entitled and obliged to discharge his obligation.
>
> As a result, even the complete collapse of one currency would not have the disastrous consequences which a similar event has today. Though the holders of cash of a particular currency either in the form of notes or of demand deposits might lose the whole value, this would be a relatively minor disturbance compared with the general shrinkage or wiping out of all claims to third persons expressed in that currency. The whole structure of long-term contracts would remain unaffected, and people would preserve their investments in bonds, mortgages and similar forms of claims, even though they might lose all their cash if they were unfortunate enough to have used the currency of the institution that failed. There could never occur such a complete disappearance of any common standard of debts, or such wiping out of all monetary obligations as has been the final effect of all major inflations in the past. Long before this could happen everybody would have deserted the depreciating unit and no old obligation could be discharged in it.

Such a semi-automatic regulation of the supplies of the main kinds of money, insuring that they keep their purchasing power constant, would eliminate *all* the causes of the alternation of inflationary booms and periods of depression and unemployment which have plagued mankind ever since deliberate attempts at a central control of the quantity of money have been made. This is too difficult and complex a matter to pursue further here.

Let me therefore make a last point, which is that the pursuit of a monetary policy is really a very new idea. Until some sixty years ago monetary policy simply meant securing a gold equivalent or silver equivalent or a particular money in circulation. My interest in monetary policy began when I found in the 1923 Annual Report of the United States Federal Reserve Bank a statement which said that the control of the quantity of money could be used to assure the stabilization of economic activity. At that time, that was a new idea. It is only over the last sixty years that money has come to be regarded as one of the prime instruments of economic policy in general and a useful way by which political authority could contribute to prosperity. I must confess that, over the years, I have become increasingly doubtful that a monetary policy in this sense has ever done any good. My opinion is that money is not a suitable instrument of policy and that it ought to be taken out of the hands of political authorities.

The money we now have is not a fully fledged product of our cultural evolution, but a deformed child which suffers from having been unduly restricted and prevented from unfolding its full potentialities. Our money has been made to serve purposes to which it was not adapted. Money is neither a suitable tool of economic policy, nor an honest instrument for securing greater means than the people are prepared to grant it. Our money is only a still imperfect link in the self-steering mechanism of the market. We should endeavour to learn how to make it function better.

NAME INDEX

SUBJECT INDEX

9 780415 035187

For Product Safety Concerns and Information please contact our EU representative GPSR@taylorandfrancis.com
Taylor & Francis Verlag GmbH, Kaufingerstraße 24, 80331 München, Germany

www.ingramcontent.com/pod-product-compliance
Lightning Source LLC
LaVergne TN
LVHW011121300926
849160LV00008B/469
* 9 7 8 0 4 1 5 7 5 5 2 9 0 *